Applied Puppetry

Applied Puppetry

The Theory and Practice of Object Ecologies

Matt Smith

methuen | drama

LONDON • NEW YORK • OXFORD • NEW DELHI • SYDNEY

METHUEN DRAMA
Bloomsbury Publishing Plc
50 Bedford Square, London, WC1B 3DP, UK
1385 Broadway, New York, NY 10018, USA
29 Earlsfort Terrace, Dublin 2, Ireland

BLOOMSBURY, METHUEN DRAMA and the Methuen Drama logo are trademarks of
Bloomsbury Publishing Plc

First published in Great Britain 2024

Copyright © Matt Smith, 2024

Matt Smith has asserted his right under the Copyright, Designs and Patents Act,
1988, to be identified as author of this work.

For legal purposes the Acknowledgements on p. ix constitute an extension
of this copyright page.

Cover design: Ben Anslow
Cover image: Bunny made from scrap materials 2003, PickleHerring Theatre
Photograph @ Jonathon Purcell

All rights reserved. No part of this publication may be reproduced or transmitted
in any form or by any means, electronic or mechanical, including photocopying,
recording, or any information storage or retrieval system, without prior
permission in writing from the publishers.

Bloomsbury Publishing Plc does not have any control over, or responsibility for, any
third-party websites referred to or in this book. All internet addresses given in this
book were correct at the time of going to press. The author and publisher regret any
inconvenience caused if addresses have changed or sites have ceased to exist, but can
accept no responsibility for any such changes.

A catalogue record for this book is available from the British Library.

ISBN: HB: 978-1-3502-7940-7
ePDF: 978-1-3502-7942-1
eBook: 978-1-3502-7941-4

Typeset by Newgen KnowledgeWorks Pvt. Ltd., Chennai, India

To find out more about our authors and books visit www.bloomsbury.com
and sign up for our newsletters.

Dedicated to my brother, David

Contents

List of Figures		viii
Acknowledgements		ix
Notes on the Text		x
Introduction		1
1	Objects speaking for themselves: Mapping the field of Applied Puppetry	19
2	Thinking with ecology: New paradigms in material performance	35
3	Thingness, puppethood and violence: The materiality of performing objects	51
4	Puppet power in intercultural practices: Communities, ethics and representation	69
5	Plastics talking about plastics: Marlsite projects and ecological puppetry	87
6	Puppetry in HMP Haslar IRC: Working with marginalized and vulnerable participants	111
7	Toy Theatres, Kamishibai and Puppet City: Participatory ecologies	127
8	Talking to objects: Kinship with the more-than-human and envoi – sharing spaces with objects: Listening, caves, ephemera, popularity, reciprocity and chimaeras	145
Exercises		167
References		171
Index		181

Figures

0.1	Humphrey the puppet	15
2.1	Matt Smith and Humphrey performing street puppetry, Hyde, Manchester	47
5.1	Plastic fish	89
5.2	Plastic octopus with bottle tentacles	89
5.3	Workshop for Marlsite project	90
5.4	Crewe Marlsite project puppets	96
5.5	Headteacher puppet, Marlsite	97
5.6	Whale puppet on beach	98
5.7	Clinkermen puppets in the hands of audience	100
5.8	The Bunny, Marlsite	101
5.9	Bush baby puppets, Marlsite	103
5.10	Plastic bottle bear, Marlsite	104
5.11	Audience with rope, Marlsite	105
5.12	Canal barge transformed into a giant fish	106
5.13	Workshop puppets, Marlsite	107
6.1	HMP Haslar puppets	114
6.2	HMP Haslar puppets	115
7.1	Puppet City, Journeys Festival Portsmouth	132
7.2	Puppet City, Journeys Festival Portsmouth	136
8.1	The Root	146

Acknowledgements

First of all, I would like to thank the puppets and performing objects who have helped me write this book, especially Humphrey and the malignant root. I would like to thank all the people who have participated in helping me understand puppetry through workshops, including some people caught in very difficult spaces. I would also like to thank all the objects and more-than-human things that have shaped my life to this point. A heartfelt thanks to everyone who has helped with this project. Next, my family Caroline, Martha and Sylvie, who I love very deeply and have supported me through good and bad. My sister Anna Brown and my nieces Nekane, Twyla, Corrina, Sarah, Carmel and Yasmin. I thank my colleagues at the University of Portsmouth, Brooke Waine, Vincent Adams, Guido Robazza, Louis Netter, Tom Sykes, Greg Smith, Russ Percy, Roy Jordan, Tom Byrne, Phoebe Rumsey, Kit Danowski, George Burrows and especially Ben Mcpherson and Nik Wakefield for reading drafts of chapters and for their great advice. I would also like to thank the global community of puppeteers who I have got to know during the writing of this book. I would also especially like to thank my collaborative colleagues in the Odesa Polytechnic, especially Natalia Borodina who I recently became involved with in an exciting project looking at Ukrainian puppetry, and Hary Praveen for his collaboration on my PhD. I would like to thank two great influences no longer with us that were very important to my development: Penny Francis MBE and Henryk Jurkowski. I have many close friends who have supported me over the course of the book but I want to particularly thank Anna Barzotti and Pete Jarvis for their humour and company. My fellow students from the puppet course at CSSD: Sharon, Joanne, Adi, Garry and Moira. More great friends including Rory Miles, Gavin Hodson, Paul Rogers, Katherine Sandys, Derek Lee, Walid Benkhaled, Ben Priest, Chris Curran, Darren Daley, Jeff Young, Michael Thorne, Tim Hobbs, Rusty Sheriff and Magda, my yoga teacher. I have some great collaborators and friends in the puppet theatre community including Matthew Cohen, John Bell, Paulette Richards, Joanne Oussoren, Wendy Passmore and WP Puppetry, Livija Kroflin, Cariad Astles, Mervyn Millar, Karen Torley and Banyan Theatre, Goran Zelic, Riku Laakkonen, Claudia Orenstein, but I would like to thank in particular Laura Purcell-Gates. The community of Applied Theatre has also been very important to the development of this project, especially colleagues involved with Theatre and Performance Research Association (TAPRA). I was greatly inspired by the great Baz Kershaw like many others over the years. In the Applied Theatre community, I would like to thank for their inspiration and collaboration Matt Jennings, Karl Tizzard Kliester, David Grant, Caoimhe McAvinchey, James Thompson, Helen Nicholson, Kay Hepplewhite and Kate Massey-Chase.

Notes on the Text

Some of the ideas and discussions in Chapter 4 appear in Smith, M. (2015), 'The Practice of Applied Puppetry: Antecedents and Tropes', *Research in Drama Education* 20(4): 531–6.

Some of the ideas and discussions in Chapter 6 appear in Smith, M. (2016), 'Thinking through the Puppet inside Immigration Detention', *Applied Theatre Researcher*, 4(2): 147–59.

Introduction

My personal context, Hands On, Broken Puppets, Objects with Objectives, Definitions, Power and Theories, Borders, Psychogeography, Waste, Ecology, Scale, Anthropomorphism and Materialism.

I set out in this introduction a definition of Applied Puppetry based on my years of advocacy for this term, painting both a personal and contextual history for this field of puppet practice. I then look at the process of giving performing objects increased agency across landscapes and spaces. In this way I present puppets and objects as having the ability to help us explore our climate crisis, doing this through playful uses of scale, from the gigantic to the miniature. I argue that puppets and performing objects, in these processes in communities, anthropomorphize ecological aspects and issues in our world, reflecting back for us new ways of thinking.

What is Applied Puppetry?

Practices that could be considered Applied Puppetry have been around for most of the twentieth century. The establishment of the Educational Puppetry Association (EPA) in the British context in 1943 is evidence of this use of puppetry in educational and community practice. During the Second World War the EPA presented, through their leaflets and newsletters, a hopeful vision for puppetry with a social purpose (EPA 1945 and EPA/Wall 1953). Educational puppeteers now could be inspired by the spirit of this organization operating, as it did, during a period of global crisis. In historical documents, the idea of puppetry as a social educational force is clear, even during days of war and turmoil. Much later, in the UK context in 1992 the position of puppetry in the UK was surveyed by Keith Allen and Phyllida Shaw and they noted:

> Almost three quarters of the puppet companies surveyed work in schools and more than half in community centres; performances and workshops in residential homes and institutions are common, and a handful of puppeteers work with the

health service. For some puppeteers, a performance or workshop in a school is no more than a useful source of income; for others it is a conscious choice to work in education. Similarly, for some teachers, the puppeteers are no more than entertainers; for others, they are professional artists contributing to the educational process. (Allen and Shaw 1992: 43)

This viewpoint of UK puppetry demonstrates a shift from the social idealism of the EPA's vision of puppetry for a social educational purpose towards an economically driven necessity for educational puppetry in the 1990s, after the impact of the individualist economic changes of the 1980s. What I have noted in regard to this change in culture is that puppeteers today, when considering the examples explored in this book (especially Chapter 1), are committed to the idea of puppetry as a social educational form and not just as a handy secondary income stream.

Historically, the book *Puppets and Therapy* by Alexis R. Philpott (1977) presents early attempts to use puppetry with people. Much of the language of that book is out of date and the voices in the collected accounts lack consideration of individuals, seeming functionary and outdated, though often fascinating. In *Puppets and Therapy*, a sense of the human body experimented upon with puppetry is a rather troubling theme that ghosts the text. This use of 'puppet power' is often a concern I critically explore around discourses about puppetry in practice. This power is often left undefined and presented uncritically as one of the aesthetic qualities of puppetry. My scholarship questions the power of the puppet, analysing its effects, both negative and positive, for the human subject and surrounding ecology. One historical text that describes the use of puppets in this engaged way is Bil Baird's *Puppets and Population* from the early 1970s when the Global North was providing aid to countries wrapped within the power of population control (explored in Chapter 4). This project was conducted in India, a vast landscape with the oldest traditions of puppetry, with one of the most systematic uses of puppetry, traditionally and for education influenced by the work of pioneers like Meher Rustom Contractor.[1] So, a history of Applied Puppetry should not see this educational and community approach as rooted in Western European practices as its origins are not there.

Following the shadow of puppetry histories from its ancient roots towards the modern practices suggests that the origins are found beyond the Eurocentric viewpoint. Performing objects were used in ancient rites globally where communities attempted to make meaning, and examples like this are still found in important traditions like Indonesian Wayang.[2] In Wayang the community is assembled symbolically and this is important to the way this performance practice operates with objects. We can speculate about how our most ancient rites using artefacts in this way (as vibrant objects) make meaning through the materialist performative lens. The object world viewed from this perspective has always given communities meaning and significance in performances. As a vernacular and popular performance style, the puppet has this lengthy lineage in human culture and as part of communities globally (Jurkowski 1996, Speaight 1955, Baird and Zanger 1965, Bell 2016, Blumenthal 2005).

Personal context

I began my practice in puppetry at the time the book *On the Brink of Belonging* was published in 1992, and my work emerged in this context amidst the tension between individual entrepreneurism and making socially responsible art. This was before the contemporary shift of puppetry towards it being a mainstream art form in the UK with "mega" shows like *War Horse* in 2007. Since training to be a puppeteer at Central School of Speech and Drama, I was also engaged in lots of work and commissions influenced by my training in Applied Theatre in community settings. Through contexts like youth theatres, play schemes, street theatre, care homes, youth clubs, prisons, probation, disability groups, museums, galleries, health networks, environmental projects and education from pre-school to master's students, I led, participated in and witnessed the potential of puppetry as a collaborative process. I explore how I work with the puppet as a 'collaborative entity' throughout this book. Through my professional work as freelancer, and through my company, Pickleherring, I became known as 'Matt the Puppet Man'. I am now an academic looking back on all this practice, mapping the terrain of Applied Puppetry through practice research. My work explores the haptic ludic pleasure of Applied Puppetry through workshops, research, residencies, lectures or performances based in communities, and this experience is reflected in this book.

When I started making puppets in the early 1990s, recycling became a necessity as I was an impoverished artist in need of free materials. This necessity was mixed with the great potential that found objects represent for the maker. When I auditioned for the year-long course at Central School of Speech and Drama, led by the queen of British puppetry Penny Francis MBE,[3] the puppet I performed with was roughly carved from an old chair leg discarded by a carpentry workshop in Liverpool. The curved form of the wood presented an already formed surface to draw, then to carve out a face. The majority of puppets made in my career are from waste found waste materials. In objects, I see ghosts of other things, such as human or animal forms, and this pareidolia is a habitual process for me in the process of making puppets. Most domestic waste including vegetables, can transform into a puppet figure. (The first time I saw vegetable puppetry it was performed by a commedia dell'arte troupe called Ophaboom .) Students love the novelty of making vegetable puppets and then eating the leftovers.

After years of frustrating small-scale touring, I found joy through finding an alternative process and performance practice using junk in the Marlsite projects explored in Chapter 5, which was a key turning point. This process was about seeing the potential for making puppets on a very large scale. Spiders that covered a hillside, whales on beaches, aliens with bottle tentacles, giant flying crocodiles, cardboard butterflies, canal barges turned into fish, giant prawns made from redundant traffic cones and sea monster chimaeras that looked like the contents of a bin, all made up the trash poetics of this puppetry. These puppet figures were of different scales – for example, the Clinker Men who appeared in one of the residencies. These figures made from waste captured the essence of the Marlsite projects as post-industrial stories.

These ecological narratives were always playful making this work joyfully accessible. The performative potential in waste objects used in this way gives objects a new use value outside of the cycle of normative consumerism.

Hands On and Broken Puppets

In 2014 an initiative from the Little Angel Theatre in London[4] led towards two events called 'Hands On' that I co-developed with Cariad Astles and Slavka Jovanovic. These events started a very important conversation around how engaged puppetry is considered and that was when I began to advocate for the 'Applied Puppetry' term. The great diversity of practices was evident at these events in the UK context and it was globally represented in the second symposium. This work developed into a focused discussion represented by three Broken Puppet Symposia[5] and their thematic views of areas, such as how disability can be discussed and how it links to puppetry. Emma Fisher's work (one of the convenors of Broken Puppet) and her scholarship leads the way in thinking about how puppetry augments the human body in performance. Therapy was also well represented through one of the Broken Puppet symposia and the use of systematic therapeutic approaches like Karim Dakroub's practice (explored in Chapter 1).

Objects with objectives

There are lots of collaborators who contribute to the development of Applied Puppetry in terms of relevant literature. Livija Kroflin has created a trilogy of texts in relation to her work with the EDT Commission (Education, Development, Therapy) of Union Internationale de la Marionette (UNIMA),[6] and these are spaces for discussions about how the application of puppetry to groups can be successfully developed. Another great project which developed the idea of Applied Puppetry was Objects with Objectives (2016) led by David Grant. This project was based around a residency in Cape Town, South Africa, and involved scholars and practitioners of Applied Theatre and puppetry. What was indicated by this project is that there is potential for an exciting dialogue between Applied Theatre practices such as that of Augusto Boal, a popular practitioner whose ideas constitute a wide influence in Applied Theatre. Boal's practice was mixed with the developing work of artists like Aja Marneweck who work intensely, developing highly skilled puppeteers and performances in the townships of South Africa. Boal's revolutionary practice is an anti-Aristotelian attempt to offer spaces where people can change and find solutions to social issues. Forum Theatre is one of the key and most popular forms he invented. His practice has effected and 'ghosted' Applied Theatre globally and his ideas and techniques have changed the way I approach practice. This practice and subsequent publications are explored in Chapter 1 as a mapping of the field of Applied Puppetry recognizing some of the important emergent voices.

Towards a definition

The puppet is an accepted form in community art making that is found in all manner of spaces and is an accessible art form that attracts participants. The majority of these participants are children, as puppetry is often popularly seen as a playful childish pursuit. In my experience puppetry enables play and the development of narratives through crafting puppets and making performances. I have found puppetry is usually easy to encourage in all kinds of groups. Puppetry does interesting things to the bodies of participants in these workshops (one of the themes of this book) and in its performances. It focuses the attention at different scales into unusual 'imaginariums' that are at once surprising, disturbing and often funny. The puppet is an 'anarchic conduit' for messages that, depending on the intention, are inclusive, therapeutic, interventionist, activist or sometimes problematically dogmatic. The puppet becomes 'applied' in these processes when it is operating outside of the usual cultural spaces for theatrics. This space is found in schools, prisons, festivals, youth centres, old people's homes, on the streets and generally outside of the specialized drama studio.

The puppet in some of these contexts works with specific agendas – for example, projects about exploring human health or the narrating of stories of the traumatized and marginalized.

Applied Puppetry can be organized as though it is 'done to' the bodies of the participants or it can be employed as something made and controlled by those bodies in a community setting. When the 'done to' model is employed, messages are delivered didactically or simply towards groups in communities. This didactic form can appear very instrumental in the way the puppet 'tool' is employed and so this 'done to' method is not always effective at including community participants in the narratives. An alternative principle is the 'done with' model where the puppet comes from the hands of the community, and through this book I make the case that this is an ideal way to approach practice. Controlling the means of production gives power to the group experience in Applied Puppetry. Throughout this book the idea of *community-centred making* is presented as a best practice model for Applied Puppetry. Another related theme explored in this book is how the puppet affects people and how we recognize this in practice, positively or critically. The power puppets have in this practice is often found in their resistant silence. Puppets can say and produce powerful affects without words and that is why they are effective, for example in street protests.

Like Applied Theatre, Applied Puppetry is an umbrella term that contains an ever-expanding group of practices, including therapeutic approaches. This is where I need to note the lack of attention to the therapeutic approaches in my experience and writing. There is a well-established field of puppet therapy that takes an approach based on psychological principles.[7] This approach fits well within the space of Applied Puppetry but is specific in how it approaches the participants' identity and psyche. In my practice the understanding of the participants in terms of psychology or therapy is not an intention or part of the practice. There may be therapeutic benefits in Applied Puppetry, but in the practice that I conduct and analyse, the intention is not to transform or pathologize the participant directly. In this book I will not take a psychological perspective on the way puppets affect bodies.

Applied Puppetry, as a practice, is a way of thinking through networks of objects exploring the opportunity for alternative approaches. It is also important to note that I do not advocate that puppets are always 'good for you' as in certain contexts and with certain people they actually are powerfully uncanny beings which need to be introduced with care. Some people find puppets very disturbing due to their uncanny bending of realities and grotesque potential. Over the years I have met many students who do not like and are disturbed by some of my puppet progeny. Also, there are settings and projects where there is no point in using puppets as the group is not interested in the form. Even when there are no puppets, there are still a multitude of other objects in Applied Theatre that significantly alter the participants and the ecology of practice. This influence is often ignored and left unacknowledged. This network of objects and things is the focus of this book. Applied Puppetry draws on a wide array of disciplinary fields and like puppetry in general is inherently interdisciplinary. Drawing from the fields of anthropology, identity politics, disability studies, queer studies, psychology, post-human thought, ecology, radical pedagogy, experiential education, post-colonialism, feminism, new materialism and the whole array of critics who consider objecthood allows us to reconsider the often elusive problems that puppets pose for the human thinker around issues of power, representation and ethics.

A position presented in this book, in the process of Applied Theatre, is the use of devising Applied Puppetry as a more inclusive community process than the staging of already written plays. In the workshop spaces the puppet is a great facilitator of improvised stories. Children use puppets to tell complex and unique stories with enthusiasm . The puppet in this context produces in children a strong desire to make narratives often without a starting point or prescribed stimulus. These stories are influenced by the child's environment and this makes them all the more funny or rich in content. The puppet in this space gives licence to say what is often a bit hard or too naughty to say without the puppet. Children love puppets when they do bad things and especially when they hit each other. Repairing puppets after these kinds of violent narratives is a consideration for the Applied Puppet workshop facilitator.

Puppets encourage improvisation through devising in a way that shifts embodiment of the narratives, this changes their dramaturgy encouraging visual-based narrative development and this is one of their strengths. Puppets represent ideas that are difficult to express – for example, describing the process of conception in a sexual health workshop for teenagers (Smith 2009).

Aim of the book

The aim of this book is to see puppets as more than just instrumental tools used bluntly to impart messages towards community audiences. Puppets in Applied Theatre are important agents opening up participants to discuss, on their own terms, issues and narratives they are interested in discussing. Puppets elicit play, like the way good toys elicit play, and a special level of participation exists with this play with puppets shown to an audience. This performance is where poet Samuel Taylor Coleridge's 'suspension of disbelief'[8] occurs and the puppets' life grows in the minds of the audience through their 'poetic faith'. The puppet 'trickster'[9]in this process shifts the focus, building bridges across the void of experience, between people, through performance. Puppetry also employs a myriad of styles from traditional tangible puppetry (glove, marionette, shadow) to the world of less matrixed performing objects in popular culture (dolls and avatars). Puppets are continually entrancing groups, even when recently certain traditions are dying out, like Punch in the UK and puppetry in contested places like the Indian Kathputli colony.[10] Against this dwindling of some traditions, Applied Puppetry is a vibrant form, growing and developing, as it is used with new community groups and in the ever popular space of amateur art making.

Power of puppetry and relevant theories

Theories explored in this book to frame discussions of practice are drawn from a number of post-war philosophers including Michel Foucault as a way to approach politics of the embodied subject, Jacques Derrida in his deconstruction of concepts like hospitality, Emmanuel Levinas and his transcendental ethics, John Gray in regard to freedom and puppetry, Roland Barthes's semiotics in relation to popular myths and Gilles Deleuze in respect to understanding multiplicities and experience. I only look at one ancient philosopher, Plato, whose cave allegory seems to ghost ideas of puppetry as an artificial human practice. In relation to performance ecology, the key reference points and theories are drawn from Baz Kershaw, Lisa Woynarski, Wendy Arons, Theresa May, Carl Lavery and Clare Finburgh Delijani. Tim Morton is explored in detail in relation to their concept of 'being ecological'. There are other theories I refer to that are very important in considering the puppet, including Masahiro Mori's uncanny valley, John Bell's performing objects, Kenneth Gross's literary view and Henryk Jurkowski's histories. One of the largest schools of thought drawn on for this book is the recent 'object turn' in thinking developed by Graham Harman in relation to Object-oriented ontology (OOO), Jane Bennet's vibrant materialism, Bill Brown's thing theories and Ian Bogost's use of litanies and OOO.

There are a number of important practitioners referenced and used as examples within this book. Many of these are artists not just working in puppetry, such as the visionary eco-artist Joseph Beuys, the artist Kara Walker and her explorations of racial violence through installations, Suzanne Lacy's socially engaged feminist practice with communities, William Kentridge's use of objects in installations exploring the politics of the twentieth century and Wael Shawky's installations using puppetry to critique Eurocentric histories. The work of famous performance practitioners is referenced and presented as important influences on puppetry and object theatre, including Tadeusz Kantor's visual theatre of objects, Eugenio Barba's embodied and intercultural physical theatre, Mike Pearson's exploration of the spaces of performance and Augusto Boal's radical dialogical theatre for communities using Forum Theatre. I also explore my personal relationship with an important visual community company, Welfare State International (WSI).

Specific practices in puppetry are explored mainly through my own practice but also in reference to other companies and practitioners. Peter Schumann's work as activist and visionary puppeteer has been a continual influence, the now global practice of South African puppet company Handspring has changed the landscape of puppetry especially in the UK with *War Horse*, Bil Baird's historical practice is used as a key example and Gary Friedman's pioneering Applied Puppetry in Africa is also another influence. Other companies of note considered are Rouge 28 Theatres reuse of the Japanese Kamishibai form, Banyan Theatres' engaged puppetry and the enmeshed object performance of artists like Duda Paiva's puppetry and Jeong Geum-Hyung's object performance art.

The approach in this book is to use these examples to frame my own embodied experiences of practice using puppetry and objects to develop practices with communities. Chapter 1 uses the work of innovative practitioners and academics to map the field of Applied Puppetry and then the rest of the book centres more around my practice and its effects.

Puppets break social or conceptual frames splitting apart and mocking human interactions in fascinating ways. Their power is often found within very specific biopolitical situations that critical thinking helps us to understand the way through which this power is distributed. Michel Foucault and his concept of the biopolitical (Foucault 1991) forced me to reconsider many of the assumptions about how bodies are disciplined, positioned and affected by the power of the puppet. Foucault's critical thinking is one type of critical perspective adopted in this book to unpick the practice and its meaning within human interactions with objects. This criticality is provoked by my experience of practices, and this use of practice reconsidered, in relation to ideas and theories, is the approach in this book.

One field of knowledge that is brought to bear on the practice in this book is the growing philosophy of Object Oriented Ontology (OOO) and New Materialism. This relatively new turn in thinking about object relations is enriching for the practitioner and scholar of puppetry. It opens up ways to think about the vibrancy of objects within networks and changes the traditional ontologies we have used to explain the object world. The approach in this book uses this thinking to frame and analyse practices that valorize the object as doing more than being a passive prop for humans. Influenced by this 'object turn', in my practice and scholarship, I don't just take for granted the non-human, more-than-human (Abram 2012) networks of objects that affect and shape my ability to conduct practice.

Morton's ideas of the ecological are an important reference point for thinking about the practices I discuss. Morton's combination of OOO and ecological thought are a great gift to the puppeteer and activist. Seeing potential in the object parts that make up the globe is connected to seeing the potential in everything. Expanding this to the practice of theatre-making reinvigorates the field of performance. I see my work here in this book as part of a reinvigoration of the field of performance through a renewed attentiveness to the whole network of objects in theatre and performance. The 'non-human ensemble' in performance practice is more important than ever and even more vibrant as a space of consideration. There are many ways of thinking ecologically through performance and this book offers up some of these practices for critical inquiry focusing more on how particularly objects enable this practice.

Employing theories and viewpoints freshens the way the puppet is discussed, but we have to be careful not to mythologize puppetry like Roland Barthes did in his *Lesson in Writing* when the Japanese puppet form is explored from a Eurocentric position (Barthes 1977: 170–8). Barthes compares Japanese Bunraku with Western ideas of antithesis and suggests that 'Bunraku cares nothing for these contraries, for this antonymy that regulates our whole morality of discourse; concerned with a fundamental antilogy, that of the *animate/inanimate*, it disturbs it, dissipates it to the advantage of neither of the terms' (Barthes 1977: 171). These fascinating theories and critical thinking can help us to consider the puppet like Barthes, but this mythologizing never fully appreciates Bunraku within its context or community. This elusiveness when reading puppetry is a reason for its popularity as a useful metaphor for philosophers and political commentators about semiotics, freedom, being, or human experience (think of all the uses of puppetry to visually symbolize 'control'). The issue of control is part of puppetry and how it is often used as a metaphor. The art of puppetry can also be working with the object opening up how the object can appear less controlled and more autonomous. Exploring the way that puppets are controlled is part of the technique of puppetry.

Puppet borders

During 2020 a giant refugee puppet travelled across Europe to arrive back at its source, the UK. The puppet was attacked by far right racists in Greece and celebrated by communities across Europe (Gentleman 2021). Born from the desire to raise awareness of the plight of refugees or asylum seekers crossing, or often dying on our borders, this puppet encouraged the best and worst in human reactions to migration. I had the chance to ask one of the creative team from Good Chance[11] if it was easier for the puppet Amal to cross borders than the puppeteers and they stated it was definitely easier for the giant puppet. One episode recounted involved a short boat trip for the puppet (not subjected to passport controls), but for the puppeteers and crews the journey was a major detour. This puppet of a displaced girl called Amal built on a large scale highlights the cruelly absurd way we try to enforce spatial boundaries around our bodies. In this way the puppet as object other physically circumnavigates the issues around the border zone. Amal, the giant puppet girl, also elicited powerful reactions, as the *Guardian* reported this impact on audiences:

> As Little Amal prepares to cross the Channel to the UK on Tuesday for the final stage of her journey, producer David Lan says the exercise has forced thousands of people along the route to reflect on their attitudes towards refugees, particularly towards the hundreds of thousands of displaced children forced to flee their homes because of conflict over the past decade. (Gentleman 2021)[12]

As Applied Theatre scholar Kate Duffy-Syedi suggests, puppet spectacles like Little Amal 'raises important questions for our field about political neutrality in refugee engaged theatre, and the power of spectacle' (Duffy-Syedi 2022: 225).

This 'free' movement reveals the border zones materially and puppets interact symbolically with the other objects of the border zone creating new meanings and unusual identities.

Puppets can do much more than just merely represent the oppression of the border; they allow us to play with the very notion of what is a border as an assemblage of objects full of performances. Puppets find it relatively easy to cross the border zone as I have found when they are travelling with me through airport security without question across continents. In Chapter 6 I discuss my explorations into puppetry in the nexus of border performances. The experience of making puppetry in an Immigration Removal Centre (IRC) was at the limits of what I then felt was possible with Applied Puppetry.

The desperately hopeless existence of the men I intersected with in the project at HMP Haslar IRC, like Little Amal, brought glimpses of joy in an altogether shameful disciplinary carceral human environment. The puppets I took through the Haslar prison security zone were never checked or processed in the way that human bodies were, like the way Little Amal could 'freely' cross border zones on her journey.

Puppet psychogeography

> The city and puppet both depend on human animation, but they are a particular kind of object that dictates and controls its movements. Cities and puppets interact with humans to generate meanings and to negotiate identities (Goodlander 2020: 8).

In 2018 I explored the ways that puppetry and cities could interact with each other through the project Puppet City, initially conceived with the title Puppet Psychogeography's (explored in Chapter 7). As Goodlander suggests above, puppets and cities can interact in surprising ways in relation to the ways that humans perceive themselves in their environments. These meanings are fluid and unfixed, troubled by the anarchic spirit of the puppet. I discuss the Puppet City as a site for playing with human concepts of urban space using puppets as surrogates for our experience creating a ludic space for thinking and more importantly playing. The cardboard cities built in this project indicated that puppets elicit play between children and adults, provoking questions about how we live with objects interacting with our environment.

Waste puppets and questions of ecology

Throughout this book I return to the concept of the ecological as a way to understand the intersections and issues surrounding and contextualizing Applied Theatre practice. This does not mean that the processes discussed are always speaking about or to issues of the environment. My work with people caught within the border zone of immigration does not relate obviously to recycling but is ecological in thinking through how certain human identities are traded as a waste or surplus with democracies like the UK. Applied Puppetry that does not exclusively use recycled waste materials is still ecological as it is working in a multifaceted interdisciplinary way that gives a very specific focus of the object and materiality through its exegesis or development.

Thinking ecologically about Applied Puppetry is a holistic approach to understanding the levels and contextual framings around this form of practice. It challenges us to both consider the identities of human participants as well as the objects they interact with – surrounding discourses, places and spaces, preceding expectations, underlying positions, performance remains and their after effects. The ecological approach presents a challenge to the practitioner to be cognizant of this whole array of aspects involved in practice. This might at first thought seem an impossible task and more of an aspiration, but this book offers insights into how this ecological approach can be employed.

Puppet scale

Scale is a very important aspect of puppetry in regard to its audience or environment. The range of puppetry in this book can be understood through considering scale. I explore how this practice can be developed in various scales and often using cheap materials. Playing with scale is also one of the delights of puppetry from tiny Thumbelina to the giant awe inspiring puppets of companies like Royal de Luxe.[13] Scale in puppetry can be a magic realist experience when a character shifts from one size to another in different planes of existence. For example, in one of my shows – *Pandeamonium* (1999) – by playwright Jeff Young, the character of Humphrey appears floating on an umbrella into a landscape of hills until the birth of the Industrial Revolution when the earth is literally split onstage and Humphrey reduces to a fifth of his size in relation to the chimneys and monstrous machines that grow out of the earth. In this vision of the Industrial Revolution the hyper objects (Morton) of landscape and heavy industry are animated with rudimentary objects like rusted tin cans and old dust sheets. Playing with scale in regard to the puppetry like this allowed us to bring to life the visions of the man-made hell of *Pandeamonium* by visionary British artist Humphrey Jennings (1987). In this way performing objects offer the ability to explore the Industrial Revolution theatrically through a scale that made this epic narrative a possibility.

Puppets in this manner provide us with scaled performed models that are animated and through which we revise our positions in regard to the ecological. In this touring show I mimetically compared our bodies to the multitude of rusted tin can people puppets rattling in lines across a ripped apart landscape.

Anthropomorphism, materialism and ecology

Anthropomorphism relates well to puppetry processes, but it is problematic when used in relation to ecology because it describes the human-centric drive to shape the world in the human image. Putting eyes on an object is an attempt by a human agent to reduce the otherness of the object so that the human can mimetically approach the object, especially in the performative realm. By animating the object, the puppeteer can give human qualities to the object and this is much more intense than seeing faces in the design of cars. When I look at the video document of the root, discussed in Chapter 8, I cannot stop seeing a face in its image after the ten minutes of video. Anthropomorphism presents issues for the way we look at the meaning of puppetry and performing objects in relation to ecology as it highlights our need to mirror ourselves in natural forms, an age-old problem of what we now see as part of the Anthropocene. Another way of looking at this is that if the process of anthropomorphism allows us to reconsider the object other with fresh eyes, we can speculate differently about our ontological positions and maybe produce sympathy for objects. If the process of anthropomorphism allows us to think about wood, paper or plastic, it can allow us to think through our relation to these things in an ecology. For example, David Nash's sculpture of *Wooden Boulder* (2003) which floated away downstream for years, finally disappearing from view, reflects human-centred ideas of temporality and agency. We can't help ourselves from humanely characterizing the wood on its journey. Similarly, the brown paper workshops and performances of South African artist Aja Marneweck produce a strong sense of object presence that produce human empathy.

Recently, I voiced a plastic bottle puppet which talked about how it felt, as the playful notion in this skit was that 'plastics could talk about plastics'. The plastic bottle discussed its ubiquity and that you could find its kin on any beach in the world. When I hold a plastic bottle that has been sliced in the middle for a mouth and I begin to speak through the plastic, it presents a funny monologue of turning up on beaches everywhere and it quite obviously performs like a human-style clown. All of these examples produce anthropomorphism on different levels, but all of this also provides a way to approach the object or ecologies. So, there is nothing necessarily wrong with anthropomorphism, especially in puppetry, as it is a very useful process through which to encounter the non-human world then possibly understanding this realm in ecological terms.

Materialism is also not inherently 'wrong' for authorities like the social scholar Daniel Miller when he considers our relationship to objects.[14] His exploration of 'stuff' presents the human need to accumulate objects around us as a positive and important part of how we create and reinforce our sense of identity (Miller 2008). The creation of a puppet by an individual in a workshop can say a lot about their identity and the way they like to interpret or make meaning of the world. This can be interpreted psychologically or socially within the frame of therapy or Applied Theatre. It can also develop into a way of commenting on the processes of new materialism and ecology. Objects performing roles in new ways draws attention to the nature of the object's material situation. This focus on materiality is an exciting outcome of playing with objects in Applied Puppetry.

As you read this book, reconsider the objects we use in our practices as part of this ecology of practice. This practice of repositioning makes us more cognizant of our place within a wider ecology and network of entities. This book is grounded in the experience of objects affecting the bodies of participants through embodied ecological effects. But where does the ecology fit into this exploration of puppetry?

Well, it doesn't, as all of this practice with consideration of bodies and objects fits into the wider ecology.

The work that I have made as a puppeteer is always ecologically intersectional as it usually has an audience within a context reacting to the material others that I create and perform with. Since the early days when I was an artist on the dole making odd shows in Liverpool, the need to use scrap trash materials was a necessity. Finding scrap plastics to make a loose adaptation of Ted Hughes's apocalyptic children's fable *The iron Man* (1968) was because of my economic constraints. Finding resources on the streets from the waste of industries or domestic spaces was my modus operandi during those lean years and still is today. I am well attuned to seeing the potential pareidolia, or other life, in litter and found objects. These objects found in human waste have always been part of the network of my practice. This use of waste was more explicit at the turn of the twenty-first century when I created the Marlsite projects explored in Chapter 5. This practice is inspired by the era-defining book by Suzi Gablik, *The Re-enchantment of Art* (1991). She exposed the need to make work as if the 'world really mattered' against the irresponsible arrogance of modernist artists' autonomy, and this critical viewpoint of Gablik's reinvigorated my work. Gablik's view of art within the social realm is a theme throughout this book and I return to her feminist approach to intersectional listener-centred practice throughout my discussions.

Using the already defined life of an object in a new way is implicit in all puppetry, but when the puppet is made from waste this process is pronounced. A plastic bottle puppet carries within it the narrative of overconsumption and the miasma of waste in advanced capitalism. These puppets are made by groups and in this making is a new way of thinking about consumption. These narratives about trash and consumption using puppetry as pedagogical tools are explored in Chapter 5. Also, in this book the discussions of ecological puppetry are interwoven with other narratives, but the practice involved in these pages is always already ecological, implicitly and sometimes explicitly produced.

This concern with the non-human and more-than-human has meant that I now talk to malformed roots and blobs of discarded expanding foam (explored in Chapter 8). This dialogue with objects appears a meek response to the climate crisis, but I persist in this performing object-based practice. I performed for the first time my dialogue with a malformed root in front of Baz Kershaw and it was a kink in the path of my research.

The root was not animated or manipulated like a puppet. It mostly sat still on top of a step ladder. This assemblage of objects heightened and focused the attention onto the root object into a collective act of anthropomorphism. Throughout this event at an academic conference, I looked only upon the root. I spoke only to the root and was attuned to the root. The context was the applied working group at Theatre and Performance Research Association (TAPRA) in 2019. The root performance was well received and opened up a great dialogue with Kershaw who I refer to as he has and continues to be an important authority on the possibility of eco-performance.

The experience and continued collaboration with the root have established in my practice a method through which to expand notions of how objects are also embedded in performance. This has changed my workshops, performances and teaching of Applied Theatre developing an attuned and enmeshed approach. In Applied Theatre objects are enablers and conduits through which creativity can be encouraged. Objects act as bridges through which the group or individual gain confidence in articulating their own story or point of view. Widening this view, quotidian objects like chairs should not be taken for granted in applied practice as they offer support and establish a dynamic space for practices like the drama circle or 'chair games'. In teaching I often emphasize the way that a facilitator can allow these objects to enable the work in the space with the participants. The network of objects in applied practices enabling human sociality is most often forgotten within this network of things. A prop, a chair, the floor, light, air, clothing, phones, are all enablers in the temporary transformations of workshops. The puppet used in Applied Puppetry transforms to an even more explicit and 'magical' degree. It presents an opportunity to focus away from the direct 'face to face' of human performance practices and intentionally playfully valorizes the things in the space. The focus of this book is often the process of making puppets in workshops rather than the study of puppet shows. This is because for me the major changes and deep experiences of puppetry can be found in these processes.

Branches, roots and nodes

To map this book, imagine an organic series of branches, roots or nodes and this is the shape of this book. The format develops through thinking about Applied Puppetry as a field in Chapter 1. Chapter 2 opens up ideas about materialism and ecology as a way to place puppetry within the network and spaces of ecological practices. This chapter draws on Morton's important thinking that brings ecology and materialism together, a perspective on how we can 'be with' objects performing or otherwise. Then Chapter 3 follows a theoretical branch following new materialism through the ideas about art objects in Bill Brown's scholarship. These two chapters, though theoretical, are filled with important examples of art, puppetry and projects of my own making. I discuss historical puppetry for a purpose in Chapter 4 as a way to open up issues that ghost Applied Puppetry practice, including the example of Bil Baird's *Puppets and Population* (1971) project. This problematic example is then compared with my experience recently using Theatre for Development (TfD) in Nairobi, working remotely and importing puppets from the UK. In all of this work, as well as valorizing the potential of puppetry, I critically trouble the practice. In Chapter 5 I explore a period of practice where my work with Pickleherring blossomed into the Marlsite projects as an example of working with waste in an ecological framework. The reflection on Haslar IRC in Chapter 6 is a fulcrum around which my critical appraisal of Applied Puppetry grew in depth and this experience was a part of my PhD. This research experience explored in Chapter 6 had a powerful impact personally and professionally in regard to what is possible with puppets in a demanding and traumatic prison environment. The ethical idea of the 'hand to hand' is a key outcome of this practice and reflection. This discussion of objects and bodies then moves into the urban space of the city in Chapter 7 where the Puppet City project encouraging free play with a city-building kit and puppets grew out from a research collaboration with a geographer and architect. Play is emphasized

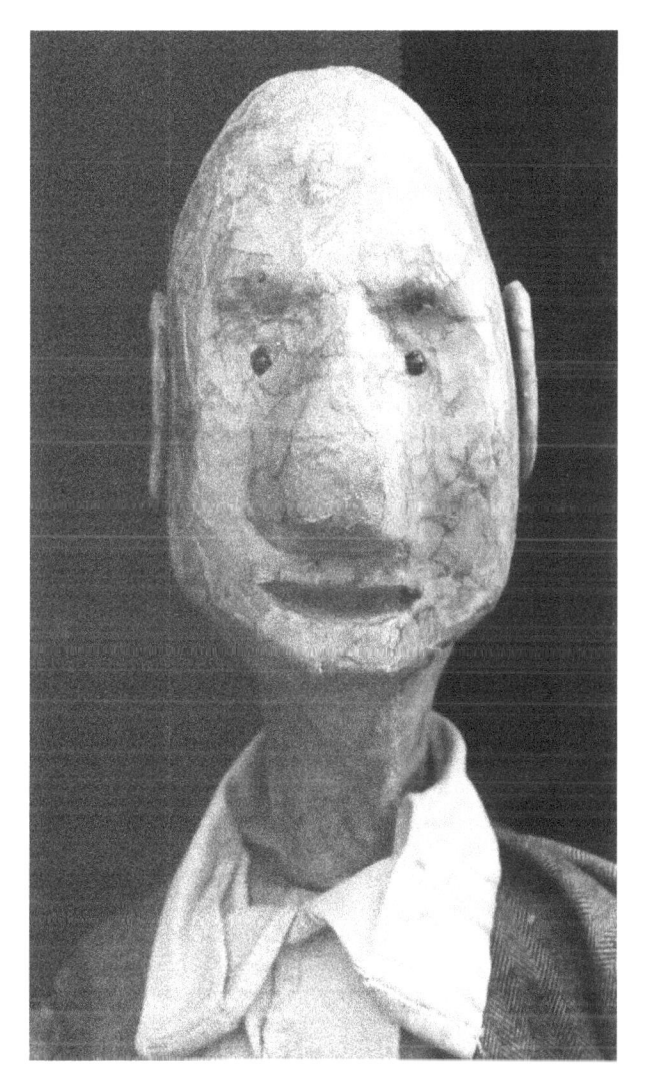

Figure 0.1 Humphrey the Puppet, 2008. Photograph by author.

in this chapter as an important building block for any kind of creative collaboration or participation using puppetry. In Chapter 8, I arrive where my practice and scholarship has recently found its place, in dialogue with the mystery of an abandoned malformed root and waste foam blob. This chapter is framed by the ecological ideas that influence the chapter's heart, through the performance texts about objects. These performance texts with the root/blob are a defining moment of my thoughts and concerns about how we can become more attuned to the world through object play. My hope for this book is that it will encourage explorations of the object world through performance as a part of a cultural shift of seeing things as not in service to the human puppet 'master'.

I hope you enjoy the multilinear branches, ideas, stories and critical reflections within this book.

Notes

1. There is a great deal of educational puppetry in India with Contractor as a key figure in its history. Meher R. Contractor, *Creative Drama and Puppetry in Education* (NBT: India, 2001). A more recent appraisal of how puppetry works in rural communities in India is covered by Claudia Orenstein – C. Orenstein, 'Women in Indian Puppetry: Negotiating Traditional Roles and New Possibilities'. *Asian Theatre Journal* 32, no. 2 (2015): 493–517.
2. A fascinating study of the politics of messaging and propaganda using Wayang is found here: K. A. Nugroho and L. Sunarti,, 'The New Order Play: Wayang as a Medium for Development Messages, 1969–84', *Pertanika Journal of Social Sciences & Humanities* 27, no. 2 (2019): 2017–32.
3. Penny Francis has captured her ideas and thoughts about puppetry in this wide-ranging text – P. Francis, *Puppetry: A Reader in Theatre Practice* (Basingstoke: Palgrave, 2012).
4. More information about the company and history can be found in the website of Little Angel Theatre – https://www.littleangeltheatre.com/.
5. Documentation of these important symposia exploring Applied Puppetry can be found here – C. Astles, E. Fisher, Laura Purcell-G and P. Sextou, 'Broken Puppet Symposia', *Journal of Applied Arts and Health* 11, nos 1 & 2 (2020): 200–7.
6. An important international group who is developing the field of Applied Puppetry are the EDT Commission (Education, Development, Therapy) of Union Internationale de la Marionette (UNIMA) and information can be found here: https://www.unima.org/en/commission/education-development-and-therapy/#.U5bOK3J_tsE%20%20.
7. A puppeteer I discuss and who has developed a very clear system of puppet therapy is Karim Dakroub. Also the company Awesome Puppet Company https://www.awesome-puppets.com/ and the work of its founder Daniel Stolfi are examples of puppet therapy.
8. A detailed recent view of Coleridge's phrase now a common performance concept based on poetic faith is found in M. Tomko, 'Politics, Performance, and Coleridge's Suspension of Disbelief', *Victorian Studies* 49, no. 2 (2007): 241–9.
9. The trickster figure is a character that is found in many cultures as an entity who can shape-shift (Loki), cross boundaries and playfully disrupt life. They disobey normal rules and often have secret knowledge and a contact with the sacred. They inhabit a liminal space like puppets between myth and chaos and oftentimes the puppet-like trickster can give narratives and puppeteers a force through which to escape the quotidian rules and contextual power structures.

> However necessary, Trickster, that shifty, crafty archetypal symbol found across times and cultures is a particularly tricky concept to resolve. Archetypes are, by their nature, hard to define and relegate to fixed, static definitions. Trickster is all the more challenging to describe because it is the embodiment of contradictions. The Trickster archetype represents the dualities and polarities that directly confront our desire for clarity, certainty, and stability. Trickster is unpredictable and has a pluralistic, shape- shifting nature that defies rigid structure. It is a liminal, or transitional archetype associated with boundaries,

edges, and places of transition (Hyde, 1998). It serves as a balancing agent, an equalizing force that challenges us to grow, oft times employing discomfort to motivate the process along. (Azaria 2015: 30).

10. Information about the plight of artists in the Kathputli community can be found here in an article by Nahla Nainar: https://www.thehindu.com/society/pushed-out-of-kathputli-colony-its-magicians-puppeteers-and-acrobats-wait-endlessly-for-a-new-home/article34664575.ece. 'Pushed out of Kathputli Colony, its magicians, puppeteers and acrobats wait endlessly for a new home – Some have found new audiences and are teaching courses online with the help of student volunteers' (Nainar, 29 May 2021).
11. Good Chance Theatre Company details: https://www.goodchance.org.uk/.
12. The issues and challenges of this large-scale puppetry project crossing borders is captured in this article – Amelia Gentleman, '"People Felt Threatened Even by a Puppet Refugee": Little Amal's Epic Walk through Love and Fear', *The Guardian* (2021) https://www.theguardian.com/stage/2021/oct/18/threatened-puppet-refugee-little-amals- epic-walk.
13. The website of this French large-scale puppet company can be found here: https://www.royal-de-luxe.com/en/.
14. A study of people and their things in one street in London is captured in D. Miller, *The Comfort of Things* (Polity: London, 2008). Throughout his scholarship Miller presents human collections of objects as positive life affirming and identity forming acts

1

Objects speaking for themselves: Mapping the field of Applied Puppetry

Throughout this chapter I explore how artists and practitioners can rethink with objects and form a new paradigm of engaged practice called Applied Puppetry. This paradigm decentres the human within the complex terrain of objects and entities, exploring what objects are able to do within communities. The proposition is that by allowing objects to speak within practices, new dialogues and narratives are unlocked about experiences. To open this discussion, I use imaginative 'object speculations' and these texts are drawn from my experience of a research network event in Cape Town, South Africa, led by David Grant.[1] With reference to the wider global field of Applied Puppetry, this chapter explores how puppets are more than tools within practice when we use them in sensitive and even transgressive ways with groups. This chapter is a glimpse into the developing ecology of practices that constitutes Applied Puppetry. A guiding question in this chapter is, how do speculations about object agency provoke a new intersectional view of practice in communities when using applied approaches?

In 2017 I was part of the project Objects with Objectives led by David Grant from Queen's University, Belfast, in which puppetry and Applied Theatre was considered. This project was part of the UK Arts and Humanities Research Council's international research network. Grant is a great enabler of very important discussions and outputs about how objects are gaining significance in Applied Theatre within scholarly performance studies networks. What follows next are these reflections after the experience of the visit to Cape Town imagined through the speculative lens of some of the objects I met in that experience. These are presented as short responses, then developed afterwards in relation to the practices and some of the practitioners involved with these objects. This practice, of 'voicing objects', is a method through which to understand the practice of materialism and attunement to objects. It is also a twist on ethnographic responses highlighting, in particular, my position to the objects, and it is my personal selection of significant things that I focus my attention towards.

Shoe

There's a shoe at the side of the road. It never made its way out of the township and into the city. It sits there empty. Did the foot that once walked in that shoe make it into the city one foot shoeless? The roadside dust covers the empty shoe. A signpost of absence.

Brown Paper

You massage me with your hands into your body. Your sweat impregnates me. You transfer energy into my seemingly inert form. You attempt to animate me. My resistance frustrates you. How can you transfer your concept of breath into me? I have no body. I am brown paper. Scrunch me up and flatten me out. I then play at being a puppet that haunts you. My performance troubles you and your sense of you. Fold me away in a box. Your trace is left on me.[2]

A Cardboard Box

I am saying 'blah … blah … blah' over and over. I open my flap and oppress the human body that comes towards me as part of this drama exercise inspired by Augusto Boal. I am grotesque and totemic. You struggle to resist my presence. How can you get past me? How do you solve the problem of the oppressive giant puppet which is an assemblage of things? Can my puppet logic only be matched by more puppet logic?[3]

A Plastic Bag

Knot me and form me. Animate me. I am more alive than when you tore me from my brothers and sisters. I walk like a bird and I am balanced like a battery powered segue. You watch me with wonder. The puppeteer projects their thoughts and skills onto me until the performance is over. Then you can fill me with trash.[4]

A Feather Boer

I have visited more prisons than many criminals. I have caressed the necks of offenders (as they call them). I breakdown institutional spaces through my camp presence. Why do human bodies move differently when I am around your neck?[5]

A Resuscitation Doll

I have felt a thousand kisses. All of them are blowing life into my artificial chest. The alcohol wipes have bleached my mouth from when you sanitize me. I embody countless deaths and you can leave me here without empathy or love. Do you care for me? Can you nursemaid an object? Zip me up in a bag and call me 'Annie'.[6]

Broken Accordion Bellows

I was waiting to become the belly of a wolf. All the time I was broken inside the music shop. I was waiting for this moment. A breath of new life in this puppet parade.[7]

Elephant Puppet

My skin flaps in the wind so I don't blow over. I can feel this African wind blow right through me. How did I become part of something that brings this community together? I am an elephant but I am also a bridge in this community celebration.[8]

A Stone

I am a stone picked up in the Township. A witness to the street next to the community centre, post office and church. A hard cold reminder of remembered and forgotten days. You were meant to use me in a ritual about change as instructed by the young woman. Instead, you left before the ritual and took me away in your bag. What changed? I am still here. Is that not enough? I crossed the equator going north and you didn't know what to do with me. Put me amongst the pebbles on Southsea Beach in the UK.

Dompass

Taken out of the drawer in the Dompass centre in the township. A trace of trauma. A witness to history. Inside the pages of the dompass there is a passport-sized photograph with the face of a man. He blankly stares back. Do I sense a tear in your eyes? In this object, in this setting you're transfixed by a miniature artefact of historical tragedy. This man's stare confronts the inhuman racist processing of men's bodies. This object does not speak, it silently screams this history.

These creative fragments responding to objects are presented here as a way of glimpsing into the networking events in Cape Town in 2017. These fragments present the object as central to the experience of these recollections and practices. This foregrounding of the object or puppets' imagined experience is my reaction to the 'object turn' in theory and practice. One point I discussed as part of this networking project was that this form of materiality in Applied Theatre is an underdeveloped research area. This materiality is pronounced when objects are employed in practice in Applied Theatre, like the feather boa in prison theatre. The variety of this selection of objects and puppets from the networking event indicates the multifarious techniques being employed by practitioners. The other objects explored in the fragments above speak for themselves about how they are active participants in knowledge-making and how these objects change the subject in practice and experience as much as humans attempt to change them.

The idea for a research network about Applied Puppetry emerged from the 'Whose Voice Is It Anyway?' symposium at Queen's University, Belfast, in March 2012 (Grant 2020: 14). The origins of this project were born from artists and academics coming together with people whose lives had been affected by the Northern Ireland 'Troubles' considering the ethics and practices associated with retelling stories in a society coming out of conflict. The idea of the artist, as a kind of ventriloquist mediating the real-life stories of others, led to considering puppetry as a metaphor for applied drama, and there was discussion about the puppet as an effective distancing device, in the

Brechtian sense. The Objects with Objectives research network set out to investigate these propositions, and the initial findings of the Cape Town Symposium in May 2017 suggested that it may be more accurate to view the puppet in applied drama as a kind of conductor (in the sense that the term is used in Playback Theatre) – a means of transferring narrative energy.

One of the most profound experiences during the week in Cape Town was in the context of the Langa Township. In this example puppetry enabled dialogue facilitated by puppeteer Karen Torley. Torley of Banyan Theatre and her description of how her Granny puppet performed in the Langa Township with local children serves as an example of how puppets and objects change social relations.

Karen's story

During our visit to Langa Township I spent the afternoon with the local children. My puppet 'Granny' was the pull to get the children to engage with me as we danced to the music of a tin whistle and played. This broke the ice with the children, who had no problem joining in once I took Granny out of her bag. After showing the children how to work the puppet, I was amazed to witness Granny turn from Scottish/Irish into an African Granny through movement and dance. The children played with the puppet, using their imaginations, creating their own scenarios, and entertaining each other with her. She was passed around and disappeared for almost an hour with a child. If only she could talk!

I showed them how to make origami boats using paper leaflets the drama company had with them. We did magic tricks with an elastic band I found in my bag. The group of children grew and they were deeply engaged with both the materials I had brought, including Granny, and those we could find in the space.

At the end of the day a child came over and took my bag. He gently placed Granny inside, tucked her in, and zipped the bag. (Personal correspondence 2017)

Torley's approach as puppeteer, commissioned by a varied list of clients, is focused around the way that playing with objects and opening up possibilities for interaction with this play is a key aspect (Torley 2020: 149). She also emphasizes the need for belief in the autonomy of the puppet figure mixed with fun for the process of puppetry to work in communities (151). Her approach is later explored in this chapter in relation to animating medical mannequins. Next, I explore the practices connected to the object fragments above and my reflections that grew from the research networking in more depth, as a mapping of the field of Applied Puppetry.

Brechtian distance and metaxis in practice

In his research into Applied Puppetry Grant explores the idea of the puppet in relation to the idea of distancing or Brecht's v-effect and he found, through his interaction with puppeteers, that puppets actually act like bridges as well as distancing figures in practice. The puppet both oscillates from both distancing to connecting the participant. Grant sees Applied Puppetry as 'negotiating doubleness' in this process (2020: 16).

This process involves the separating of character from material mixed with the double coding of Boal's Metaxis between the social and the aesthetic. Grant sees this process thus:

> I like to think of applied drama as drama with an ulterior motive, in the sense that each performance seeks to serve an objective beyond the act of performing itself. When puppetry is introduced into this process, this becomes even more evident as the subject of the drama becomes literally separated from the performer. But the audience's 'double vision' allows it to fuse together the presence of the puppeteer(s) and the puppet, facilitating the experience of radical empathy and sympathetic presence. (Grant 2020: 27)

Grant's observations about the practice of Applied Puppetry root is within the genealogy of twentieth-century performance practices of Brecht, Meyerhold and Boal as a dialogical form able to facilitate narratives of witnessing and trauma for individuals and groups. For him there is great potential for the puppet not only as a political theatre method but also as a conduit for sensitive emotions or narratives in participants. His overall findings drawn from practice connected to the research in South Africa and Northern Ireland is that the Applied Theatre puppet enables groups and communities to explore 'vibrant materialism' (Grant 2020: 27) when using puppets in performance.

Medical mannequins as puppets and enablers of simulations

An unusual application of puppetry is in the work of Jennings, Tizzard-Kleister and Torley when working with nursing students, looking at simulated role play using medical mannequins. My experience of their workshops involved seeing a remarkable reinscribing of worn medical mannequins into the role of surrogate patients that then encouraged sensitive and empathic responses in the training of nurses. The mannequin/puppets in this practice remained mute and rather uncanny as animated figures helping to shape the response from the simulation. The mannequin figures in this practice of Jennings, Tizzard-Kleister and Torley were medical training figures, recognizably a plastic and latex approximation of a human figure, obviously animated by the clearly present puppeteer Torley.

Simulation using puppetry is a novel use of Applied Puppetry to develop responses in human participants. Jennings and Tizzard-Kleister emphasize the issue of care which has been an important theme for Applied Theatre (Thompson 2022) and is also important to Applied Puppetry. Looking at their practice with medical mannequins, I was struck with how care is imparted and it reminded me of the work of Eric Bass. The puppeteer Bass emphasizes this careful approach by the puppeteer as a 'nursemaid' supporting this imaginative space and appreciating the autonomous inner poetry of the puppet:

> As puppeteers, it is, surprisingly, not our job to impose our intent on the puppet. It is our job to discover what the puppet can do and what it seems to want to do. It has propensities. We want to find out what they are, and support them. We are, in this sense, less like tyrants, and more like nurses to these objects. How can we help them? They are built for a purpose. They seem to have destinies. We want to help them arrive at those destinies. (Bass 2014)

The issue of how the puppeteer coexists presented by Bass emphasizes the puppeteer as 'nursemaid' in the landscape of performance meaning. These problems of co-presence extend beyond the relationship between the object and the performer and into the relationships of other objects and bodies present in the space, especially in medical settings. The 'propensities' of the performing object as described by Bass as part of the inner language of the object is what the puppeteer often seeks in their craft. Through a practical workshop in 2015, *Living in the Puppet's World* with Eric Bass and Ines Zeller Bass, I experienced this development of an awareness of the object, exploring this notion of feeling through the puppet which was central to their approach to practice.[9] In Applied Puppetry, the facilitator is attempting to understand the propensities of all participants, whether they are objects or people through an application of care.

> In order to enable our medical mannequins to perform as patients, they need to be anthropomorphized, impersonating human norms by having a clear and believable 'character' and performing appropriate diegetic actions. In contrast to digital animation or literature, this live anthropomorphism emerges through puppetry, requiring direct human interaction, evoking a slew of consequences explored throughout literature on objects, things and materiality. (Jennings and Tizzard-Kleister 2020: 79)

In Jennings's and Tizzard-Kleister's project, with nursing students, the use of mannequins as puppetry provoked many unforeseen consequences that are compelling to witness as Applied Theatre. Issues of the agency of the anthropomorphized figures given character and life within this project suggests that paying attention to objects can develop better care and more resilient interactive responses in nurses. Jennings's and Tizzard-Kleister's research, with the skills of Torley as puppeteer, provide evidence of how puppetry can actually promote powerful feelings of empathy to 'artificial others' in practice. Torley in her practice as puppeteer imparts techniques and particularly the application of Breath, Belief, Focus and Touch (BBFT) (Torley 2020: 150) to impart in the puppet the ability to produce empathy in the nurse who is training. Tizzard-Kleister and Jennings draw on Deleuzian theory in their discussion of puppetry and nursing students in order to understand the issues of animating artificial bodies, with the interface between human and non-human. The provocation to apply the Deleurzian concept of the 'body without organs' to puppetry provides a rich source through which to theorize Applied Puppetry. These ideas make us reconsider agency and complex personhood and how they are connected inexorably with human or non-human rights.

This ongoing project indicates how adaptable puppetry can be in non-theatrical contexts. Animating already anthropomorphized medical mannequins appears to bring a whole new exciting and innovative quality to these objects. Tizzard-Kleister, Torley and Jennings explore how the performance of the mannequins enables participants in learning about the way people develop knowledge from performing objects. This is an example of how universities with practitioners can deploy interdisciplinary approaches that use puppetry to augment new ways of thinking and learning.

In my own university's simulation practice, I have come across other medical simulation mannequins that have hyperreal latex bodies. A very realistic puppet of a baby infant was part of a very intense training I collaboratively facilitated in 2021 with doctors and medics looking at a case of a child's death through neglect. This project was initiated by a colleague in forensics, John Fox, based on actual cases. The company Lifecast,[10] which was testing the baby mannequin as part of the training, allowed me to see more of their cast of hyperreal mannequins including an old woman. The level of detail in these figures was compelling, uncanny and in some ways alarming as a visceral experience encountering a realistic human artificial figure. As a puppeteer I explored the potential for animation with one of these mannequins but was somewhat disappointed in the wobble in its appendages of latex.

Using puppetry within medical research and training reminds me that there is a dark history of objects linked with other species, in medical research imparting new knowledge, sometimes with a lack of care or without any sympathy. The surrogate artificial mother figures were used to torture monkeys in the disturbing research of psychologist Harry Harlow through which he explored the concept of love and attachment (Blum 2002). In this example, other species (monkeys) and medical simulation puppets (the surrogate artificial monkey mother figures) helped humans understand more fully our concept of human love.[11]

Community spectacle and positive change

Care and sensitivity in response to materiality is an implicit part of the practice of Aja Marneweck, a South African puppeteer who has developed community puppetry in Townships like Barrydale, South Africa. Working in partnership with the world famous Handspring Puppet Theatre, Marneweck takes the techniques of intense manipulation and physical understanding of puppet figures into the community context in large-scale community events using truly remarkable giant-scale puppets. These figures use similar engineering and aesthetics of the famous horses in *War Horse*. Marneweck also makes work on a smaller scale using the everyday material of brown paper. In the workshop I was part of, we were asked to physically connect and meditate with the two-metre-long pieces of brown paper. This involved touching, crumpling, folding, moving and haptically understanding the brown paper. This brown paper was then manipulated as figures exploring the tensions of rasas influenced by yogic practice. By the end of the process with the brown paper these objects felt charged and imbued with an increased sense of presence. These figures were then mixed with more tangible puppets with sculpted heads, but still with the brown paper simple human body form. These figures have a powerful presence like the sculptural figures of Alberto Giacometti. The sensitive practice of Marneweck is taken into community settings in South Africa and this produces powerful effects.

> In the context of the Barrydale parade, it could be puppetry's ability to serve public enchantment and popular magico-aesthetics that have also assisted its agit-prop efficacy, revolutionary attributes and unique abilities to agitate the powers that be through metaphor and imagination. The capacity of puppetry and the dynamics generated between puppet, performer and audience, [organizational] partnerships and co-creative processes can generate creative 'ethics of mutuality' (Taylor 2018) in a socio-economic landscape [characterized] by both hope and hopelessness. (Marneweck 2020: 43)

The sensitive practice and care for the brown paper as a training technique is amplified in the large-scale community parades discussed in the above quote. Marneweck contributes a reflection on South African community puppetry by examining the Barrydale Giant Puppet Parade, an annual community puppetry event that began in 2010 in Barrydale, South Africa, as a collaboration between Handspring Trust for Puppetry Arts, the local organization Net vir Pret and other partners. Marneweck leads the development of what has become a major annual community event for residents of Barrydale that brings together sides of this racially and economically divided town. This practice involves the role of puppets in community reconciliation, situating the event within the wider context of radical aesthetic, political and cultural transformations drawing on theories of radical political performance. Marneweck argues that the annual Barrydale performance 'raises a complex ambiguity of form, meaning, politics and aesthetics around celebration and imagination amidst social realism and economic disparity' (Marneweck 2020: 35). Marneweck links puppetry's unique capacity to Jane Taylor's (2016) argument that magical thinking opens the possibility of a reciprocal sustainability. Donna Kouter (one of the key collaborators and artists in the project) reflects on community reconciliation and the particular abilities of puppets in storytelling to create a 'magical link' – which Kouter envisions as a 'golden thread' between puppeteer, puppet and spectator (Kouter in Marneweck 2020: 43). Kouter also reflects that puppets provide a 'whole experience' for participants as a vehicle for experiencing the non-human world (Kouter in Marneweck 2020). The large-scale events in Barrydale using the awe inspiring puppet styles of Handspring are a great example of how spectacles in communities can use performing objects to focus collective narratives, often around other species like giant elephants.

It is one of the distinguishing features of Handsprings practice that they explore interspecies interplay in their theatrical visions. This is also part of their important community work in Barrydale, which is not as celebrated or visible as the global phenomena of shows like *War Horse*. In a touring production of *Ubu and the Truth Commission* by Handspring and William Kentridge in London in 2015, I experienced how Handspring use the puppet as a powerful 'witness'. In relation to the traumatic violence of apartheid, the puppets in the *Ubu* production took on this role of 'witness puppets' telling verbatim stories of terror. Art theorist Jill Bennett explores how the puppet can be perceived in this way arguing that 'witness puppets' are effective in addressing trauma in her review of Handspring's *Ubu* (Bennett 2005: 119).

Puppetry and the body

Laura Purcell-Gates's development of ideas about embodiment, disability and affect are important reference points for the field of Applied Puppetry. In a collective review of the Broken Puppet series of symposia in collaboration with Persephone Sextou, Cariad Astles and Emma Fisher, they developed a 'manifesto' of important points raised through their scholarship.

1. Puppetry is inherently interdisciplinary and so can 'meet' any other discipline. Its power lies at the interdisciplinary intersection of psychology, sociology, pedagogy and the arts.
2. Applied Puppetry has the potential to use emergent technologies and robotics and work with the intersection between technology and health.
3. A puppet is not a puppet without its puppeteer – without a human being holding, caring and intending it; training in emotional skills is therefore important.
4. Applied Puppetry training has to include open-access workshops, but fundamental theoretical input is needed for rigour and understanding.
5. Several training options could be possible, such as short courses, more academic courses, training aimed at practising professionals, diploma, seminar and placement courses, postgraduate training. (Astles et al. 2020: 205)

These sets of demands for the field are encouraging and emphasize particular themes inherent around care, emotional awareness, the need for scholarship, interconnection with emergent technologies and the interdisciplinary potential of Applied Puppetry. One important aspect from Purcell-Gates practice and scholarship is the need to recognize the embodied and affective potential for puppetry especially in regard to bodies that are othered like disabled bodies (Purcell-Gates and Fisher 2017). With Fisher she suggests that the puppet offers a form of 'rupture' from which we can rethink our bodily ideas and experiences (2020: 363). Fisher's practice as puppeteer performs in this transgressive way, as we see in performance both her disabled body augmented with a bespoke device attached to one of her arms and further articulated through the puppet as an extension of her body. The puppet in this transgressive way does not mask disability but actually celebrates bodies and otherness.[12]

For Fisher and Purcell-Gates 'puppetry is a form with potential for multiple modes of intervention in both lived experience and cultural constructions of disability, linked through the puppet's status as constructed body' (2020: 371). In this practice the combination of an embodied approach combined with an appreciation of the material object seem key elements of Purcell-Gates important points about Applied Puppetry. It is more appropriate and enriching to work with puppets to open up spaces of rupture than to reinforce oppressive normative narratives about bodies. This approach also emphasizes the need to be focused and aware of the ecology and space within which practice is workshopped or performed within community groups. In our work together, Purcell-Gates and I emphasize the idea of Applied Puppetry as a way to negotiate between the spaces of communities, identities and transgressions (Purcell-Gates and Smith 2020). Puppets can be strange talismans that allow a way into community practices that can affect participants' identities (Goodlander 2020) and if used in a transformative way can offer potential alternative transgressions against contextual normative values. Conversely, if used like a weapon as explored in Chapter 4, the puppet is able to reinforce narratives used against specific identities, bodies and communities. Generally, Purcell-Gates encourages the intersectional way of mobilizing puppetry where the practitioner is cognizant and aware of issues of race, gender, disability and material ecology and then imparts this knowledge in the community.

The experiences and explorations of the Objects with Objectives network in Cape Town led many network members to a place of inquiry looking at objects in Applied Theatre, as we repeatedly noticed and commented upon the potential of puppets and performing objects to connect or mediate while foregrounding their materiality. This led to two key areas of further inquiry as we worked to locate theoretical models deepening our understanding of the mechanisms at play when puppets or performing objects function in these ways. Affect theory is one such model, with the potential to unpack the mediating function of puppets/performing objects through attention to the ways in which affect enacts connections between human/non-human matter, as in art critic and scholar Simon O'Sullivan's description of affect as 'the matter in us responding and resonating with the matter around us' (2001: 128).

One of the central points of inquiry that emerged from the network activities in Cape Town was a shift from a focus on puppets/performing objects as distancing devices – figures that allow people to examine stories and issues at a remove – to one on puppets/performing objects as mediators that function as bridges between people, stories, or even social issues. In this framing, affective resonances between types of matter are transformed and, in some cases, heightened through the participation or mediation of puppets/performing objects. The role of puppets/performing objects in the circulation of affect is one example of the ways in which a focus on puppet/object materiality, drawing on and contributing to emerging work in New Materialisms, allows for alternate engagements with multiple bodies. This has the potential to deepen our perception of what constitutes bodies, voices, subjectivity and agency. It can expand understanding of multiple and porous boundaries between types of bodies/objects/matter, with potentially transformative effects in Applied Theatre contexts. We moved forward with network activities and discussions traversing the fields of Applied Theatre and puppetry, but overall, in these practices we often let the objects speak this alternative discourse towards power.

From the impact of Object with Objectives and its events including symposia and workshops, a network developed beyond the group that travelled to South Africa. Next, I will explore some of these practices and scholarly activities as it helps to give a deeper sense of the field of Applied Puppetry globally. I am sure it will become clear these practices are diverse, working as they do with all kinds of groups of people. The work can be explored in more depth with reference to an edited edition of *The Applied Theatre Research*, edited by Laura Purcell-Gates and myself (2020).

Trauma workshops

Karim Dakroub produces a compelling case for the use of puppetry in relation to trauma in the context of the Syrian crisis, and his practice brings us close to the way that puppetry can provide a bridging mechanism for people suffering powerful bodily effects (Dakroub 2020). His work in traumatic ecologies crosses the terrain of how puppetry is used as a therapeutic and community-based method. The puppet's function in his work as an interface between the body and trauma is explored through scenes, events and a very clear structural model of intervention. His use of puppetry presents a format through which positive changes can affect the lives of displaced people. As much as a medium of expression, Dakroub's style of Applied Puppetry is a way through which people can heal embodied traumas like sleep deprivation. The puppet in this practice becomes a site for projected anxieties that can be explored in a distanced manner through developing new discoveries using performing objects for participants. Dakroub offers practical approaches towards the use of puppetry with vulnerable groups in the most volatile and precarious of contexts.

> Puppetry helps people to travel to the dramatic reality of nostalgia, then return safely to the daily reality of refugee status. The return is safe because this process sets clear and tangible boundaries between imagination and reality, between nostalgic yesterday and here and now. These limits can be controlled in space through the miniatures of people and places, and in time by setting the timing of the travel in the imagination by the puppet manipulation. What happens in the dramatic reality is a symbolic transformation process. (Dakroub 2020: 61)

One of the stages of the process of Dakroub's therapeutic puppetry is the improvisations using the uninvited guest puppet (Dakroub 2020: 62). This small, relatively characterless puppet enters the space of the group and immediately shifts the dynamics of the space towards exciting new potential events. This puppet embodies an innocence but also a vulnerability that reflects the experience of the fragile groups and individuals that Dakroub works with. The interventions of this practice adopt a psychosocial approach to building the reliance through this kind of puppetry, art-making and object play. Much of the play and creativity becomes symbolic narratives of trauma that are projected towards the objects. This type of practice is possible, only with a trained therapist aware of the development of safe practices. What Dakroub offers in his very useful article and powerful practice is a systematic and structured therapeutic process through which to adopt puppets with groups (Dakroub 2020).

Puppetry and migration

Husam Abed and Réka Deák from Dafa Puppet Theatre use puppetry with refugees and other communities, positioning puppetry and performing objects as sites of both expression and enactment of community and identity, allowing us to 'break out of time', reimagine histories and create new and layered memories for objects.

> Another great imaginary thing that the puppet can give is the idea of a substitute narrative – how to access and reimagine the history of a community. At the last party at Baqa'a refugee camp in September 2019, we did a site-specific performance about home demolition using objects. In this performance, there were Palestinian, Syrian and Sudanese refugees and one Indian participants. We used an object representing a Caterpillar bulldozer, which is used to destroy the houses, and we changed the meaning of this object. It is no longer a Caterpillar; it can be a shaving machine – it can be anything. And this rewrites the history, rewrites something that happened. (Abed and Deák 2020: 137–8)

Abed in his practice finds new metaphors and ways to rewrite narratives of the migrant identity with people who are caught within a displaced position. Puppetry opens up this space of new metaphors and stories in the context of this practice. As I discovered and is described in Chapter 6, puppetry can enable discussion and performances in the traumatic space of the border. Abed's practice and research is one of many explorations of how puppetry is reacting to the space of immigration like Erica Sapir's company Puppeteers Without Borders.[13]

Palliative puppets

Riku Laakkonen's puppetry practice has explored the vulnerable space of palliative care in Finland. His work is both poignant in its approach to the subject of end-of-life and sensitive in the way it facilitates delicate co-construction and interchange using object theatre. Laakkonen initiates with people in palliative care an exchange between himself and the patients using objects to elicit narratives or open up dialogues. This intimate practice includes a novel reworking of Augusto Boal's (2008) spect-actor into Laakkonen's idea of the spect-animator, a relationship elicited when he plays with objects and the patients in a one-to-one performance experience. This practice treads the path linking Applied Puppetry as therapy, respecting the agency of the participant.

> To make this form of art together with a palliative care patient also transforms the patient into a spect-animator of their own narratives. Every time I witness this, I recognize the possibility for the patient to be part of the moments of the expressive objects, but I also see their agency increase in these creative meetings. The interplay of the three elements – object animator, spect-animator and objects – creates a space to discuss, to remain in dialogue. Equality is a fluid state that, in practice, has to be produced or discovered over and over again.
>
> Throughout this approach towards a shared space, the facilitator must keep in mind their approach to otherness because this is the way to respect the other in intimate practices. (Laakkonen 2020: 115)

It cannot be underestimated how sensitive this practice with vulnerable individuals in palliative care has to be, to form these creative acts of storytelling with objects.

Laakkonen is an innovator of puppetry and object theatre for older people which proves that puppets can be accepted in this context with adults when sensitive facilitation is adopted. He enacts a deep respect for both the agency of the object and the participant. The adoption of Boal into this context, like Grant's evocation of metaxis, shows that puppetry can be adopted within the Theatre of the Oppressed form and Boal's therapy models (Boal 2008 and 2013). Even at the point of facing death, people can play with narratives and not be ruled by fate, adopting instead, dialogical Boalian transformative techniques. Objects in this practice are also part of the 'care' of the person facing the end of their life.

Shadow puppetry

Joanne Oussoren's practice explores how the use of shadow puppetry enhances the experience of older people in the care system of the Netherlands. This way of working is an effective way to open up new experiences for older people who are often isolated and vulnerable. Oussoren offers us some key points to consider in relation to using puppetry with this type of group in the community.

> Sometimes the caregivers attending comment that, for the first time in their lives, they see their loved ones engaged in activities like colouring a drawing. Often the nursing staff hear special memories and thoughts from their clients during these activities, which they never knew about before. In this process, a new way of looking at each other's personal memories develops itself, and opens the door to unusual conversations between participants. (Oussoren 2020: 146)

Her company Droomtheater[14] has developed new approaches to how to connect to local communities and they craft bespoke sets to be able to take puppetry outdoors including table top shadow puppetry inspired by traditional Chinese shadow puppet forms. This practice is a celebration of colour and like Handspring explores other species, when they make and perform exotic bird puppet characters. What is compelling about this practice is the way that it opens up new conversations amongst older people who can be isolated and lack cultural stimulation. Sometimes the wonder of Applied Puppetry is in these valuable conversations and dialogues as it stimulates and enables more than just the puppet performances.

Summary

A thread that runs throughout this chapter's exploration of the field of Applied Puppetry is the importance in sensitive facilitation and consummate people skills needed as part of a practice that is able to operate in specific communities or with individuals. It is intensely demanding for the practitioner, skilled in both understanding then listening to the needs and identities of people involved in these practices. Adding to this skill is the ability to listen intently to puppets and objects within this practice enabling their magic and wonder for groups. It is apparent that the practitioners highlighted in this chapter are skilled puppeteers, but this is secondary in value to the ability to facilitate participants in a mutual and equitable manner. All the practitioners here see the value in Applied Puppetry not as a secondary income but as a vocation that is separate from touring shows. This is a more positive picture than the one portrayed in the introduction where I described the individualism of the 1990s as identified and observed in the *On the Brink of Belonging* report about the situation in the UK (Allen and Shaw 1992).

Applied Puppetry, as this chapter indicates, is a well-established form within the umbrella of Applied Theatre practices. What is also encouraging and clear is that Applied Puppetry is a global practice mirroring its heritage in community events. It is also a practice that speaks to issues as part of globalization like migration and borders. Much of this book is an exploration of my own practice in Applied Puppetry, but I hope through this chapter to indicate that there is a plethora of work by committed artists and scholars globally. All of this practice aims to allow a space for people's narratives to emerge but it also is a space for objects to speak.

Notes

1. Objects with Objectives was funded by the AHRC. Useful resources including videos can be found here on Queen University Belfast website – https://mediasite.qub.ac.uk/Mediasite/Channel/objectswithobjectives/browse/null/title- az/null/0/null.
2. Brown paper as a material to explore technique was part of a workshop technique led by Sara Matchett of University of Cape Town and Aja Marneweck of Cape Town's Paper Body Collective, in which network participants and local puppeteers collaborated to locate rasas in puppets constructed from brown paper.
3. The cardboard box was part of an experiment in Forum Theatre using giant assemblages of objects representing oppression led by Dr Elliot Leffler of Reed College and Tamara Lynne, cultural worker, educator and artist. These puppets emerged from a provocation by Leffler and Lynne on the potential of puppets and objects to allow Forum participants to move beyond the neoliberal framing of oppression as grounded in individual choice, in order to enable engagement with material representations of systems of oppression.
4. The plastic bag puppet was improvised in a hotel bar for me and other members of the group by puppeteer David Morton from Australian puppet company Dead Puppet Society when he was demonstrating techniques of puppetry animation.
5. This object voice relates to Caoimhe McAvinchey's description of the feather boer as an example of how objects in Applied Theatre can develop in significance, in this example, in prison theatre. She reflected upon a feather boer that was a prop in women's prison theatre and how this prop activated the bodies of the women to be more animated, playful or even camp.
6. The example of the resuscitation doll animated is part of the research of Matthew Jennings and Karen Torley working with training nurses in patient care. This was a very interesting example of how puppetry can be applied to the context of medicine and nursing practice as a form of role-play simulation.

7. The reused accordion bellows are part of the street puppet 'wolves' performed by Mexican company LaLiga Teatro Elastico (laligateatro.com) and these puppets processed in Cape Town with groups of children following who had made their own puppets from waste materials. This is an example of how children's workshop puppets can be integrated into a larger-scale street procession with the company's more crafted puppets like the wolves.
8. The puppet voiced here is Handspring Theatre's stunning life-sized elephants used in the Barrydale Township festival in 2016 (discussed by Jane Taylor (2017: 29–31).
9. This workshop was at the Little Angel Theatre, London, UK on 8 February 2015. Eric Bass company Sandglass is a well-established puppet theatre company based in the United States. https://sandglasstheater.org/.
10. The commercial company Lifecast make simulation mannequins in a hyperrealist style. https://www.lifecastbodysim.com/.
11. D. Blum, , *Love at Goon Park: Harry Harlow and the Science of Affection* (London: Merloyd Lawrence Books, 2002). This text gives an account of how Harlow experimented on monkeys and effectively tortured them to explore psychological ideas about affection.
12. I have discussed the potential for puppetry to celebrate otherness and disabled bodies in a previous article about street puppetry with a group from a special school in Portsmouth. My account of using puppetry in this way can be found in M. Smith, 'The Sentient Spoon as Broken Puppet: Celebrating Otherness with Performing Objects'. *Journal of Applied Arts & Health* 11, nos 1–2 (2020): 49–58.
13. Link to website for Puppeteers without Borders: https://www.puppeteerswithoutborders.com/.
14. The extensive community puppetry of Dutch company Droomtheater can be looked at this website: droomtheater@online.nl.

2

Thinking with ecology: New paradigms in material performance

For theater to matter at all, we must think of it as an ecological actor, and cease producing work that privileges the metaphoric over the material to such an extent that the plight of the material gets lost in the spectacle itself. (Arons and May 2012: 6)

In this chapter I present a personal vision and theoretical approach to objects in performance, focusing on how current trends in philosophy have repositioned objects in relation to traditionally human-centred practices, like theatre. I explore the issues of materialism in performance combined with the crisis ecology of our current malaise, relating this to how we think *with* objects. Morton's rallying call of 'being ecological' (2018) I adopt as a point of departure for new practices that use puppetry and objects in practice, responsibly and in an intersectional manner. Additionally, I explore how employing these recent developments in philosophy informs a new consideration of objects through a process of valorizing objects as participants in performance. This revisioning is a perspective about how practice functions between objects and subjectivities.

Thinking *through* or *with* performing objects and puppetry

Let's venture…that performance can include and recontextualise things unexpectedly drawn out of their customary milieu: displacements of found and fabricated in illogical ordering. With excessive repetitions, subversive of generic codes and unconventional animations. (Pearson in Bleeker et al. 2019: 119)

The methodology in this book is one of approaching the object by both listening and feeling, haptically speculating about the propensities of things. This means understanding the context around objects allowing us to rethink the object as a theatrical thing. This is an active pursuit that involves experiencing and embodying the elements of the object that are available to apprehend, then attempting to understand its presence. This type of method is part of many disciplines including archaeology and is also found in performance cultures beyond puppetry. Mike Pearson, the authority of site-specific and experimental performance, vibrantly describes in the above quote creative approaches in how to think *through* things in performance. His manifesto, of sorts, offers ways of approaching thingness in practice.

> Let's conjecture … that, after philosopher Bruno Latour, things - non-human objects and environmental effects - have *agency*, serving as actants, sources of activity; that they possess distinct powers and capacities, such as effectivity, efficacy, volition, causality; that they can do things, make a difference, alter the course of events. (Pearson in Bleeker et al. 2019: 121–2)

This position and practice, suggested by Pearson, could be considered as a way of thinking *through* things by cathexis, towards the thing, through its presences and 'body'. The possibility of this process, of thinking *through* things, is attempted through lengthy experience of materials shaping our thinking, like for example when the sculptor David Nash 'thinks wood' in his practice (Thornton 2019). If I suppose that I am 'thinking through' the puppet, I am positioning my nervous system and thinking body as extended beyond my skin. The puppet becomes some form of prosthesis.[1] This seems to happen in practice, but when the puppet is left alone not connected by the human operator it still has presence and an uncanny life independent of the puppeteer. When I pontificate about the puppet, this thinking suggests an 'other' operating independently, not imitating my life nor just as an extension of my body. Object others enable me to imagine thinking like a puppet but also to rethink my position on objects in general.

Adrian Kohler uses the notion of 'thinking through' when considering his skills as puppeteer and joint artistic director of Handspring Theatre. This thinking becomes apparent for the audience through a very intense development of the use of movement, stillness and the emphasis on the breath (Kohler 2009: 140). This technique became globally celebrated through the accomplishment and embodied skills of puppeteers in *War Horse*. Transference of breath is a key technique of this puppetry. Chronicler of Handspring Puppet Theatre and puppet expert Jane Taylor suggests that this process could be one of prosopopoeia.

> Prosopopoeia is generally conceived of as a rhetorical device through which the speaker projects herself into the being of a second person or thing, in order to communicate obliquely, to a third term. The puppet, which can be anything from a sock to a bundle of sticks and cloth, in some ways is akin to the prop but rather radically veers toward personhood, becoming a materialization of the rhetorical device, prosopopoeia. It thus provides an object-based site for the projection from a speaking subject. The puppet is that other being or thing onto which a speaking/thinking being is projected. Yet the puppet is a particular kind of illusionist, wedded to maintaining the fiction of its autonomy. A puppet would rather die than admit that it is not alive. (Taylor in Posner, Orenstein and Bell 2014: 231)

Taylor here is describing a process originating in the human subject projected towards or into the puppet. I would add to this and suggest the puppet has its own rhetoric to speak as an object other; it is just that we don't always listen intensely enough to what it wants to say. In my practice I suggest that the puppet veers towards puppethood and not just a human-like estimation of sentience or presence.

Part of the endless beauty of the puppet is its puppet-like falseness as a complex artificial object framed and reframed by performance. In workshops I train students by transferring their breath into a small piece of muslin material, giving to that object the very convincing subtle appearance of life. Even simpler, when just holding a puppet figure the interconnected blending of the human performer and the puppet means that the puppet figure has a new energy or presence. These techniques are rather convincing 'tricks' through which to emulate life in the puppet rendering the puppet figure through physiological emphasis but not a cognitive transference. So here I am calling into question the idea of thinking *through* the puppet or object as a way of categorizing practice in relation to ecological ethics. Is it more reasonable to say we are 'thinking with' the puppet in performance and human spaces of culture?

Ecological positions

Baz Kershaw looks at the paradoxes when we consider the possibility of an ecological performance culture. The issues of the way that performance involves both materiality and the spectacle are intertwined in this problematic space of performance.[2] Kershaw presents that there is a possibility in companies like WSI and others committed to ecologically creating art, to form spaces in which people are involved in a new type of cultural exchange; 'participation must be of kinds that are continually renewed through humans courting, as it were, the non-human "other" in themselves and others' (2007: 238). This is a responsive, responsible and reflexive participation 'courting' with the non-human and problematic ideas of 'nature' and performance. There is the possibility in this space for spectacles that deconstruct and challenge contempt and curiosity of the non-human other, a recognizing of the capacities of those things anew (2007: 238). Within this frame of ecological performance Kershaw continually reminds us that we cannot shake off the ephemerality and materiality of theatre which presents an important paradox for him. This combination haunts all dramatic performances for Kershaw (2007: 41).

Later in this book I look in depth at a performance where I enacted Kershaw's idea of 'courting' with my root performance piece. In many ways he inspired my confidence to renew my research into puppetry using the frame of ecologically thinking and being. The ephemeral nature of performance was also part of the methodological approach of Marlsite projects (Chapter 5) in which the performances were uniquely contained within a one-week residency, never to be repeated. For me, this use of the ephemeral was also a way out of the established systems for making theatre in British culture. This is a theatre that is not built to last, apart from some remains, which is then partially recycled into another unique spectacle.

Kershaw's groundbreaking contribution as well as being critical offers a hopeful landscape to explore ecological 'sane' practices in which we understand we are intertwined with 'the Earth's environment, acting *in* it rather than *on* it' (2007: 318). Similarly, Arons and May, when introducing the idea of ecological performance, point towards the paradoxical issues involved when meshing materialism and human cultures:

> A fundamental transformation of values with regard to the more-than-human world, one that includes a full acceptance of our enmeshment in the larger ecological community, is long overdue. But here we come to a fundamental paradox: one of the key means of shaping and transforming human attitudes and values is the arts, but the arts (in the West, at least, …) have traditionally been conceived as the activity that most divides humans from 'nature'. Moreover, theater in its present form – with its emphasis on human conflict in the context of human institutions – occupies a space at the far end of that spectrum. (Arons and May 2012: 1)

Another eco-drama scholar Lisa Woynarski emphasizes the need to think ecologically in an intersectional way when considering what she describes as ecodramaturgies (2020). When we consider performing objects within their milieu they are interconnected with intersectional issues around humans and more-than-human concerns. Theatre and performance amplify or dampen this emphasis in practice through either highlighting or ignoring the relevance of objects to intersectional politics. Woynarski calls this interplay 'bioperformativity in practice' and as a process through which 'bioperformativity counters [this] anthropocentrism by understanding the biological/material and the performance effects of things' (2020: 71). Her concept of bioperformativity seems apposite in relation to puppetry as she further defines this new process for performance; 'Bioperformativity is intended to critique and interpret the way the human and more-than human are categorized and constituted in performance, acknowledging more-than-human performances through drawing attention to embodied ecological relationships, emotions, ideologies and political effects' (2020: 72). Adding to this I would argue that the puppet has no place within binaries or boundaries and often slips between, in an interstitial space problematizing categories of bios, matter and animacy. Woynarski looks at the performativity of trees as having 'agency' in their performances by referencing artist Beuys's *7000 oaks* (2020: 75–6), a sculptural eco-installation which involves planting oaks next to ancient stone. Woynarski presents this possibility for non-anthropocentric performance culture towards the messy organic landscape shifting the focus (2020: 77). Often made of wood, the puppet has a similar non-human possible agentic potential, like the tree, as described by Woynarski, in its vibrant performativity.

In practice I often ponder about the spaces where the puppet and I begin and end and find this mysterious space does not easily exist through experience. I am enmeshed and intertwined with the puppet in performance, exchanging atoms through skin to wood or other materials. Parts of puppets are left on me and me on them in a bodily collaboration that reinscribes us in a complex palimpsestuous mixing. A splinter, a sweat stain or a layer of skin, write this set of traces. Some puppeteers and performing artists exploit this practice explicitly like in Duda Paiva's *Bastard!* (2011) in which he creates an existential world onstage where foam puppets and his body intermingle.

Duda Paiva's puppet and dance performance is described by critic Oriane Maubert as 'a shared body, and shared movement, reinforced by the concept of intercorporeality' (2019: 44). Scholar Lynne Kent calls the work of Duda Paiva and the practice a type of 'mesh-theatre' drawing from the use of mesh to describe ecologies from eco philosopher Morton (Kent 2022: 7). This intercorporeality is part of all puppetry in different degrees from the puppet operated on long strings above the stage to the performing object intimately enmeshed with the human in the work of Duda Paiva.

Similarly, the human body is mixed with the non-human in Jeong Geum-Hyung *7 Ways* (2017)[3] in which she erotically and intimately moves with DIY objects, masks and hoovers. 'The objects determine how the performance turns out' she is cited as saying in an article by Lee Woo-young (2016) in the Korea Herald.

In my own practice this intermingling feels functional, bringing life to the puppet and also generating a powerful bodily experience. When teaching puppetry with students the emphasis on the first touch with the puppet or performing object is acknowledged and given a particular intense focus. In this moment and experience the performer is exploring the contour of the object viscerally through touch, trying to understand the possible propensity of that thing in performance. In this sense the first touch is a charged act and ultimately an exchange between the human with the object actant. This intermingling can be further understood as an ecological exploration within the interstitial spaces of networks and things.

Morton asks us where we draw the line in this mesh of matter and experience (2018: 87) when they suggest that we are always already ecological, whether we like it or not. This meshing is connected to another key concept of Morton's which is attunement to things, a word used throughout this book, as it so clearly describes an ecological positioning, but also describes the practice of the puppeteer. In Applied Puppetry this attunement is meshed or mashed up for the practitioner, as the elements of facilitation, ethics and participation all form part of this network of forces. For Morton attunement to things feels like veering around the thing that is considered and explored, as they suggest that objects cannot be known in their totality (2018: 139). For example, science cannot fully know a thing as there is no interpretation or phenomenological understanding, so the process of attunement is necessary to explore that thing further. This new form of 'uncanny intimacy' with things involves for Morton a newfound kinship with the material world and objects (2018: 145). The experience of puppetry following the concept of attunement is intentionally intertwined, as a practice between embodiment, materials and imagination. Objects have a timbre (2018: 144) that we meet, explore and intermesh with in performance allowing us to understand these mysterious qualities better. Puppets can be 'research buddies' who join us in exploring the taken for granted world of OOO where objects are like the allusive essence of perfume. Morton argues that ecological aesthetics is formed through our interaction with the material world beyond our human prejudices and that we can see objects as more than just 'objectified, static, manipulable lumps of pure extension decorated with accidents' (2018: 149).

Morton warns that in our attempts to understand and interpret things we run up against a problem, because 'the execution of a thing is not the thing' (2018: 26). The experience of objects as a complete whole is closed off to us and we study them from the outside, which for Morton is not necessarily a problem (2018: 32). Morton's combination of OOO and ecology are so enriching as they bring into question our attitudes to ecological facts and our relationship to objects. For ecological thinking Morton suggests 'OOO tries to let go of anthropocentrism, which holds that humans are the centre of meaning and power (and so on). This might be useful in an era during which we need to at least recognize the importance of other lifeforms' (2018: 34). This is the opportunity that a more 'object-oriented theatre' offers, found through the practices I explore in this book. Theatre study and practice is enriched through this alternative attuned viewpoint. Drawing from Heidegger, like fellow OOO philosopher Harman, Morton reminds us that things aren't directly present to us until they malfunction (2018: 45) and that the terrain of attuning and understanding things is a bumpy landscape. In this way for Morton 'things are unspeakable' (2018: 47) – a point I discovered when exploring objects in applied performances. Objects in the OOO sense can be anything at all and for Morton have the potential to be 'radically mysterious' as well as open for us to interpret (2018: 48). We have to be careful to consider that it is the normalization of things that has led to great distortions and we should look towards the uncanny in objects and things to think beyond the anthropocene (2018: 49). This is a reason why the puppet is a good companion in the journey towards the mystery of things, as they inhabit the uncanny world betwixt and between entities so well. In their company other objects reveal themselves in performance and imagination. There is also the possibility that puppets, in the way they inhabit what roboticist Masahiro Mori calls the 'uncanny valley' (Mori, MacDorman and Kageki 2012), offer a research companion in the futurescapes relating to non-human robot humanoid others and autonomous technologies.[4]

Even though all art (whether popular or high art) could be considered ecological, some art talks through and speaks about its substances and works towards including its environments as subject and narrative and Morton situates this practice as ecological art (2018: 52). The investigation of Morton's dark ecology is to understand that 'we and other life forms exist in an ambiguous space in between rigid categories' (2018: 56), and throughout my writing I present how puppets can play with us, navigating and meandering around this space of blurred categories. This space involves what Morton valorizes as 'a realm of unspeakable, nonhuman beauty not confined to normative anthropocentric parameters' (2018: 60). Throughout Morton's philosophy there is a dance, when looking at objects, between seeing them as things in themselves and as part of the entanglement and mesh. This is part of the dance with intersectional awareness that needs recognition and listening to, through highly attuned practice, encompassing both human and non-human elements. Morton posits that through solidarity with non-human entities there is the opportunity for an art that is ecologically explicit as it brings this 'solidarity with the nonhuman to the foreground' (2018: 121). Nonviolent solidarity with the non-human can be a basis for democracy as well as an arts practice. After thirty years of working with puppets I have seen the possibility for solidarity and enhanced relationships with performing objects in theatres or in communities. Part of understanding the network is to listen to the way that art is doing things to us more than as just a representation and as Morton puts it, recognize that the art 'might have designs on you' in this entangled loop (2018: 132).

For Morton the experience of attunement involves 'charisma', as well as 'veering' where the experience of art can be both demonic and magical (2018: 157). This set of affects on the human is part of the experience of puppetry and often I have had discussions with groups and individuals about the 'magic' of puppets. I have also met some very charismatic puppets over the years. Early in my career I was suspicious of the word 'magic' as shorthand for 'I don't really know', but now it seems an appropriate term for the interaction with the incommensurable being of the puppet. Ways of investigating the puppet involve a movement around or in between the categories of known/unknown, seeable/unseeable and normal/paranormal. Morton makes a pop cultural reference suggesting that everything is like Dr Who's TARDIS when we are in the act of attunement. The humility of exploring this mysterious space for Morton is one of possible transcendence for the individual; 'the self transcending subject is underwritten by a mysterious power emanating from the non-subject (the 'object')' (2018: 162). In this process we start to appreciate what things are doing to us and not what we apparently think we are doing to them. Eventually the puppets and performing objects shape my being and allow me to imagine thinking like a puppet. I cannot project my thoughts into the materiality of the puppet in a transference as the wood, glue and cotton are already resisting and affecting me. This is where the magic of puppetry is to be discovered – through the ability to listen and react to what the puppet wants to say in both performance and experience. Purcell-Gates, in her process when training puppeteers with small figures made from scrap newspaper, enables the puppeteers to discover 'what the puppet wants to do' in workshop practice. This practice is both deeply focused and liberatory for the performer.[5]

Morton's philosophy is much more expansive than just as a way to invigorate the process of puppetry through attunement to objects and is intended here to offer an idea of care to the ecology in general. This care is towards the ageless problem of human interactions and the eventual crisis which is the anthropocene. Morton is suggesting a 'playful seriousness' with care towards object others that could then become a collective consciousness beyond anthropocentrism and the ecology of the planet as a service industry (2018: 186).

A way into this consciousness could be through an emptying of the self, or Kenosis, as Morton posits. Kenosis is part of the practical warming up in puppetry before working with the puppet as a performer. This then shifts towards the intense focus of cathexis towards the performing object, which is part of how the magic of puppetry is realized.

This is much more apparent in contemporary styles of puppetry where we see both the puppet and puppeteer in clear view. So, puppetry as an ecological practice echoes this approach to materiality but more importantly the ethos of Morton and of 'being ecological'. We can pull ourselves out of the 'misanthropocentrism' that Morton frames as part of religious heritages around ecologies (2018: 203) in this enmeshed process and mentality. Morton continually reminds us that we are already ecological and that there is an opportunity to become more sensitively attuned fully embodied beings by increasing our awareness of our kinship with object others. I use puppetry as a practice to help me understand this positionality and embodiment.

Animated cancer experiences

Morton suggests that cancer cells are more alive than we credit and this is why they kill us (2018: 155). In 2006, as part of an Arts Council–funded research and development project, I explored my own experience (when I was a young man) of cancer cells, specifically testicular cancer. In collaboration with Paul Rogers and Gillian Knox we made a puppet show about my experiences, as a form of dark cabaret, at Liverpool Institute of Performing Arts. The performance began with a shadow puppet show, representing my insides, replicating the scans of my abdomen, that I repeatedly undertook before and after treatment. Inside my belly, we presented on the shadow screen a magic realist world of sea life and other absurd shadow puppets. I then introduced the unfeasibly large testicle puppet that had been removed, which I called Frank. This puppet of a testicle sang songs in a Country and Western style and spoke with a New York accent (I found the tumour in New York). The puppet was a large ball of scrap foam (upcycled from an old sofa) with eyes, teeth and an arm formed in a cubist style at unusual angles around the puppet. The intention for this performance was to bring awareness to audiences about testicular cancer, but the piece was received by some guests in the audience try-out as 'too weird'. Feedback after the showcase suggested the show would struggle to reach out as an educational performance. From a more personal reflective perspective, this experiment explored how I attuned to something as unknowable as a tumour in a puppetry show. I veered around the experience of cancer and its trauma using objects to help me understand my own being and the way my embodied experience mutated in my earlier life with cancer. Recycled foam, fashioned into a tumorous testicle, helped me to do this. This process did not add anything to scientific knowledge and I did not find a cure for cancer, though it did unpack the way that medical cultures often 'make strange' illnesses for the patient. I discovered through this bizarre performance a new kinship with my removed testicle, which is a more positive mindset than the contextual messages about cancer I often saw in wider popular culture. This research and development of a performance gave me a way to think beyond the disempowering medical metaphors that Susan Sontag so eloquently attacks in *Illness and Its Metaphors* (2009). By a strange attunement to my removed testicle, I was able to understand my experience of illness and create my own playful metaphorical world to understand cancer. The testicle puppet had a strange agency and spoke to the even more strange agency that was afforded to my own cancer cells in this dramaturgy. It is also an ecological story, as it points towards our limits of knowledge of objects like cells, which make up our anatomy within the wider culture of the medical infrastructure and the world that it inhabits. Attuning to these cells, by using puppetry and not fighting the material conditions of my own body, is part of how I healed from this traumatic episode in my life.

Taking the notion of agency further in regard to objects in an ecology, this materialism rubs up against some problems when puppetry is considered. How can a puppet consent to being a performer or how can any object consent to being contextualized within a performative framework? A colleague of mine, Nik Wakefield, looked at the idea of consent in relation to the classical sculptural figures of Apollo and

Daphne as part of a research-sharing event. In the story Daphne's refusal to consent ends in her transformation into a tree. To avoid violence, she becomes an object. Is the blank stare of the puppet a refusal to consent to being part of the meaning-making spaces of theatre? Is an ecological practice one in which we leave things alone? Most of the material life of a puppet is spent not performing and for some historical puppets in museum collections they are no longer performed with or played with. These exhibited puppets could be within a different matrix of performance when they are not performing.

Piano-part puppets

Recently in 2022 I made twenty puppet figures from upcycled piano parts. I found the broken piano on the street and during lockdown made a prototype puppet without a show or performance in mind. The twenty puppets were then made for an exhibition in 2022 at Treadgolds, Portsmouth, an old Victorian forge. I made duplicate puppets from the piano parts, with wire hands and the piano hammers as legs. These small puppets inhabited the space of the exhibition hanging relatively motionless as marionettes. This process of making puppets, not for performance, but purely for exhibition, was a new point of departure for my making. They still clearly represented a puppet figure, but did they appear to have more agency because I did not animate them? They worked within a different aesthetic realm, being produced not for the usual purpose I experience; of performing in a show. They also seemed to hang in harmony within the ecology of Treadgolds, a historical Portsmouth building. These puppets had had a performative presence and maybe more agency because I left them alone to hang around. Puppets trouble the idea of apparent, implied or imagined agency through both their performance in a mobile mode and also in their still inanimate state. This is part of their aesthetic appeal for famous critical thinkers like Roland Barthes who considered the Japanese Bunraku or Ningyo Joruri puppet form.

> In dealing with a fundamental antimony, the animate/inanimate, Bunraku muddies it, makes it fade, without benefitting either of its terms. In the West, the puppet (Punch, for example) is expected to offer the actor the mirror of his contrary; it animates the inanimate, but the better to show its degradation, the indignity of its inertia. A caricature of 'life,' the puppet thereby affirms life's moral limits and presumes to confine beauty, truth, and emotion in the living body of the actor, who, however, makes of this body a lie. Bunraku, though, does not put its own stamp on the actor, it gets rid of him for us. How? Through a certain conception of the human body, which inanimate matter rules in Bunraku with infinitely more rigor and trembling than the animate body (endowed with a 'soul'). The Western (naturalistic) actor is never beautiful: his body would be of a physiological, not plastic, essence. He is a collection of organs, a musculature of passions, whose every spring (voice, facial expressions, gestures) is subjected to a sort of gymnastic exercise. But by an absolutely bourgeois reversal, although the actor's body is constructed according to a division of passional elements, it

borrows from physiology the alibi of an organic unity, that of 'life'; it is the actor who is a puppet here. (Barthes 1971: 78)

The Japanese puppet form of Bunraku gave Barthes the semiotician the opportunity to have an example that countered Western aesthetics which he wished to critique. The Ningyo Joruri form in which sign systems are separate; with storyteller, musician and puppet spectacle inhabiting separate spaces, is idealized in Barthes's assessment, but it is also partially viewed, because he is so interested in binaries. This means he misses the slippy materialism of puppetry and its place in the uncanny valley where it disrupts categories. He also avoids the important spiritualism and animism within Bunraku/Ningyo Joruri which is part and parcel of this beautiful art form. Part of the mesmerizing technique of traditional Bunraku is the way the puppeteer appears to think and move through the puppet figure and to some degree understand the potential animacy of the object. So Bunraku/Ningyo Joruri for Barthes is a handy exotic form through which a semiotic lesson in language is delivered. He misses the attunement the puppeteers learn after many years of practice and craftsmanship. Barthes projects onto the Bunraku/Ningyo Joruri, a European logocentric set of semiotic points that allow him to critique culture. His view essentializes this art form and offers a partial view that ignores the ecology of the practice. As puppet authority Jeremy Bidgood suggests, 'Barthes is more interested in using the Bunraku Theatre as a springboard for his own theorising than discussing Ningyo Joruri's particularities on their own terms. He is frequently derogatory about aspects of the performance that he finds hard to stomach' (2014: 176). In this way Barthes makes very interesting points about the sign systems of how performance can be understood, but very little about the ecology of the Bunraku/Ningyo Joruri theatre.[6] Barthes in his important historical essay, which was part of the Western fascination with Bunraku, is neither thinking through or thinking with the puppet figures that provoke such fascination in Western eyes. This process is a projecting of ideas onto the practice.

Thinking with

Sociologist Sophie Woodward presents a very clear method and approach in how to research material cultures in relationship to the object. She cautions against projecting ideas and meanings onto objects; 'we cannot just impose meanings onto things, as they are not passive but instead are "vibrant" (Bennett: 2009) and may resist, surprise, challenge or excite us' (Woodward 2020: 1). The processes that Woodward describes in her book *Material Methods* provoke the researcher to accept the entanglement with the object world and understand the way that objects, when resisting, can affect us in our journeys to produce meanings. Object beings are part of the social world of relations and we have to adopt a creative and integrated approach to working through these cultural spaces (2020: 5). Her use of 'thinking with' the object as participant or maybe research collaborator indicates a reaction to the 'object turn' in ontological terms and as a social theorist. For Woodward, a key issue is how you orient yourself to things in research terms (2020: 12). If you are particularly attuned to the object then you could both creatively and practically feel you are thinking *with* that object. This approach seems to be in some kind of opposition to the idea of 'thinking through' the object in practice and research.

Hours of training as puppeteer were given over to focusing my being, as though I was pushing my attention through the puppet, as a surrogate, in my performance. I have spent hours looking at the back of the head of puppets projecting my thoughts towards the materiality of the thing in front of me. It is the basis of puppetry training to use your peripheral vision to be able to keep the focus on the back of the head of the puppet and understand where the puppet's 'look' is pointing, so an audience can believe or 'suspend their disbelief' because of this entanglement of the puppeteer and puppet. It is a technique that I have now developed as part of my muscle memory, like a musician in regard to their instrument. I also imagine the inner life and poetry of the puppet, as I approximate this 'apparent' thinking through.

At this later stage in my career this 'thinking through' method seems inappropriate to approaching the performing object or as a model for a relationship. Thinking through is as inappropriate as if I said that I 'think through' human participants in my Applied Theatre practice. As though participants are a vessel through which, as a 'desiring machine', I project my being, not just onto them, but through them. The puppet, like the person, resists this attitude to practice, as this idea of 'thinking through' is impossible. When I am manipulating a puppet, it is not passive, as it resists my attempts to understand its being, as I deal with its surfaces as an object. The puppet consistently challenges me to adapt my position and preferences for ideas in relation to its blank stare combined with its beautiful stillness. When I allow myself to playfully engage with the puppets' position within the entanglement of the social and the material, it takes me on a surprising journey as a fellow traveller. This is when I am 'thinking with' the puppet as part of performance research.

The apparent autonomy we ascribe to things like objects is an issue when we think that a puppet can, or cannot, resist both our gaze and our manipulation. Who is doing the controlling in this relationship? In this strange interstitial space these object beings can look more at home when they are still, away from human touch. 'Thinking with' seems the appropriate position to adopt, when exploring the relational problems that puppets create for puppeteers and researchers of performance in these interstitial spaces. It seems ethical to problematize the notion of attempts to manipulate the puppet and, instead, think about what it does to us. Another approach is to give the puppet object space like a thing with autonomy in its own ecological domain. Is it a cruelty to use the puppet as a metaphor, within a human-centred meaning-making space, when there's so much more potential for these objects? This question arises when puppets or performing objects are considered as intermeshing with our ethical ponderings and ecologies of practice. These knotty thought experiments are brought to my attention by my faithful companion, collaborator and researcher Humphrey, the puppet. He has followed me around the world to conferences, events about puppetry and as part of Applied Theatre. As well as being highly illuminating in presentations, he now openly challenges audiences to think with him about puppetry. His effect on me is profound, as he not only gives me the opportunity to speak about puppetry but also gives me the confidence to speak. His presence in my hands, or sitting at my side, allows a space for this vocality to be made through both of our bodies.

Humphrey's monologue (from *How to Explain Immigration Detention to a Puppet Goat*, 2017)

HUMPHREY

I resist your attempts to define me. I contradict knowledge formed about me. I stare blankly back at you, knowing you do not fully understand me. I am material, I am metaphor. I am Humphrey. I confound your attempts to rationalize my existence. I laugh at your meagre language that confuses the experience of me…

    I can help you if you like. Looking at me you can begin to understand what it is to be human, though you will never understand how it feels to be a puppet. My otherness is uncanny and playful. Welcome to my world.

    I hold out my hands to you. My artificial hands. I feel the hand of the puppeteer inside my body. I feel the puppeteers hand touch and move my artificial hand. I am animated by the puppeteer and given the appearance of an autonomous object. Your active gaze animates my presence and I seemingly come to life. Try and make this process work with a human being and not a puppet and it is impossible. I remind you of how complicated it is to relate to each other. I am an enigmatic problem for you to solve. I welcome you through my artificial body tainted by the sweat and skin of my puppeteer's hands and through my body of sponge paper, cloth and polystyrene and two black beads for eyes.

[*Singing in the style of the blues*]
    Two black beads for eyes
    Two black beads for eyes
    I can see you sitting there
With two black beads for eyes[7]

Humphrey is crafted from polystyrene; scraped, sculpted and sanded into a head with a foam and leather body with feet weighted with lead to aid tension through movement, with a skin made from brown parcel paper (influenced by Polish puppet theatre styles), with cardboard hands and with two black beads for eyes. He is thirty-five centimetres in height and is lightweight, using a style of making influenced by Lyndie Wright at the Little Angel Theatre[8] (the style is called table top puppetry). He is directly manipulated with a rod inside his back to operate the head, and the other appendages are directly moved by the puppeteer's hands. He is named Humphrey after the artist Humphrey Jennings who inspired the performance. He was constructed for *Pandaemonium* (1996) by Jeff Young, a theatrical adaptation of a book by the same name by Jennings. In this performance Humphrey the puppet appears as a human-scale puppet which is his double. The big Humphrey lies on the earth (represented by old sheets on the floor which then splits apart) and he is reborn as the smaller-scale version. The smaller Humphrey then travels through the landscape of the Industrial Revolution growing out of the ground, through the old sheets. *Pandaemonium* was a small-scale touring production in the 1990s when in British theatre culture puppetry was a rather marginal form. After this first show, Humphrey was then a street performer in festivals across the northwest of England where he would climb out of a suitcase and draw really bad portraits of anyone who would sit for him. He even won a prize at one of these festivals. The manipulation of his body is always obvious, with me towering over his form, but his unique charm is obvious and inviting to audiences of all ages. One woman in Rochdale commented to me that she was impressed with the trickery of the moving 'little man'. He was also the main performer in *ShedHead* 1999 as part of a WSI creative collaborators experiment. He has also more recently spent a lot of his time travelling and teaching humans about what it is like to be a puppet at international symposia and conferences.

Humphrey as a companion is shoulder to shoulder with me in my journey through the indeterminate spaces of looking for meaning in puppetry (Figure 2.1). We are together in the process when I animate him and he looks as if he is an extension of my body with a sense of consciousness and thought. It looks like I am 'thinking through' him as a performing object. But laced within the performance is also a sense that Humphrey has autonomy separate to me as a signifying presence. This autonomy is also part of my training, which is a paradoxical process to work with as a performer, as I have to feel interconnected to the puppet, but also seemingly give the figure its autonomous presence. This dialogue and tension between these intentions opens up an alternative space in practice which is where the puppet 'magic' is found. This process is like the way I encourage novice puppeteers to explore the tension between the feet

Figure 2.1 Matt Smith and Humphrey performing street puppetry, 2000. Photograph by Caroline Broadbent.

and the top of the head of the puppet, to give the illusion of a spine. This tension and creative space are also a way of looking at Applied Puppetry practice. Practitioners intermingle with their participants in the workshop space, but with an important emphasis on the individual's autonomy. If this practice is too 'led' by the facilitator, it is like a puppeteer pushing a puppet around the space in an awkward controlled practice. Puppets pushed in this way look dead, and practice that pushes participants around feels deadly.

Another lesson that Humphrey has taught me over the years is to be reactive to the environment surrounding our performances together. Concentrating on him as an object 'other' in performance actually develops a heightened sense of the ecology surrounding me in terms of other objects, humans or the more-than-human environmental factors. As an active agent in my practice, he becomes my guide to the non-human possibilities in performance, but also through being and difference in these spaces. These agentic possibilities outside of my skin now take forms beyond my collaborations with Humphrey into other spaces, including when I talk to a root and I am immersed in the hug of a Yew tree. These are performative acts beyond the usual space of performances.

Summary

In this chapter we have explored the performing object as a vessel through which we can imagine 'thinking through' our concerns and issues and this positionality has been troubled. The puppet can be more than a metaphor, unlike the countless times it is used to symbolize human systems of power and control. This tendency is akin to the way we also metaphorize nature. The puppet can be considered more than a prosthesis (Cappelletto 2011) for the human in rhetorical voicing or prosopeia (Taylor 2014). To fully appreciate the puppet's sense of puppethood and agency, this process is through recognizing performing objects' paradoxical presences and their ephemeral parts to play in drama. This practice is always intersectional within an ecology of practice and the wider ecology. This often messy space of practice is a mesh theatre (Kent 2022) where performative acts and techniques enable people to explore attunement to things in a space of care and 'playful seriousness' (Morton 2018). Objects affect us in ways that are appreciated following this perspective, including our own embodiment. My cancer cells were in this process more apparent and accepted as part of my embodied ecology through the entangling with puppet-making. This process combined with not seeing cancer cells metaphorically, as some alien invading force of evil. We project metaphors and binaries onto objects like cancer cells and puppets, but this method obscures the complex meanings these things have to offer to us. Whether witnessing a moving puppet or a still exhibited marionette we should consider these things as resisting objects following Woodward's material methodologies (2020). In this way the process of attempting 'thinking through' is a speculation and 'thinking with' is a practice. The possibilities of objects, following this thinking with viewpoint, is that their potential is to be more than instrumental props in our anthropocentric practices.

Notes

1. Chiara Cappelletto discusses the issues of puppetry as a form of 'organic prosthesis' and as a paradox – C. Cappelletto, 'The Puppet's Paradox: An Organic Prosthesis', *Anthropology and Aesthetics*, 59/60 (2011): 325–36.
2. Kershaw and my history are intertwined around the important heritage of WSI and their ecological spectacle-building with communities, often with puppet figures.
3. Jeong Geum-Hyung solo performance piece *7Ways* (2017) – details can be found here https://www.tate.org.uk/whats-on/tate-modern/tate-live-geumhyung-jeong.
4. Mori's 'uncanny valley' has developed a renewed interest in the reception of human-like beings such as puppets, dolls and robots. This is rooted in Freudian ideas of the uncanny and feelings of figures being out of place. The puppets' ability to disturb is an ever-present issue in practice. Bell explores this Freudian view of the uncanny and its relationship to animistic beliefs (Bell in Posner, Orenstein and Bell 2014: 47–9).
5. Purcell-Gates's practice with puppetry was captured in a training video as part of the Objects with Objectives project and is listed as '3(2)' on the website. Brown Paper Puppetry and the Celebration of Imperfection are also found here as part of Queen Mary Belfast digital archive. https://mediasite.qub.ac.uk/Mediasite/Channel/objectswithobjectives/watch/3deb759030 9b421d9db374f4a32339fc1d.
6. Bunraku/Ningyo Joruri has been a very important reference point for practitioners in European theatre and its use of three puppeteers to one puppet is very influential in the west. Part of its appropriation as a form of object manipulation has often resulted in mythologizing the practice.
7. This script is part of the performance after working in Haslar IRC explored in Chapter 6. I have used the text a number of times to offer the puppets perspective.
8. Little Angel Theatre, London, is the home of British puppetry with regular shows for mainly children since 1961. https://www.littleangeltheatre.com/about-us/our-history/.

3

Thingness, puppethood and violence: The materiality of performing objects

This chapter discusses how new materialism can be employed in flattening ontologies, away from privileged human-centred viewpoints. At this crucial moment in the Anthropocene, these ideas of new materialism have become relevant to rethinking how puppeteers operate in an ecology of practice. This approach to objects in practice I present as releasing performance from the tired power systems inherent in theatre cultures (when it privileges the human over ecological factors), especially in the use of theatre in the community. In these cultures, 'material actors' in practice have been ignored in systems of power. This chapter proposes that objects' significance can be reconsidered in the way we form workshops, performances and projects in the community. This vision for practice considers an ecological approach to the entities in performance spaces. The two questions explored in this chapter are the following: How has the emergence of new materialism affected the way we consider the object in performance? How does this make us reconsider the human and more-than-human in culture?

Meta objects

In new materialist Bill Brown's taxonomy of objects and things (2016) he defines certain objects as able to speak or force humans to pay attention to them, as something new. These objects have a pronounced 'objectness' that denotes that they are not normalized things within the general object 'noise' in our environments. Puppets and performing objects fit into this object taxonomy, where the ontology of the object is writ large onto the surface skin of the performing object. Polish theatre pioneer Tadeusz Kantor brought these kinds of 'enhanced objects' to life in his shows, like his constructivist marionette theatre work *Macchina dell'amore e della morte* (1987), his internationally successful show *The Dead Class* (1975) and generally in his self-conscious stage designs exploiting 'poor objects' collected in exhibitions. Kantor introduced a stark vision of theatre that employed modernist ideas drawn from Edward Gordon Craig's essay on the Übermarionette and the futuristic practice of Bauhaus pioneer

Oskar Schlemmer. He drew on these ideas but created a post-holocaust vision of a theatre where objects and bodies combined to produce the 'bio object'. His practice experimented with the space between the dead and alive in performance. The worn, second-hand nature of wood and steel, conjoined to make cruel images in his theatre.[1] In this theatre he reminds us of how we are always already intertwined with objects in life and dramaturgy. Visiting Cricot 2 Museum in Krakow in 1997 (when it was in the main square) gave me an insight into his theatre spaces and aesthetic, but it was also an introduction to the performing objects of his theatre which sat vibrantly present in the dark spaces of the theatre's basement, a shrine to a 'master' of twentieth-century theatre. Kantor's marionettes look like deconstructed antique shop offcuts, stiffly angular like broken constructivist automatons. These marionettes are not representing humanity, instead they represent their essential nature as objects for the audience or witness. The mannequins in *Dead Class* offer up to the audience strange deathly doubles, like a morbid lesson in troubling myths of object and subject relations.

The actors in Kantor's theatre attempt and fail beautifully to deaden their humanness like mannequins or puppets. The actors try to be as inanimate, still, stiff and as without life energy as the other poor or cruel objects he employs. The 'poor object' was a part of Kantor's total aesthetic, but it was also the signifying glue that held together his challenging artistic theatre. Before and after Kantor's theatre the human actor has explored the impossibility of being as 'dead' as a puppet throughout performance histories, but humans are always doomed to failure in this task. I have explored the 'dead acting' that is part of Kantor's world with masters' students and found it is both a difficult and a troubling experience. Similarly, one of the most disturbing and emotionally draining exercises I have been subjected to in my puppet training was to look at my hand as alien to my body and as a separate object. Humans actively objectifying their own bodies is as disturbing as the uncanny puppet expressing its meta object status. Brown defines the meta object as 'an object that seems to investigate its own status as an object' (2016: 372) and though he does not include the puppet in relation to this concept of meta object the puppet certainly displays this 'meta quality' in performance. Kantor's stage objects are involved in this process and this is why they appear so vibrant and so present.

In 1996 associated with a project inspired by Italo Calvino's *Invisible Cities*, I was commissioned as part of a residency in an abandoned school, Liverpool Collegiate, to collaborate on a short film that responded to the abandoned school's broken fire and rain damaged architecture. I found charred planks and door frames, mouldy mouldings and splintered scraps, and I made a child-sized marionette operated by strings from a stairwell. This puppet ghosted the entrance to the school and welcomed the documentary video's audience to the damaged history of the school. The charred scrap wood child puppet displayed clearly what it was made of, but it also produced the results of its investigation into its 'apparent being' as relic and presence as actant. This puppet was a temporary life until later Urban Splash turned the school into gentrified flats for cosmopolitan inhabitants. Strangely and mutely, this puppet was also investigating and demonstrating this odd human process of urban renewal through cultural reignition. It became a meta object in this process of animating the inert detritus of the building.

Brown's things

Brown describes in *Other Things* (2016) that he is exploring how 'literary, visual and plastic arts fashion questions about the object world and our relationship to it, about the mutual constitution and mutual animation of subject and object' (2016: 19). Within the practice of puppetry this 'mutual' relationship is at the heart of the practice, if never resolved. In the puppet workshop the experience of exploring subject and object relations is a dynamic situation where the puppet can speak about subjective experience even if it's often doing this through a mute visual animated form. In workshops I have witnessed the way puppets express intersubjective narratives around sex, violence and power directly. The 'mutual relationship' between subject and object in practice creates a blurring between these categories but also opens temporary portals into this interstitial zone where the unspeakable is found. This is why in puppetry workshops it is important to discuss with participants the surprising meanings and strange outcomes of making and playing with puppets. At times the uncanny puppet, blurring usual normalized positions, can disturb and upset the individual person who finds it hard to disentangle the process. If I sense this disturbance in practice, for an individual, I intentionally break the focus and chain of signification that brings the puppet to life. In this process the mutual relationship between subject and object needs sensitive negotiation between the facilitator and participant in collaboration with the object.

Brown presents a schema for objects, subjects and things in which the relation between the object and the subject produces 'thingness'. This process for Brown also produces what for Barthes is the *punctum* or moment of feeling that is the power of the object's expression received by the viewer (Brown 2016: 20). This term Barthes used in relation to photography when explaining the visceral effect of the still image on the viewer (Barthes 2000: 27). Objects for Brown express this punctum when the object connects with the subject and displays its thingness beyond quotidian experience. This is a process where the object forces the subject's attention. Brown's schema illustrates how, through processes and relations, the interrelation of subject and object is formed around the nexus of the thing. Drawing from Heidegger, Brown presents the object in this process as one in which 'the thing things' (Brown 2016: 30). This object-subject relation brings attention to the way the thing produces 'in itself' sameness the thinging thing gathers' (2016: 30). This process for Brown indicates a potential of objects and things in relation to Marx's commodity fetishism. He suggests the thing has the potential, through the activity of thinging, to have 'independent agency and voice before commodification generates the illusion of such agency and voice' (2016: 32). The puppet explores the space of how it presents its thingness and represents its agency even though it is manipulated by a puppeteer. Part of the unique joy of puppetry is exploring this imaginative space where the object seemingly has a voice and a tale to tell inside and outside of human relations or commodity exchange. The puppet voices its unique thingness to audiences as subjects and has the potential to both inform, entertain or disturb in this process of becoming. As part of Brown's exploration of thingness, he surveys the twentieth-century phenomenon of the surrealist object. Art at this point played with the inherent possibilities to disturb our sense of the fixity of objects in both cultural artefacts and the everyday. The object was in these practices othered and purposely made uncanny through odd assemblages or juxtapositions of jarring artefacts. Salvador Dali's *Lobster Telephone* (1936), Man Ray's illogical iron *The Gift* (1921) and Méret Oppenheim's sexual pun in a fur teacup *Luncheon in Fur* (1936) are all iconic meta objects from this period of surrealism. In all of these objects there is a playful disruption of the use value of the object that produces meanings in the viewer as an experience of reconsidering the object's status anew. There is also something very performative about these objects, as sculptures producing punctum, vibrancy and magnetism, because of their bold putting together of different object forms in free associations. Brown in his exploration of thingness focuses on Man Ray's metronome with eye sculpture as a key example of an art object that is doing a great deal to excite and disrupt the viewer's usual comfort in things. For Brown the work represents an 'other' looking and surveying the subject that is experiencing the piece. Man Ray's *Object of Destruction* (1932) holds the viewer as though 'the subject is constituted – that is, the way in which inanimate objects and not just human subjects hold us in their gaze' (Brown 2016: 132). Man Ray's sculpture as a mechanical assemblage is also animated and kinetic like a puppet. Man Ray exploits the performative dynamic of the movement and anthropomorphism of the metronome to produce what Brown suggests is an apparent viewing object. Puppets similarly can often be as simple as a very obvious object with eyes stuck onto them then becoming a viewing object looking back at us.

Puppet-like

It is a regular trope of puppet performance that the everyday object can be 'puppet-like' in performance. Torley from Banyan Theatre Company has in her collection of puppets a wolf puppet that she assembles for the audience, physically conjoining a bicycle seat and an old leather bag. This puppet and Torley's animation of the puppet draw the audience into a relationship with a wolf that seems to apprehend our presence as viewers. This could be perceived as a surrealistic wolf and this puppet form seems to display the unusual quality of speaking about its object status and thingness through its own performance. In my practice the putting together of multiple objects produces surrealist chimaeras. Chimaeras produce a disruption of species distinctions, in the way that puppets produce disruptions in what we see as object distinctions. Puppetry can produce a viewpoint which is positioned as the object's viewpoint and this can be used metaphorically or literally to speak to human subjects about the object's perceived reality. This practice I used to comment on the traumatic positionality of human bodies in immigration detention discussed later in Chapter 6. Considering the object's view allowed me as a researcher to understand a different perspective on this cruel carceral traumatic context in the prison. More recently I have directly used puppet chimaeras to explore the process of breaking down plastic waste. In the Puppet Enzyme project in 2023,[2] the puppet is literally enabling scientists to communicate the material thingness of plastics with community groups as part of engagement.[3] The puppets in this project describe the process of using enzymes to break down plastics like little monsters producing a quicker solution to the breakdown of the monumental amount of human plastic waste. In this way, puppets as assemblages of objects explore the potential of their performance about the experiences of things.

One important critic of the tendency in art to theatricalize objects is Michael Fried. His attack on minimalism in *Art and Objecthood* is an influential text that critiques the essentialism of minimalism and artists like Carl Andre including his infamous brick installation *Equivalent VIII* (1966) as some form of theatrical trickery. The basis for Fried's argument seems to suggest that there is a hierarchy of art where theatre appears as a lower form in the network. He also describes a tendency in art to take the ready-made object to its natural conclusion in some form of artistic atrophy, 'This "negation of art" ensues from the work's theatricality: its attention to the encounter with the embodied, spectating subject, and thus its concern with space and the situational subject' (Brown 2016: 85). Brown's summation of Fried here sums up some of the important qualities of puppetry as an art form; the way that the puppet calls the subject into a relationship of noticing, both drawing attention to material, spatiality and situation. In my practice, I valorize the theatrical process of engaging, through the body with puppets, as we can through this process recognize and then demonstrate objecthood.

Brown in his historical and philosophical expression of thingness presents the object as a place to reside for the human subject in what could be described as a sublime experience of things. 'The object in other words, has the form of no form; it is a kind of formless form, having taken the shape of shapelessness; it's more sublime than beautiful, in the sense that it lies beyond comprehension and yet is neither threatening nor terrifying but simply soothing' (Brown 2016: 143). This soothing journey into the sublime space of objects can also be found in the more intentionally crafted object 'as the abstract other thing-manifests an energetic release from mimetic form; so doing, it serves as a kind of conduit to a world that is not this world … it is the source of some kind of immanent transcendence' (2016: 143–4). Puppets, though intentionally made and crafted as actors, can be made with the aim to interrogate this thing-object world for the human. The puppet can also produce in the maker or the audience of the show this pleasurable experience of 'immanent transcendence' into the magical world of puppetry. Another aspect of puppet theatre is object theatre where the object is animated and imbued with narrative or meaning in performance. This practice with objects can be developed further into conceptualizing the practice of playing with the exciting materiality of things. Puppets that explore the nature of materiality can appear in museum collections like the next example commenting on human/object temporalities.

Kiki the monkey puppet's monologue

My name is Kiki. I used to live under the stairs. Then you died and I came here to the museum. In the museum I am a celebrity. You inscribed your history on my silky back. I was frightened back then of the children's faces, behind the wire.

You never spoke about our time in France. The war and the pain. The bodies. I was left under the stairs, but you knew I was there. You never spoke about it all, but now I shout out loud about our history. Staring back through glass now, not wire. My back is still marked by the words you put there.

In 2009 the family of a Second World War US army private donated the puppet of a monkey called Kiki to the US Holocaust Museum.[4] The puppet's description in the online archive gives no real indication of the puppet's experience of the war and the camp in Vittel in occupied France. The monkey is literally inscribed, with pen marks, its surface etched with information about the events that were filmed as part of a newsreel shot at the camp, now part of the exhibition and reported in the newspapers in the United States at that time of the war. The puppet is clearly shown entertaining the children and adults of the camp with the monkey puppet in photos in news archives. The puppeteer, an army private and ambulance driver, did not tell his family about why he felt the need to perform for the children or who made the puppet, according to the museum curators. This lacuna does not diminish the uncanny power of the monkey puppet viewed now from another century, representing the context of trauma and suffering. This puppet, like Walter Benjamin's Angel of History, looks back at this historical episteme (Benjamin 1999: 249). After the death of the puppeteer, Kiki the monkey puppet still remains, not just as an artefact in a museum but also as a vibrant witness to the trauma inflicted on bodies. The monkey does not need to speak or move to be able to say something about the power of its original context. The wonder of this object is that it embodies a narrative trace of humanity and the violent biopolitics (Foucault 1991) from a time when the state of exception (Agamben 2005) was in operation during the war. This is how this monkey puppet speaks about the war as an object witness.

The puppeteer and artist Dennis Silk poetically discussed the powerful status of the object and puppet as a witness (like Kiki the puppet) in his provocative texts about puppetry. In the following extract Silk provokes the reader to give time to appreciate the agency of objects:

> We say animism. Then we put it back on the shelf with the other relegated religions. Maybe our flight from animism is our flight from madness. We're afraid of the life we're meagre enough to term inanimate. Meagre because we can't cope with those witnesses. (Silk 1986: 44)

The fear of the inner life of objects expressed here by Silk becomes a dynamic realm for new knowledge about the object world. In addition to the puppet's speculative internal vibrant potential and its role as witness, the puppet represents characters, categories, stereotypes and identities.

Brown describes the way that objects and things comment on history as an 'unhuman history' and this history provoked by the thing envelops the human subject within deep time. Kiki the puppet functions in this way as an object that comments upon 'unhuman' and human history as a mute artefact that speaks volumes about the artefactual and the inaudible trauma of history. For Brown, the 'other thing can compel you to consider the inhuman dimension within which humanity takes place'

(2016: 154). Fay Tsitou, a puppet researcher, explores how museum artefacts and puppets for her develop this renewed understanding in participants about heritage and history through objects (Tsitou 2012). Puppets in museums are vibrant talismans for historical time even when they usually stock-still as they animate narratives of things exploring time.

As a freelance artist I have been employed to animate exhibition spaces in places like the Science and Industry Museum in Manchester (making puppets of animals that reflected a natural history exhibition), Bury Art Museum (animating the stories in Victorian narrative paintings with puppet figures including a puppet of Wriggley, the collection sponsor) and The Lowry, Salford (using shadow puppetry to animate the figures in Lowry's paintings); in these experiences I witnessed how puppet making enlivens experiences of artefacts and art in the museum context. Closer to where I live now, in my native Portsmouth, a ventriloquist puppet in the D-Day Museum mutely comments upon being a witness to the Normandy landings and liberation of Europe. The museum's description presents Bertie the puppet thus: 'Bertie, [which was] used by Captain Edward Harold North (known as Ted). After he went to Normandy in 1944 as an officer with the Royal Warwickshire Regiment, shortly after the D-Day landings, he used Bertie to entertain the troops. He landed on Juno Beach'.[5] I have often considered what horrors this ventriloquist puppet witnessed with his artificial staring cartoon eyes and fixed rictus smile while under the care of Captain North.

History now has morphed into a space where object and subject positions have been questioned by theorists like Bruno Latour. Brown critiques this democratizing project of Latour's with the object in relation to Actor Network Theory (ANT) (Brown 2016: 168). The issue for Brown is that there has never been democracy for subjects before widening and flattening of this concept for objects as well. Even so, this flattening of ontology in analysing systems and cultures does offer up unique positions for objects in history.

Brown sums up other contemporary attempts to flatten the subject/object positionality when considering OOO and critiques Graham Harman as attempting to treat 'objects whose mysterious depths are comparable to the depths of human subjects' (Brown 2016: 167). I share Brown's concern for the issue about the process of flattening ontologies as it potentially homogenizes entities in some way, when good practice would eschew that respecting the unique status of individuals is paramount. Certainly, using ANT and OOO in the context of communities and engaged arts practices has to be applied very sensitively. In workshops, care for the participants and a deep respect for them as autonomous people is a primary condition for good practice. What I am suggesting based on readings of theories such as Brown's, Latour's and Harman's is that this 'care' can be extended to the objects in the room. In fact, a regular comment about puppetry is that it often displays, in the way the puppeteer works with performing objects, a great deal of care for the object or puppet.[6]

Brown does not neatly conclude the issues of subject and object status, and in the practice of Applied Puppetry blurring the boundaries in these categories is often where some interesting practice emerges. Out of practice and its rubbing against theories of thingness, my suggestion is to use this incommensurable space of the mysterious nature of things, objects and humans to enable new narratives. Working with the mysterious beauty of participants and the unique qualities they bring to Applied Theatre can be enmeshed with the beautiful mysterious qualities of objects. Often, I have given voices to puppets and suggested with their help they can enable us to explore what it is to be human, even though we never understand what it is to be an object like Humphrey. This type of paradox is playfully meant as a way to explore our often simplistic views on agency and freedoms. It also reinforces the power of the puppet which is complex and can amplify the agency of people, or in some negative cases reinforce powerful narratives of violence against subjects in racist puppet forms.

This violence of puppetry in relation to race has been challenged and discussed by Tobi Poster-Su (2021) and Paulette Richards (2019) as well as collected in an exhibition at the Ballard Institute of Puppetry in 2022.[7] This evidence of the power the puppet object delivering messages about identity in regard to bodies is part of the traditions of many puppet forms. It is also exploited to great effect by contemporary artists to critique historical racist narratives as in the shadow works of Kara Walker, for example her shadow work *Grub for Sharks: A Concession to the Negro Populace* (2004). Much of the recent interest in race and puppetry suggests that in practice the othering of others is as much part of actor-based theatre as it is in puppetry. So, understanding the propensity of performing objects to conduct this violence against human subjects is part of a responsible Applied Puppetry practice understanding its intersectionality.

Objecthood and puppethood

Critic Maria Walsh summed up the issues of the 'new objecthood' in her article *I Object* (2013). According to her reading of the object zeitgeist she declares that 'artists are rushing to become objects or to side with the object' (Walsh 2013: 9). This change in focus is encouraged by digital technologies which can network subjects into a system of objects. She sums up OOO as a way to see that 'every object has a different durational potential which allows it to occupy different realms outside human consciousness' (2013: 9). This seems good news for the puppets in a world where their unique position can be more accounted for, if not fully understood. Walsh appears alarmed at the agency given to objects as things in works that displace the human experience and particularly their 'limits of identity' (2013: 10). Even so, she does offer her own critical appraisal of the ideas of Harman when she warns us to take care when approaching the object world in arts practice.

> Object oriented philosophers such as Graham Harman suggest that all objects, including humans, enter into surface relations with each other, but retain a dark hidden core that is outside of all relation. This is not an essence, as essence would refer the object back to identity, but rather an autonomy, which I find hard to weigh up with his insistence on how objects transform one another in their encounters with other things in the world. (Walsh 2013: 11)

This concern for a lack of essences from Walsh does suggest that if we regard the mystery of objects in this way it would trouble a lot of the ways we aesthetically apprehend art in the future. She is suggesting that without essences the sublime experience of the artistic other is rendered empty because we cannot break through its surfaces. Though, autonomy for objects can also be part of how we approach apparent subjecthood for objects in our practices and art-making. Objects can be given more autonomy and respect for their mysterious core in this process. Walsh offers a way to explore this landscape where the shifting of ontologies in which humans have a privileged position is over suggesting that 'the question to be asked is whether the gathering of "quasi-objects" and "quasi-subjects" might allow instead for a different kind of participation, one in which the life of things is shared rather than subdued or feared' (2013: 12). In the shifting sands, that is the practices of Applied Puppetry, this new approach to the object and participation offers an exciting potential. The shared potential of objects explored with participants is an ethos that is at the heart of puppetry with groups but often overlooked in the same way as the theatrical prop becomes forgotten as an actant in the stage drama. This questioning of subject and object positions using performing objects as guides opens up a new politics of object 'decentred' practice.

Performing objects and animated things

A term now used interchangeably with puppet is 'performing object' and this term draws from the scholarship of John Bell (1997 and 2016). In his comprehensive view of American puppet modernism (2016) he deploys the term 'performing objects', in relation to the politics of historical social events like floating effigies as part of the Macy's Parade in New York. In his example of large-scale street performance Bell uses the term 'performing object' to classify non-puppet objects that clearly perform as part of these dramas. Marlis Schweitzer and Joanne Zerdy (2014) also employ 'performing objects' and add 'theatrical things' to the developing discourse that is part of the object turn in performance scholarship. This important shift shows subjects akin to puppets in the reconsideration of sets, props and costumes with much more importance and presence than just as inert aspects of theatre cultures. Schweitzer and Zerdy present this practice as a process where 'Onstage stuff provokes the critical attention of scholars scrutinising theatrical objects as discrete entities and as part of a collection or network' (Schweitzer and Zerdy 2014: 11). The contexts that are considered as part of this collection of different entities is very important as it allows us to take into account different aspects within the network of objects which are vying for power. This can be seen in a workshop space as the interplay between bodies, minds, mobile phones, lunch pizza, institutional framing discourses in notices, air quality, atmospheric noise and the like (this list or litany could continue ad infinitum). Schweitzer and Zerdy assert that performing objects and theatrical things are 'active agents performing alongside rather than behind or in service to human performers' (2014: 6). Their book echoes this point but also suggests that in the new epoch of the more-than-human hyper objects, these entities have the potential to be more performative than human beings. Our entanglement with performing objects reconfigures relationships in theatre and drama and this can be negotiated in applied community performances as well. Borrowing from Latour and ANT, Schweitzer and Zerdy provide a pathway for the anti-anthropocentric study of performance cultures where they see 'physical materials not as inert human possessions but instead as actants, with particular frequencies, energies, and potentials to affect human and nonhuman worlds' (2014: 2).

Tree standing

Q: What did you do in the workshop?
A: They made me stand in the space like a tree.

When I trained in puppetry a very serious puppeteer made us imagine we were hugging an invisible tree for a very long time. I loathed this exercise as a pretentious waste of time and effort. I think my problem was that I was not actually hugging a tree. Since this workshop I have now become interested in Yew trees which are often to be found in churchyards as well as woodlands and have incredible ages that can reach thousands of years. Some form hollows in which you can be enveloped by their trunks and they hug you. In literature trees have become prevalent and I had the pleasure to listen to a presentation on arboreal feminism by Catriona Sandilands in 2022. She began her discussion with Apollo and Daphne (where Daphne becomes a tree to avoid rape) from the tales of Ovid and his opening gambit in *Metamorphoses* – 'Let me sing to you now, about how people turn into other things' which is quoted in the novel about trees and humans, *Overstory*, by Richard Powers (2019: 147). Contemporary arboreal literature has reacted to recent science in which plant signalling and networking trees are understood as forming communities in which they share resources in kin networks and this is now part of ecological thinking. For Sandilands this 'interspecies fluidity' is part of a Deleuzian possibility of becoming something else. She also suggests that it is part of the human death drive facing the ecological. This literature she explores as navigating the arboreal drives of writers and is found in novels such as *Overstory* by Richard Powers (2019) and *The Vegetarian* by Han Kang (2015). Sandilands also cited in her discussion the historical group of Chipko tree huggers in Northern India[8] and a theatrical play in which trees appear and speak onstage – *Estado Vegetal* (Vegetative State) by Chilean theatre artist Manuela Infante (2019).[9] This fascination with the performative nature of trees Sandilands ascribes to a reaction against the modernist valorization of speed and power over the inert and for her there is a possibility to appreciate that mental exceptionality can be found within bodies that are passive and still, like trees.

When a puppet is still, after or before a performance, it is not really inert, but full of Schneider's performance 'remains' (2003) and this was a recent discovery I found when thinking about puppetry workshop practice. Previously the displayed puppet I found to be of less interest when I was in my youthful speedy state of bringing objects to life through live animation. Puppets in those days were functional beings given meaning only through their instrumental use value in entertaining an audience, bringing joy to groups through play and creative haptic joy. I now find that the still inanimate puppet has a great presence, especially after being crafted and left as part of the archiving of performance. The puppet within the archive festers with the stain of human hands and sweat. Many of my puppets are now well over twenty years old and they gain gravitas through their years of service and redundant stillness in cupboards or suitcases.

The puppets of Wael Shawky, an Egyptian artist whose works have been shown worldwide in galleries like the Tate Gallery, display this gravitas in their stillness.[10] In his video work Shawky's puppets possess a vibrant presence especially his appropriation of an antique group of Italian puppets from the Lupin collection. After the performance in his epic films, which retell orientalist histories from the eastern perspective, these objects have presence and vibrancy, which is part of their appeal and attractiveness in exhibition spaces. For critic Omar Berrada who discusses Shawky's oeuvre,

> marionettes embody a paradox of representation: they stand in for the human figure while abstracting it from itself. They challenge our categories of subject and object, our distinctions between beings and things. They model our perpetually denied yearning for political autonomy: the strings are conspicuous, their pullers invisible. (2015: 29–30)

Puppets are imbued with this paradoxical meaning through performance, but they are also containers for this meaning. Their problematic status as objects in transition continues to hold this presence for the viewer. So, using puppets as still representations of ideas or the knowledge of a community group can extend the reach of the practice beyond the theatrical event. Puppets that were made in the context of my practice in HMP Haslar (Chapter 6) held this presence when displayed as performance remains and as objects that questioned our ideas of political autonomy in direct relation to identities of men caught within immigration detention. Idly hanging from their strings or captured in a still image, these representations made within a painful environment did not stop provoking the viewer to think of their status as object others commenting upon human others, silently.

For Victoria Nelson the puppet is a form of conduit for imagination and creativity and like human simulacra they are 'not just a passive vessel but a magnet for attracting [divine] power' (2001: 40). Performing objects hold this power long after the event or playing.

This is an important point to address when objects are made with and for communities, as they carry narratives of identity and power within their artificial fabricated parts beyond performance. Nelson in her historical study reminds us that early English puppeteers were called 'motion men' and 'motion masters' (2001: 49) which connects to my youthful desire to see the puppet only as a moving sculpture. I now know that puppets can say much more in their stillness and this quality is what human performers cannot effectively embody, unless they are dead. I nurse the performing object to life with motion and an approximation of characteristic shapes or gestures, though actually it already embodies a beautiful stillness that I have no control over. The stillness of the malformed root in performance (Chapter 8) still animates through its 'apparent passivity' as a vessel of secret mysterious knowledge. This mysterious inner life of the object is what translates into performativity when networked with human audiences and interpretations. This stillness, like that of the tree, is an object lesson in how to think ourselves out of the paradoxes of the human-centred binaries that trap us within culture. This is not just the rule of philosophers but also the prevalence of children playing with 'material others' in puppet workshops.

Navigating towards the meaning of objects as a new materialist enterprise has grown in volume recently, and one of the great gifts to this enterprise is the collected volume *Object Reader* (2009). In this book is the object lesson of Carolyn Thomas de la Peña, where she explores the meaning of a saccharin sparrow, a domestic ornamental object. Her approach she describes as 'through a combination of close material observation and a careful re-imagining of body encounters' and in this way she is able to show that 'it is possible to suggest a means of decoding what I term "experiential" material culture' (2009: 506). She suggests that objects like the ornamental container as a bird produce meaning for her through the encounter with the non-human. The object becomes imbued with this merging with the human body and then for her 'objects must be considered equal parts "stuff" and sensation' (2009: 506). The material experiential culture of puppetry involves an intense objective to affect the body of the end user, which is both the puppeteer and the audience. Also, part of this embodied experience is the trace of the maker and puppeteer on the surfaces of the puppet. Add to this the unknowable mystery of the object's inner secret life and the puppet is a heady mix of meanings and signifying levels. Carolyn Thomas de la Peña calls her investigation into these kinds of object lessons as an 'intimate entanglement' that affects her sense of embodiment (2009: 509). Part of the study of Applied Puppetry involves this investigation and awareness of the entanglement with objects and their performance affects.

A good puppet bash up: Questions of violence

Hiding behind an upturned desk, then performing with junk puppets over its edge, gives children a means through which to change their embodied social configurations and amplify their vocality in pronounced and surprising ways. I often warn, when teaching how to lead puppet workshops for children, that it is very hard to contain the release of verbiage that comes from children in a workshop when they talk with a puppet in this way. I warn that it is hard to get the child puppeteers to stop or end their usually quite incomprehensible vocal improvisations. My practical suggestion, so that there is some way to end the skits by children, is to make sure the children have devised a good ending and if that doesn't work, I use the blunt tool of a round of applause to end the performances. In these performances, often very quickly put together, children cannot contain the desire for violence the puppet produces in them. I have had to pointlessly intervene in many sessions when puppets bash each other to bits and pieces against the infectious delight of laughter-induced jollity in a group of children. The haptic joy of making the puppets often descends into the haptic pleasure of a good puppet bash up. Most of these young children are not really aware of the heritage of Punch and his violent murderous narratives.

> The puppet's new brutality significantly modified the portrayal of his marriage, as the hen-pecked buffoon of the eighteenth century was transformed into a

murderous wife-beater. Puppet historian George Speaight attributes this violence to the mechanics of glove puppetry as, given the limited actions of glove-puppets and the difficulties of dialogue within the showman's box, violent fights provided the lively action necessary to attract an audience. But whatever the reason for high levels of violence, the new Punch and Judy show rapidly proved to be a success. Audiences enjoyed Punch's violent conquests. Although the increasingly common name given to the thuggish puppet was clearly an abbreviation of his eighteenth-century appellation, 'Punchinello', 'Punch', in the context of his new role, was also certainly suggestive. (Crone 2006: 1058)

Rosalind Crone, in her article, offers as her explanation of the violence in Punch shows of the Victorian era that it was a reaction to the displacement of middle-class ideas of behaviour and bodily experiences that children could not participate in or adhere to (2006: 1082). Often the puppet workshops (that I led and witnessed as a freelance artist) which displayed the most violence were found within the disciplinary context of primary schools and this may go some way to explain the unleashing of the tide of violence in the little skits. This behaviour and experience are also attributable to what the great puppet scholar Speaight suggests is produced by the puppets' material conditions and 'mechanics' (Speaight 1970). More recently, during the pandemic, the problem of violence for the Punch professors in seaside locations during lockdown seems to have spilled into the audience's aggression.[11] The Punch professors deny that it is the fault of the Punch and Judy shows' barbaric dramaturgical content and heritage that encourages violence but is instead caused by what is found in the audience.

Beyond the cycle of violence that Punch elicits[12] historically, on the geographical margins of the seaside booth, there are ways to approach this puppet violence in a restorative way. In Cape Town, South Africa, the puppet is used to discuss and educate around gender-based violence[13] of the kind that Punch relishes and performs in his slapstick performance. This initiative by the Mothers Union uses puppetry to educate about violence, because according to their website 'puppets are magical creatures in the minds of children. They can give instructions, turn tears into laughter, and be used in imaginative play by small hands and large. Using puppets to engage early learners offers multiple benefits' (Mothers Union 2023). The experiential material culture of the puppet show can elicit a strange visceral pleasure in violence or even create an educative platform to discuss this extreme bodily trauma. In my previous experiences as an overworked freelance puppet artist in a school, I found it hard to contain the desire of the children to enact violence of this kind. All I offered was quick first aid to decapitated puppets with sticky tape. It certainly was not an intention to enable or encourage violence or violent acts in my puppet workshops with children, though it did feel like an intervention in thwarting play to ask the children to stop the puppet bashing. As Matthew Cohen suggests when looking at puppets and violence, 'Puppetry's distinction comes from the fact that its objects of performance are already designed to be destroyed' (2007: 8). Cohen's novel way to draw us into the paradoxes of puppetry ends with a useful suggestion of the puppets' value: 'Though destroyed in play and fantasy again and again, puppets survive this destruction to allow us to take responsibility for emotions, ideas and actions in society' (2007: 16).

My approach to children's puppet workshops is very open and I give little emphasis to a 'design phase' for the puppet making or puppet show devising. When I brought this 'loose' model to master's students at Goldsmiths University, they seemed shocked at this lack of a plan or structure to the making and doing. My justification for this looseness is that a workshop should be a very open space that leaves lots of room for the individual's idea of how to proceed. An ideal of this workshop method is to let the objects do the work for me as the facilitator. This freedom for the individual does mean that they can decide to make whatever they desire without hopefully causing harm to other people. This was often the case, and in unique situations this was an important possibility. For example, in my time as tutor in, what was then called the care system (for young people who were beyond mainstream education and a danger to others and themselves) I used forms of puppetry or material workshops that were adopted to reduce the risk of harm between bodies. In this context I was concurrently commissioned (while working many freelance jobs) by a local secondary school to collaborate on a production of Ted Hughes *Oedipus* (1969). The making of puppets for this production allowed a collaboration between the care home and the school as the puppets were made remotely and then delivered to the school-based production. The risk of violence from the young people in care meant that the puppets became a positive conduit through which the vulnerable disturbed young people could engage with the puppets at a distance from the young people in care.

Puppets in this way enabled difficult human relationships to be negotiated beyond physical risks. The puppets made for this production of *Oedipus* also represented the tragedy of the context and system that young people find themselves within, represented in the bodies of the puppets.

Literary critic Kenneth Gross when considering puppetry points us to many of the themes of puppetry and materiality, including violence, covered in this chapter when he assesses the disturbing sexually deviant puppeteer in Philip Roth's 1995 novel *Sabbath's Theatre*:

> The violence latent in a puppet's mimicry; they echo that power to translate and affront human meaning latent in the puppet's shiftings of human scale, its manifest madeness, its readiness to be manipulated, its invulnerability...Puppets offer a refuge for fantasies otherwise exiled. Endlessly accessible to touch, puppets attach us to the most ordinary objects, the most tabooed gestures. They are by turns trashy and talismanic; they survive through the deliberate polymorphousness of their identifications, joined to an unyielding rigidity of character...The opacity of puppets, their fantastic poverty and secrecy. (Gross 1997: 68)

The power of the puppet, captured here by Gross, is what is important to attest to in the use of these objects in workshops and community practice. The potential violence of the puppet is part of this network of vibrant experiences and meanings.

Puppets are assemblages that trouble notions of the real and the sensual in the beholder and this has made them very relevant objects to the philosophical practice of OOO. Harman asserts in his attempt to make OOO lucid for a wider audience that 'objects come in just two kinds: *real objects* exist whether or not they currently affect anything else, while *sensual objects* exist only in relation to some real object' (2018: 9). An apparent simple category is asserted in this definition but this becomes unstuck when you take into account that the inner mystery of the object is never possible to fully apprehend or know. The puppet object further troubles these categories and ways of speculating about reality through OOO or related fields of ANT or new materialism.

Harman in his defining 2018 volume *Object Oriented Ontology: A New Theory of Everything* speculates about aesthetics and experience and draws on Stanislavski's' acting technique in relation to developing a level of 'becoming' the object. He then boldly claims that 'theatre lies at the roots of the other arts' and that masks are at the beginning of this genealogy of human artistic practices (2018: 85). I extend this claim about masks towards the puppet, as a root form at the beginning of human cultural deep time.

Mabel the chimaerastic dog

Mabel the puppet is made from a dead dog's skull, old rusty screws and nails, a gnarled stick for a spine, copydex glue, stained plastic trash, scraps of fur, dried out tape and a purple felt tongue.

The puppet Mabel described above, has the skull of a real dog and so contains, in biological terms, the DNA of a dog (built during lockdown and then performed with in a surrealistic show for Portsmouth We Shine Portsmouth arts festival 2021). These material facts do not help us to understand this object as she is a chimaera of parts assembled together. She moves in an uncontrolled and awkward manner as if her legs have no knee joints, like Beckett's character Clov in *Endgame* (1957). Mabel yawns and reveals her purple tongue and rusty screws for teeth. In the construction of this puppet, my aesthetic choice was to accentuate the inner poetry and mystery of the performing object and sensually provoke that experience. Mabel doesn't return your gaze as she has no eyes, she has just empty sockets and so you do not contemplate her gaze when confronted by her presence. I wouldn't take her to meet children in a puppet workshop, though adults do find her beautiful. She is ultimately spooky and uncanny in appearance, whether through her stillness or awkward moving gait. These qualities of uncanniness are also to be found in the community workshop puppet, roughly constructed with fixed eyes and simple movement systems. This style of puppet often in my experience has a plastic bottle head and scrap material body. So, in this way adults and children through inclusive workshops can also play with the fantasy world that exploits the aesthetic of the inner poetry of things through transforming found objects.

Summary

Puppetry offers us a way to engage with explorations of the inner life of objects through practice and contemplation. Applied Puppetry develops into a regard for the sensual affects of these puppets and the practice of making them and performing with them in groups. New ontologies that displace human anthropocentrism have to be approached carefully in community practices with people if we are to be 'relatively equitable'. If these practices negotiating participants and performing objects is possible it is through producing haptic joy and rich experiences. It also demands that we account for the risk of bodily changes and the potential for violence. Workshops and performances are containers for these kinds of puppet imaginariums, but the facilitator has to be prepared for the unknown and surprising anarchy that the trickster puppet can encourage in participants. Deep-rooted desires in individuals and their relationship to what psychoanalyst Winnicott (2010) would call 'object relations' are very hard to predict or account for in people. Puppets can help us do and say surprising and funny things. As Bell concludes: 'The "uncanny" power of puppets persists, not necessarily as a problem to be surmounted but as a theatrical sentiment to be felt, appreciated, interpreted, and celebrated' (Bell in Posner et al. 2014: 51). So, the problem of the puppet and performing object lives on in practice.

I have stated and continue to state that my practice is non-therapeutic and this has always been very important to me professionally because of my respect for therapy and lack of expertise in this area. This said, the field of puppet therapy is well established and practised by groups like The Awesome Puppet Company.[14] What these practitioners and practices remind us of is the profound affects performing objects can have on participants. Susan Linn recently described the positionality and category problems of puppet therapy and her thoughts about how to connect to object relations around the tricky terrain of OOO.

> As playthings, and as a form of artistic expression, puppets reside in what D. W. Winnicott (1953) identifies as transitional space, which is the intersection of the inner world of thoughts and fantasies and the outer world of actions and interactions that exists in real time and space. According to Winnicott (1971), we play 'in the service of the dream' (2010: 69). That is why children's creative play is a gift both to them and to the adults who care for and about them – it is a window into their hearts and minds. (Linn 2020: 105)

I struggle to deal with the idea that I can find a window into any other's heart or mind using puppetry even though I often speculate about the inner world of the other which is found in the puppet or object. It is clear to assume after accounts like Linn's that there is lots of evidence that puppets affect participants in very unique and therapeutic ways. This potential to affect hearts and minds is always already part of the terrain which the facilitator should be cognizant about when conducting good sensitive workshop practice.

Throughout this chapter I have explored the possibilities and impossibilities of the mysterious poetics of puppetry and performing objects. Speculative materialist philosophies encourage us to explore and conceptualize this ambiguous terrain (which is now becoming a serious force in theorizing cultural spaces). My point is to suggest that this speculative approach is also part of the way we conduct Applied Puppetry as a practice that sensitively values the mysterious qualities of people's identities combined with the potential of objects. This is a rather unfinished non-totalizing experience, like that of a workshop. Objects are mysterious containers and it's the networks around them that offer up new understanding in community and applied types of engagements. Spaces like workshops are not hermetically sealed or closely bounded things. They have great potential to be more than this when the networks are considered around them and we are working through or with these entities. The propensity of the object to affect the body of the participant suggests an ethics of using the object in workshop and community practice. Puppets can do so much more than blunt violence against each other or another perceived other. There are accounts of this violent trope like the rifle and puppet analogy from Spanish Civil War puppetry cited in Chapter 4. Promoting a more explorative and less instrumental approach is through seeing the puppet as more than just the tool like a 'cultural hammer' used to bash culture. Employing Brown's approach to thingness as an expansive practice is another alternative to the instrumentalizing uses of the art object like the puppet. This attuned sensibility in our context of climate change suggests we urgently need to revalue our material environments. Maybe puppets and performing objects can be our guides into a less destructive or violent anthropocentric relationship and into a new set of values for revaluing our object kin.

Notes

1. A discussion of Kantor's materiality can be found here: J. Juntunen, 'Human/Object/Thing: Tadeusz Kantor's Puppets and Bio-Objects', in *Theatremachine: Tadeusz Kantor in Context*, 29–40, ed. Leach et al. (Illinois: Northwestern University Press, 2020).
2. A video that describes this project: https://youtu.be/GPjPnVdoeGM.
3. This project I conducted with scientists from the University of Portsmouth Centre for Enzyme Innovation, 2022–3. The project is still ongoing during the time of writing.
4. Link to United States Holocaust Museum and description of the puppet Kiki: http://www.ushmm.org/information/exhibitions/curators-corner/a-surprising-discovery-kiki-the-monkey-puppet.
5. For details, see theddaystory.com.
6. This relates to the way that puppeteer Eric Bass calls the animator the 'nursemaid' of the puppet (2014). E. Bass, 'The Myths of Puppet Theater', *Howlround*, 2014, https://howlround.com/myths-puppet-theater (accessed 24 March 2016).
7. https://bimp.uconn.edu/alterity-symposium/. Symposium: Representing Alterity through Puppetry and Performing Objects – This Symposium was important in discussing issues of racial representation in puppetry and was the opening of this discussing to a wider audience – Website for Ballard Institute and Museum: https://bimp.uconn.edu/.
8. Description of tree huggers movement: https://eu.patagonia.com/gb/en/stories/the-original-tree-huggers/story-71575.html.
9. Discussion of the performance text *Estado Vegetal* (Vegetative State) found here: https://www.moussemagazine.it/magazine/manuela-infante-lucy-cotter-2019/.
10. 'Based on extensive periods of research and enquiry, Wael Shawky's work tackles notions of national, religious and artistic identity through film, performance and storytelling. Shawky frames contemporary culture through the lens of historical

tradition and vice versa. Mixing truth and fiction, childlike wonder and spiritual doctrine, Shawky has staged epic recreations of the mediaeval clashes between Muslims and Christians in his trilogy of puppets and marionettes.' https://www.tate.org.uk/art/artists/wael-shawky-13675.
11. Discussion of bad behaviour in Punch audiences: https://www.theguardian.com/stage/2021/aug/04/punch-and-judy-professors-decry- aggressive-audiences.
12. A discussion of puppetry violence can be found within C. McPherson, 'On the Horrifying, Hilarious Violence of a Punch & Judy Puppet Show – Who Doesn't Love a Puppet, with a Wriggling, Uneasy Love That Might Be Terror?', *CrimeReads*, 2021. https://crimereads.com/punch-and-judy-puppet-show-violence/ (accessed 10 January 2023).
13. Description of action against gender violence using puppetry project on this site: https://www.mothersunion.org/news/using-puppets-teach-about-gender-based-violence-southern-africa.
14. Awesome Puppet Company website: https://www.awesome-puppets.com/.

4

Puppet power in intercultural practices: Communities, ethics and representation

This chapter explores case studies in relation to power as a heuristic about the way objects are used in Applied Puppetry. The first example is the intervention in the 1960s in Theatre for Development (TfD) involving population control by world famous puppeteer Bil Baird. Baird's use of puppetry in relation to population control is an example of practice that positioned bodies within a unique process and power. Critically considering this practice amongst the network of other objects in the context of the Indian sub-continent indicates how puppet bodies directly affect the bodies of humans. This exploration of historical examples I first discussed in an article in 2015.[1] This historical practice is then considered against projects I conducted remotely with artists and community activists in Nairobi in 2022 using puppetry to deliver and discuss Lung Health and then Covid-19. The comparison of these historical and contemporary practices opens up ways of thinking critically about performing objects in these forms of TfD. This chapter considers the power of puppetry in education and community contexts, in particular, the focus is on how we define power.

Puppetry in the social conditions of performances and workshops can be read reflexively exploring the 'biopolitical', drawing on Michel Foucault's use of this concept in *History of Sexuality* (1998). For Foucault, power and politics is connected to and directed towards the human body and its life in social spaces. Foucault read the way that historically the body is disciplined and administered through a power over life or biopower. Biopower produces new conditions, knowledge and systems that change the individual subject within the context of their social situations. Foucault's mixing of politics and the corporeal is a way of understanding how participants' bodies are engaged in Applied Puppetry practice and how people relate to each other connected to the non-human materiality of puppets. Using this critical approach to power we can consider diverse identities and issues of biopower in order to respect participants' agency when using performing objects. To define this power, I next explore three tropes where this power can be identified critically.

Historical antecedent tropes of puppetry with a purpose

During the Spanish Civil War, puppets in republican propaganda puppet shows are described as *effective as rifles* (McCarthy 1998). In Ahmedabad, Indian children perform with puppets and pacify patients in an asylum and this is described as effective as a *straitjacket* (Philpott 1977). In rural poor areas puppeteers are encouraged to see themselves as *educational missionaries* (Crothers 1983).

A point that has continually frustrated me while reading texts about engaged forms of puppetry is the constant assertion that puppetry is 'good for you'. This assumption about the puppet as essentially a force of 'good' is often combined with self- congratulatory assessments of the effects of puppets on people. When looking at historical examples I found this uncritical view of puppetry and its power challenging to read, due to outdated political viewpoints in the sources I found. Puppetry is not politically benign, and this is especially clear when puppetry is used as propaganda, puppetry within mental health settings and as part of TfD campaigns. Despite positive intentions, there are negative events of puppetry history found in accounts when it was mobilized to stereotype and actually enforce caricatures of identity – for example, Nazi puppet troupes promoting fascist ideology (Kamenetsky 2019). When looking back at historical practices in books and archive texts I identified three tropes in puppetry practice that seemed to capture pejorative aspects of puppetry used for social purposes:

- The puppet as a weapon.
- The puppet show as straitjacket.
- The puppeteer as a missionary figure.

This reading of history is inspired by the puppet theatre authority Henryk Jurkowski and his tripartite division of European puppetry as 'spontaneous puppetry', 'artistic puppetry' and 'puppetry in social care' (Jurkowski 1996). Jurkowski explains these categories thus:

> The first referred to all those primitive puppet forms and popular puppet shows with no clear or formulated artistic concept; the second to puppet theatre resulting from an artistic concept; the third to puppetry as an instrument of certain social and state bodies for which it might serve an educational and/or propagandist purpose. (Jurkowski 1996: 5)

In addition to Jurkowski's (1996) history of puppetry in 'social care' there were three particular sources that inspired my choice of tropes as negative antecedents of Applied Puppetry. The first trope is drawn from theatre scholar James McCarthy, who explored the significance of puppetry in the Spanish Civil War. McCarthy discovered a bold claim for the violent potential of the puppet in revolutionary warfare. McCarthy claims: 'One of the most ancient theatrical forms, puppetry became for the republicans an element of contemporary struggle, adopting a role in antifascist propaganda, which, in the words of one enthusiastic reviewer, saw the puppet as no less useful than the rifle in the successful prosecution of the war' (McCarthy 1998: 44). There are archive images of this kind of propaganda puppetry, and Bell suggests when exploring puppet modernism of the 1930s that 'in the United States (and across Europe as well) all aspects of theatre began to be valued for their educational and propaganda potential' (Bell 2016: 135). So this direct purposeful agit-prop potential for puppetry is a power ascribed to puppetry historically.

The second trope is inspired by the Foucauldian perspective of the 'docile body' related to how a puppet can be viewed as imposing a pacifying 'straitjacket' for an audience. For Foucault docility is produced in the body of the subject within regimes of power and institutional frames in a multilinear way by both the subject and the system. The puppet as straitjacket appears in historical accounts collected by British puppet authority Philpott (1977). He explores the straitjacket analogy for puppetry, arising from observations in an asylum in India. Philpott cites in his book a report by one of the key innovators of Indian educational puppetry, Meher Contractor:

> As an experiment, some of the schoolchildren performed for the inmates of the local Mental Hospital. 'The puppets, without exaggeration, had moved the inmates, who were very unruly and disturbed, to such calmness, and had pacified them so completely, that the doctor later complimented Smt. Mangaldas, by acknowledging that no straitjacket could have soothed the patients better. (Philpott 1977: 42)

This idea of the potential force of the puppet as a pacifying agent is a stark example of the power of the form to affect bodies within an institutional ecology.

The third trope, the missionary, is drawn from the extensive and useful library guide to puppetry by Jessie Frances Crothers (1983). Her outdated points about imagined populations chimes with the way that power in Applied Puppetry can be played out through the controversial figure of the missionary. Crothers frames educational puppetry thus:

> The educator missionary, in the modern and confusing jungles of today's large cities or in the mountains and valleys of countries near and far, can use the power of the puppet to bring quick understanding to people long neglected ... Governments have, and should have, the use of this practical puppet tool to help teach unlettered and underprivileged people who need information on farming, family life, medicine and education. Puppets can be inexpensive, can be easily and quickly moved from location to location, and can hold the interest of child or adult students who have had little formal education. (Crothers 1983: 10)

Crothers is here showing her vested interest in promoting educational puppetry when she draws upon the missionary figure. In these three accounts puppets are clearly fighting ideological battles, promoting docility and changing attitudes. In this way the puppet is deeply involved in the contextual political ecology and biopower between human identities and specific objects performing or representing identities as part of this ecological network of power.

The trope of the straitjacket as an analogy of the pacifying educational puppet show in the asylum relates to the Foucauldian idea of the straitjacket which for him symbolizes the contradictory forces of constraint against freedom that produce both bodily experience and subjectivity in disciplinary medical contexts (Foucault 2006: 439). The dynamic between discipline and resistance is also present in Foucault's concept of biopower. Biopower, as power over life, is potentially a repressive force, restricting the individual's freedom and producing passive docile bodies. The practising puppeteer in socially engaged puppetry is connected to the network of biopower often reproduced by capitalist medical and institutional techniques that administer and control the populace. Using biopower to analyse puppetry applied to social agendas emphasizes its corporeality within the ecological power relations between bodies.

Discourses and techniques of administration control or frame human and puppet bodies mobilized by these processes. The relation of body to puppet is explicitly used by Foucault as a metaphor in his descriptions of the docile body within the history of incarceration presented in *Discipline and Punishment*: 'A body is docile that may be subjected, used, transformed and improved. The celebrated automata, on the other hand, were not only a way of illustrating the organism, they were also political puppets, small scale models of power' (Foucault 1991: 136). Automata act as puppet-like machines or primitive robots which reproduce an impression of life and were historically popular with the aristocracy. Automata-like puppets also offer a representation of the way politics and power operate on the individual body to produce a controlled, manipulated or machine-like programmable life. Programmed people like prisoners, patients or soldiers are, for Foucault, transformed into a corporeal and cerebral shape via training and manipulation. The Foucauldian idea of automata and puppets as metaphors suggest that the bodies of the puppet, puppeteer and spectator are puppet-like – manipulated into social shapes and controlled by forces unidirectionally – as this is the case in the examples of the three tropes presented here: weapon, straightjacket and missionary.

Population control as puppet power

One of the most troubling accounts of puppetry I discovered, which was used directly towards bodies, was part of the work of Bil Baird, the great performer, author and pioneer of puppetry who worked on projects that toured post-war United States as well as India (as photographically documented in *Life* magazine).[2] He designed a programme supported by the US foreign aid (World Education Organisation based in New York) of the 1960s which was tied to population control and fears of the population 'bomb'. Baird scripted the play *Small Family, Happy Family* and the project is described in the document *Puppets and Population* (1971). In *Puppets and Population*, intended for use initially by indigenous populations of India (but more generally the Global South), it was presented thus: 'The basic human qualities of "Small Family, Happy Family" give it a universality that makes it playable almost anywhere … The plays human situation is valid anywhere' (Baird 1971: 25). Baird provided a creative cultural health intervention through this set of documents and practices that aimed to reduce and control population growth. Baird was one of the most famous puppeteers in the world in the 1960s, because of the work with Hollywood making puppets for *The Sound of Music* (1965). At this time, he had also made extensive tours of India and presented puppet traditions in his important book *The Art of the Puppet* (Baird and Zanger 1965). The pamphlet he authored, *Puppets and Population*, viewed critically, demonstrates problematic qualities: cultural imperialism as a set of Western norms about sexual health; imparting and importing these ideas towards the bodies of subaltern peoples; the patronizing use of simple peasant puppet stereotypes; the instrumental approach to engaging communities and the direct propaganda style of delivering messages. Baird introduces the programme thus: 'The puppet play included in this booklet, "Small Family, Happy Family", is one example of a teaching tool to let villagers know that they can limit their families and that they will have a better life by having small families' (Baird 1971: 13). This document is ghosted by the patronizing trope of the educational missionary – an interventionist character full of good intentions towards the subaltern population aiming to change opinions and behaviour in relation to the production of life. The style of glove puppets that Baird provides as templates in the programme do not have any relationship to the indigenous traditional puppetry styles found across India. Baird presents the subaltern character in these glove puppet forms through a Western concept of Indian identities and as an abstracted simplified 'grotesque cartoon' form of the Indian peasant. Baird's puppet show exemplifies Foucault's concept of biopower (power over life) through the way powerful normalizing discourses around sex, population and control are directed towards subaltern identities. The individual is subjugated by these discourses and the associated attempt to impose an administration of their bodies that intersects with a set of Western sexual norms connected to Western development funding and foreign aid.

This deploying of biopower is apparent, for example, in the following short extract:

ARJUN: For one thing, supposing that your wife were fitted with a loop.
LAL: A loop? I have never heard of the loop. What is it?
ARJUN: A loop is a small plastic ring that is worn inside the place where babies come from. That stops the next baby from coming until you want it. (Baird 1971: 63)

The modules for the programme that appear in the document *Puppets and Population* provide directions about why it is important for the subaltern people to use the contraceptive pill, the loop (intrauterine device), condoms and sterilization. Baird articulates his missionary position clearly, leaving no doubts as to the way the population are framed as passive recipients for this programme:

> We puppeteers have an important job to do now – a job I think we can do better than anyone else. It is to tell the people that it is better for them, for their country, and the whole world if they keep their families small; and then show them how they can do it. (Baird 1971: 20)

The global ecological context of health education and TfD tied to population control was not just a result of forces from outside the country, as the Indian authorities also welcomed this intervention. The idea contained in this programme about the propagation of life also reflects US foreign policy in this period (Connelly 2006). This period stands out as a historical example of mass experimentation on poor populations. It is important to draw attention to the influence of ecological economic forces here, the brutal contraceptive and medical techniques with their associated objects as well as the ignoring of reproductive rights. The ecological context of this project is a provocative example of the use of the puppet as an object to directly shape and influence populations' bodies. This process encourages passivity in populations through deployment of this 'benign' propaganda about reproductive rights. The project Baird led suggests a repressive form of biopower embedded in the ecological interaction of the community and state authorities with local and global economic forces. In the attempt to address the serious ecological issue of human population, or as it was then popularly labelled the 'population bomb', the rural subject is objectified through performance into a puppet form embodying and demonstrating normative values relating to sexual choices and population. As subjects stereotyped, turned into puppet objects, the subaltern voice is masked and does not speak in the *Small Family, Happy Family* puppet show. Instead, the subaltern is simplistically represented as the comic glove puppet and speaks like an uncanny version of an identity. This puppet identity gives voice and bodily form to an authoritative other constructed from Indian and Western discourses of sex and 'power over life'. The subordinate group is represented, but, in this context, they are unable to speak, left as a symbolic mouthpiece for messages imported from outside the community.

As a biopolitical practice, Applied Puppetry exists intersectionally in relation to the diverse identities of the group members, affects their bodies as audience members or workshop participants and this involves them in processes within an ecology of powerful objects producing opportunities for either docility or resistance. Biopower is exchanged and developed between and within a complex ecology of economics, environments, medical objects, human subjects, globally affected local spaces (including the puppet as object), which are connected to broader discourses surrounding the practice. These elements indicate, if recognized critically, the potential power of Applied Puppetry, and a sensitive awareness of their interaction potentially informs effective practice. Puppets have power when conducting Applied Puppetry in specific communities or workshop settings, especially when agendas are brought from outside that community within the complex ecology of practice, especially when in this intercultural setting.

Burlesquing as Baird

I folded the historical example of Baird's puppetry into my performance practice when I presented *Open and Closed Hands: The Applied Puppeteer as Meek Hero* (2014) at Royal Holloway, University of London. Through this event I explored the way performing objects relate to biopolitical networks by creating an imaginary dialogue between

Baird and myself (cast as a meek puppeteer) defining Applied Puppetry. I represented Baird in this performance as a heroic missionary character, full of good intentions helping the world's ecology. I viewed him critically as a 'hero' from my contemporary position within performance culture. In this appropriation of Baird's character, I drew on the use of philosophical dialogues to develop new knowledge. At the same time, I referenced the use of dialogue as a learning form, which is entrenched in Western traditions of philosophy and also found in Brecht's Lehrstück (learning plays).[3] In this performance dialogue, I drew on the source of Baird's programme for his play *Small Family Happy Family* (1971: 11–28) and its population control agendas. Initially, the intention was to present Baird as a glove puppet, once the dialogue was written, but I rejected this idea during the process.

A tangible puppet representation of Baird in this critical performance I considered too violently satirical – a cruel appropriation to adopt – so I played with using a dictaphone with cassette and distorted playback amplification to represent Baird's character.

Mocking a dead puppeteer whose influence is important to the world of puppetry felt cruel, though I still wanted to interrogate the political problems of this figure and his practice. The dictaphone recorded my 'inauthentic' American voice masquerading as Baird's voice. This use of the inauthentic voice draws on the tradition of heteroglossia in puppet traditions, as commented upon by anthropologist Joan Gross in her study of Walloon puppets (2001: 280). I often use lots of inauthentic voices as a puppeteer, and in this performance I adapted my version of an American accent in the recording. The dictaphone was placed within a small cardboard box full of cut-up text from Baird's play, and this assemblage of box, with dictaphone, represented Baird within the performance. I struggled with the ethical dilemma of this representation of the deceased puppeteer Baird, and my invocation of Baird through the objects was, in reflection, personally troubling. This representation of Baird did prove effective in some aspects; for example, the absence of any tangible figure and the disembodied voice were effective in presenting the issue of absence in relation to the historical Baird. This use of the voice in performance explored the unfamiliarity of recorded voices commented upon by Steven Connor in his history of ventriloquism (2000: 7). Through this imagined dialogue, I dealt with a ghost representation and the spectre of Baird in my practice conceptually. This dismemberment of the voice haunted the practice through the way I invoked the dead puppeteer partially, through the recording and the impression of Baird. As well as a theatrically novel way of quoting Baird, the dictaphone in the performance became, to an extent, an effective puppet of Baird as part of the knowledge-based practice I shared. This performed version of Baird presented my struggles to understand the problem of puppetry affecting lives through both the use of absence and the inauthentic puppet voice. It also was intentionally ironic exploring how to represent Baird against his struggles to effect positive population change in the world ecology. The issues that Baird's practice evokes haunts practices for me in the contemporary environment of health action, for example, where using puppetry around bodies or objects is entangled within contexts and produces power in relation to human bodies. Next, I explore my own practice in this context after the example of Baird's project.

Puppetry sensitization projects in Nairobi

Recently I have become involved in TfD projects which cover similar ground as Baird's pioneering work from the 1960s, in using puppets in relation to human health in the Global South. Many of the issues discovered in the historical precedent of Baird's practice informed and were used by me, as a heuristic set of issues to inform a more sensitive equitable practice with collaborative partners in Kenya.

Exploring this intercultural practice, the next part of this chapter discusses community based projects in Nairobi, exploring the use of puppets delivering messages about Lung health[4] and Covid-19[5] to local people. The discussion contextualizes the process, the delivery of this cross-cultural project and the process where puppet identities changed and adapted after construction. Puppets built in the UK, in the TUPUMUE project representing local identities, changed their meaning and their cultural connotation when they were brought to life by resident artists in Kenya. Issues of identity connect in these practices to Stuart Hall's (1997) reading of cultural representations and this is employed to frame this discussion. In particular, the scholarship of Paulette Richards also frames the way we can think through the way puppetry has represented specific identities, especially in relation to race. Her argument that 'the "living object" becomes part of a community that affirms its agency – at least for the duration of the performance' (2019: 3) is a viewpoint in relation to the Nairobi projects discussed next, as the way the puppets became part of the community context developed a key change in their meaning. In relation to the ethics of representation in contemporary puppetry, Tobi Poster-Su (2020: 55) argues that this space of representation is a 'liminal' space fraught with human problems and issues because the puppet troubles fixed meanings in performance. Using puppetry does not diffuse nor even negate the issues of representation and power and Poster-Su frames these issues around identity politics when he suggests puppetry 'offers us the possibility to move beyond binary understandings of subjecthood, identity and the political potential of performance … these very possibilities and ambiguities also mean that puppetry is capable of naturalising the appropriation of identities and insidiously reinscribing dehumanising racial ideologies' (Poster-Su 2021). These contemporary ideas about representation of identity were important aspects that informed the approach in the two projects in Nairobi, which I contributed to as puppeteer discussed here.

An aim of the puppetry in Nairobi was to add to the already established practices in Kenya respecting local artists in developing their own styles of puppetry. A key factor was that the community explored their own choice of narratives, and puppets were not used in a top-down "this is good for you" model. In this 'community-led' method, puppets were mobilized as a means for cross-cultural understanding, generating community narrative, communicating sensitively important narratives and information. The choice of how the puppets were used in the hands of the local artist was part of the interdisciplinary approach. The training in puppetry techniques was delivered, by me, remotely in the UK and this left a lot of freedom for the local artists to interpret and also be in control of narratives locally.

The artistic work in these projects was within a contextual frame of health and so was positioned in relation to bodies. This meant that it was biopolitical, but with the local population less 'targeted' to make changes to their bodies. This community approach and attitude made the practice feel less invasive towards the people in Nairobi. Within the inherent problems of misrepresentation and cross-cultural engagement conducting health education art projects in this way there is opportunities, with puppets, to bridge gaps and open up creative spaces in the community practice through the reception of less direct performances made locally. Puppets can, if used in this way, present complex issues about human bodies without an exaggerated othering of characters or violently stereotyping identities when they are in the hands of community practitioners. In this type of practice, the emphasis is that the community controls and develops the narratives on their terms. Many of the recollections of these projects in Nairobi used in health education involve stating that the puppets 'had their own life'. In this sense the puppets in the project were 'autonomous entities', more than just instrumental tools used as weapons to pass on information. These puppets also worked beyond borders, before and during the global pandemic, inhabiting a liminal space between the local artists through the remote delivery. The puppets were adapted in relation to local identities, race or local gender norms which made the puppets' performances more authentic and identifiable within the communities in Nairobi. This was particularly in relation to the mother character Sally whose costume was deemed too immodest when she arrived on the ground in Nairobi.

The context of using puppets in health action

There is a great amount of evidence of educational puppetry in Kenya (Mworogo 1996; Mbugua 2004; Kei 2012; Silanka 2019). The UNIMA encyclopaedia of puppetry defines Kenyan Puppetry thus: "Contemporary puppetry in Kenya is known especially for the grand scale of its educational thrust, which is part of the theatre for development work" (https://wepa.unima.org/en/kenya/) and there is much evidence to support a plethora of projects using the puppet form, particularly in the 1990s, some influenced by the pioneering work of Gary Friedman.[6] Friedman created one of the most impressive portfolios of Applied Puppetry using the art form during apartheid and post-apartheid in South Africa, often in serious danger for his life. His work in prisons and connected to politics in South Africa is an outstanding example of the ambition for an art form that can intersect within very volatile human contexts.

Friedman, in an article by Thomas Riccio, shows that Kenyan puppeteers translated puppet forms for their own very specific uses in projects he helped to initiate. Riccio and Friedman reflect that 'Kenyan puppeteers are not simply passive and accepting of puppetry models and modes of performance. They must consider local conditions, traditions, and audiences' (Riccio 2004: 308). The situation in Kenya is that puppets are much more recognizable culturally. In this pioneering health education work in Kenya the puppets appeared to Riccio to be effective 'because there are no preconceived notions, expectations, taboos or traditional contexts attached to puppet performance in Africa, puppets remain a novelty, neutral and free to define their own place, expression, and function' (2004: 308). Mworogo (1996) similarly emphasizes the way that in Kenya the use of puppets offers more than just the communicative function, beyond the needs of information delivery, in projects like health action models: 'Puppetry represents real life, but remains one step removed from the real world ... Puppets offer the viewer and listener a nonthreatening opportunity to look and laugh at themselves' (Mworogo 1996).[7] Another Kenyan practitioner Tata Mbugua in their powerful project supporting through creativity HIV/AIDS orphans in Kenya emphasizes the potential for puppets to engage in important life-enhancing skills and emotions. 'Puppets also can offer sympathy, when needed. Community members develop the puppetry themes based on their observations and conversations with the orphans and their families' (Mbugua 2004: 308). One great organization that offers training and a very structured and well-informed approach to using puppetry sensitively is the Kenya Institute of Puppet Theatre,[8] whose director Phylemon Odhiambo Okoth offers this knowledge and insights about Applied Puppetry to a wide audience in Kenya and beyond.

Puppets have the ability to create empathy in audiences and provoke emotional responses, and this is why they need to be deployed carefully as representational figures. These figures affect the hearts and minds, oftentimes in the context of health action in Kenya, of people who are in vulnerable positions and so the puppets' power to influence should be used sensitively. This sensitive deployment is in opposition to the disciplinary tropes of missionary, weapon, straitjacket styles. This attention to power made my practice feel more grounded around the problems of the community in relation to the health awareness information.

The context of the TUPUMUE project

Discussed next is TUPUMUE, or 'let's breathe!' in Swahili, a project in which the creative methods including puppetry were contained to improve lung health. The research was led by Liverpool School of Tropical Medicine and the Kenya Medical Research Institute (KEMRI) and was jointly funded by the National Research Foundation of Kenya and the Medical Research Council, UK. The research aimed to find out how many children in two communities in Nairobi, Kenya, have lung problems and explored children's experiences of lung problems and air pollution in the very specific ecology of urban Nairobi.

The project included community members involved in all stages to ensure that the study was directly relevant to their lives and local environmental conditions. The results of this study were fed back to the two communities in creative ways that they would feel were easy to understand, including the use of creative methods such as rap, comics, puppetry, street murals and videography. The sensitization and creative elements of the project were led by Louis Netter and Cressida Bower from the University of Portsmouth.

One of the investigators in both projects, Cindy Gray, Professor of Health and Behaviour, Institute of Health and Wellbeing, University of Glasgow, indicated her thoughts on the impact of puppets in relaying health messages:

The puppet show, entitled 'Billy's Day Out', describes exactly what the children will be asked to do during the data collection (to ensure accuracy the script was co-written with the TUPUMUE scientists). The champions took that methodology into the wider community. This had an important effect on how our sensitisation work developed and the way we informed individuals about the TUPUMUE project and about lung health in Nairobi. Following the sensitisation, 900 schoolchildren were recruited to the study in a matter of weeks, before it was suspended due to the closure of schools as part of the response to COVID-19 in Kenya. (2021: pers. comm., 20 Jan.)

This valorizing of the puppet and its effects in communication in the project was echoed from a scientific viewpoint by Graham Devereux, Professor of Respiratory Medicine:

The way the puppets focused knowledge about ways to communicate urgent health issues using creative methods was very effective. I have personally witnessed, and was hugely impressed by the way the children in Nairobi schools respond to the puppets and are able to understand the message that is being communicated. The sensitisation programme for TUPUMUE opened up new modes of engaging audiences and new ways of ensuring wide-reaching public participation. This has been a very positive collaboration using puppetry and an exciting, innovative and successful way to connect to people in the communities through play and creativity. (2021: pers. comm., 20 Jan.)

It is clear from these supportive comments that in the multi-faceted project of TUPUMUE the puppets worked well in the service of both the social and scientific aspects of delivering health messages. The puppets became a focus through which the information and next stages of the project were delivered. The puppets captured imaginations through their unusual performative features and were good at passing on, mimetically, the information that could positively change the bodies of participants in performances. Next, I critically examine some of the aspects of these projects.

Puppet (mis)representation

Drawing from semiotics, Hall develops an argument that language, in all its forms, is what is key to confront and deconstruct when trying to understand representation. Hall articulates this emphasis clearly when suggesting that 'representation is an essential part of the process by which meaning is produced and exchange between members of a culture. It does involve the use of language, of signs and images which stand for or represent things' (Hall 1997: 15). This matrix of meaning around representation is a feature of puppetry, particularly when representing specific populations or racial identities. When the characters of Sally and Billy in the TUPUMUE project were imported from the UK to Nairobi they were raw stereotypes of a specific identity type in Nairobi devoid of specific meanings, until they were reshaped in the community context by local artists and community champions. These puppet characters developed further through the use of a heteroglossia of local languages, spoken by the puppets mixed with the 'attractive strangeness' of the puppets performance identity. Puppets as things should be able to represent things concretely given their unique object status, but as Poster-Su suggests, they live in the liminal space where identities are troubled and unfixed (2020: 55). Puppets continually remind us that they are more than a mere representation, because of their status as symbolic objects with an unfixed materiality. Puppets, in this way, are great forms through which to question semiotic meanings and explore how meaning is attached to things, and through this liminality we can play with stereotypes. As Hall suggests the process of representation is never fixed or finished, and in the puppet figure this incompleteness is apparent in performance as the puppet's status shifts. Representation for Hall is slippery (1997: 9) which means we have to explore visual cultures through a series of layers in the complex systems of cultural exchanges to understand this concept. In the TfD style of sensitization in Nairobi this complexity was layered through the many parts of the projects and the gaps between languages used, by both puppets and the people developing the puppetry locally, which shifted continually. This complexity and layering within local contexts meant that the puppet in the Nairobi projects was not simply used like a blunt 'tool' delivering messages.

How the puppets worked on the ground in *Billy's Day Out* and other events

Next, I discuss the importance of language based on interviews with collaborator on these projects, Howard Abwao. His role in TUPUMUE and ACT was in the use of puppetry dramaturgy developing how important messages were imparted in the drama. This dramaturgical input in how the language was used in this project was a central theme in relation to the effectiveness of the sensitization activities with puppets. The puppets, made in the UK, spoke in the performance using an important local dialect of Sheng, which is neither English or Swahili but a mixture of these languages. In the performances new vocabularies were created using Sheng communicating methods and the technical aspects of the lung health project. The puppets helped to translate the technical jargon of medical objects, for example, spirometers in the TUPUMUE project into the local context using the puppets demystifying these objects speaking local Sheng.

The local populations knew forms of puppetry in work like political puppetry on TV in the form of the *XYZ Show, The Muppets, Bunimedia*[9] and the use of Applied Puppetry projects in communities.[10] Abwao suggests it is important to understand that pre-colonial puppetry traditions also existed in Kenya, which used puppetry with mask forms to tell important stories and animate the human spirits of the departed. These wooden puppets are still reference points to visual performance-making. The rod puppets for *Billy's Day Out* changed little facially or physically from the recognizable African characters when they arrived in Nairobi. Once in Nairobi though, there were important changes to the way the puppets were dressed in costumes, in particular the mother Sally who was perceived to be immodest in her outfit when she arrived from the UK. She was redressed in a more appropriate costume by local artists. The secondary and most important change was in the voices and language given to the puppets. The voice of the puppets related to the personas on display and the voices would change depending on the part of the drama enacted. A heightened higher class of dialect was adopted in relation to scenes with health professionals, and with Billy the language echoed the idioms of lower economic classes. This modulation of language had to find a middle ground in the drama to speak beyond class barriers and was an area of conflict and compromise in the process between complex differences in artists from regions around Nairobi. Some puppeteers spoke a deeper Sheng dialect than others and some spoke in a version that could move fluidly between different types of voice. The voice of the mother puppet Sally demonstrated this ability to shift dialect between 'classes' depending on the dramatic context of the character. Sally's role became a form of mediator between the more colloquial and the higher-status language of medical information. So, there was a mix of pedagogic and vernacular idioms in these layers of language.

The context of naming the puppets was due to the common adoption of English names in Kenya, due to the influence of colonial British rule. The historical influence of missionaries meant that when people were baptized, they were given an English name as well as having a more complex African name and identity. The missionary figure also ghosts the history of educational puppetry (Crothers 1983: 10). The process of naming based on English names becomes naturalized in Kenyan culture through this period of colonial rule. So, the puppets having English names was important as a signifier of the status of the puppets as imported, but was not, in the project, jarring for the audience at all as this naming using English names is common practice in everyday Kenyan culture.

A rejection of English names is a choice in contemporary Kenya but the common practice is to continue the adoption of both names. Kenya is a melting pot of cultures that usually embraces or adopts Western influence though with differing ideologies and political frames because of the omnipresent Western influence in the complex ecology of Kenyan culture. The naming of the puppets in the project *Billy's Day Out* because of the context and the important differences in the multicultural groups meant the adoption of African names for the 'inauthentic' imported puppets was too controversial and inappropriate. The puppets are imported creations and so they were not deemed rightful to have an African family or character trait name. This was how the complicated problem of naming puppets was resolved, by adopting English names influenced by the context of colonialism.

Theatre director Matthew Hahnn who shaped the project in the *Billy's Day Out* gives another perspective on how the applied puppet can be used efficaciously in the production of 'didactic' forms of TfD:

> In the TUPUMUE project, it was very useful to utilise a puppet in the play, *Billy's Day Out*, or else the script and performance might be considered too dry or boring if delivered fully by human actors. There is a delicate balancing act when creating such a piece of didactic theatre because the play must deliver a particular message where there can be no doubt about the child's interactions with the Lung

Health Study team but it also must be engaging so that the audiences do not stop interacting with the piece.

In TUPUMUE, we found it very useful to use the puppet as the main protagonist role. By using a beautifully and lovingly created piece of art in the form of a small boy and in later performances, his mother, we were able to captivate audiences whilst delivering an important message. The use of puppetry and call and response theatre meant that the balancing act of engagement and delivering a specific message was achieved. The actors who manipulated 'Billy' pushed the focus onto the puppet by fully embracing their role and becoming the means of movement and voice for the puppet without ever overpowering the puppet nor seeking the attention for themselves. The human actors who interacted with Billy and his mother Sally. fully committed to speaking to the puppet and not the actor controlling Billy which strengthened the world that the piece created. The audiences loved the puppets; the performances were often filled with smiles and laughter because this sort of hybrid theatre had never been seen before. (2020: pers. comm., 22 May)

The context of the ACT Nairobi project

The overall aim of ACT Nairobi, the second project, was to create community resources that could enable the production of public health messages in relation to Covid-19 transmission in 2020. Public health messages in Mukuru are typically disseminated using a process known as sensitization which involves raising awareness around local health and well-being issues. The puppet element of the project was one part of the overall mix of elements. The enhancement of puppetry skills between creatives in Kenya, led in the UK by me, was achieved through online workshops covering techniques of shadow puppetry, lip sync and building junk puppets using recycled objects. The local partner, Mukuru Youth Initiative, and twenty-one community researchers were engaged in delivering these public health messages. The community researchers included youth leaders, activists, school teachers, artists, musicians and film-makers, all of whom live and/or work in Mukuru. The digital outputs were widely shared in schools, community WhatsApp groups, YouTube and other social media.

Community artists and youth activist groups continue to use the new techniques introduced during this project. Many of these methods were relatively novel to these classroom settings and were received with great enthusiasm.

Shadow puppetry was introduced in the ACT project but this was more complex to use in practice even though it had a strong impact on social media platforms. One artist champion, Rose, used this technique very successfully in the classroom context. The general principle was that these puppets were deployed using entertainment and creativity to open up dialogue. In regard to education since the introduction of puppetry as a form, Abwao has used it in the classroom where his pupils make skits about HIV, climate change and corruption. This has had a positive effect on Abwao's pedagogy influencing a more creative, less didactic and now dialogical format with the puppets encouraging what Abwao calls learning in an 'immersive' way which the puppet form enables. For example, when discussing corruption, young people can hide behind the puppet, say more honest points without fear or rebuke, talk freely, enact crimes and embody villains which the young people feel is difficult to do when cast as actors speaking without a puppet surrogate.

Kruger in her discussion of different African puppet styles emphasizes the relation of tradition and educational puppetry in the approach across the continent including Kenya:

> The puppet as a performance object with a life of its own which is dependent on the imagination of the audience, as well as on the reality created temporarily in performance which cancels out the presence of the puppeteer, becomes a safe, even protective medium through which these needs and conflicts are channelled and expressed in a symbolic yet concrete way simultaneously. (Kruger 2010: 17)

The way the puppet created a safe space to discuss health issues was an outcome of the practice locally in our project.

In the recent projects in Nairobi there was room for new techniques like lip sync sock puppets styles and this was very adaptable in this context. One of the puppeteers Jared became very successful with this form of 'muppet style' puppetry in connecting with the young people, particularly primary school aged children. This age range had no problem relating to the comic puppet forms' attractive and entertaining nature.

Puppet heteroglossia

Joan Gross in her ethnography of Flemish puppetry noted that 'speaking through puppets represents a genre of speaking that aesthetically reproduces societal heteroglossia and is maintained through mimesis' (Gross 2001: 280). This is a theme that occurs in Gross's studies of the ways that puppetry affects community linguistic codes and methods in Belgian traditional Walloon puppetry (2001). The heteroglossia of languages that the puppets could produce was definitely exploited in the projects in Nairobi. Abwao similarly emphasizes in Nairobi the importance of the use of local dialects in the mouths of the puppets to get the information across, but more importantly to open up the conversation with the community through an authentically voiced representation.

When the puppets were delivered to Nairobi, they were mere representations of the general character of a young man and an older woman. They were remade through new clothes in the case of Sally with both puppets remade through language and local discourses. Without this remaking by local artists these puppet representations would not have the power to open dialogues about health. This is because they were remade using local dialects bended through puppet performance. Additionally, puppetry in Kenya is framed by both pre-colonial and post-colonial discourses that are important to recognize when venturing into projects of this kind. Kenya has both a rich tradition outside the influence of UK and in projects, which was respected. I presented remotely in the ACT project, for example using phone torches for shadow animation, to add to the expressive tools of local artists, but I had little control over the use of this technique on the ground. Being inventive, making remote puppetry in this way during lockdown and as a distraction from the pandemic for all participants we felt positively affected well-being. The puppets, like in many other community contexts discussed in this book, became a form to link the participants when puppets were seen as useful creative tools or the conditions of the pandemic did not allow this interaction face to face. Puppetry, in this style, also left room for a lot of autonomy for artists in Nairobi to playfully 'take or leave' the techniques offered, as well as use them in their own style as a way to communicate. The responsibility of representation is shared in this way by the artists on both continents and authenticated when the puppets' voices were adapted to speak with the entertaining voice reflecting local idioms that the community can recognize.

In reflection, the projects TUPUMUE and ACT also involved a unique artistic collaboration as the puppet had a very different existence away from the puppet makers hands. As an aesthetic, using remoteness, this autonomy for the puppet is an ideal position for the puppet to inhabit, like Pinocchio, away from the original puppeteer. A hope since delivery of the puppets for *Billy's Day Out* is that Billy and Sally continue their journey independent from the Western maker and progenitors. In the ACT project the puppets and the skits they performed were made from materials and artists on the ground in Nairobi which made issues less pronounced in regard to representation of race because the community were controlling their own representations. That said, all of these puppets operated in an in-between contradictory liminal space that is hard to control or semiotically fix. In this context Sally and Billy could not be given African names as their heritage is artificially made by the hands of Western puppet makers.

Representation issues increase the need to think carefully about performing specific identities and responsibly representing, when making work in communities. This is especially pronounced when the wider context of the work being carried out is as part of a TfD model. Applied Theatre scholar Tim Prentki offers ways of modelling this tricky process when he suggests, 'it is part of the business of facilitating a TfD process to support a community in its analysis of what it can do for itself and where it is being thwarted by systems beyond its control. TfD is the process of enabling communities to explore the barriers to their self-development, be these internal or external' (Prentki 2015: 81). At the heart of the TUPUMUE and ACT projects was the belief in the community's self-efficacy.

The puppet object as trickster, joker (Boal) or fool generates a great deal of joy and entertainment as well as imparting knowledge in a dynamic and accessible format, especially for younger people. Puppets also have the potential to misrepresent identities when used as direct agents like a weapon enforcing concerns which come from outside of a community parachuted in by educational missionaries. The alternative is to introduce puppets as part of the way a community shapes its thoughts about itself and towards others. In this process facilitators of projects using puppets do not give voices to communities through a deficit model, instead these voices are amplified by the methodologies employed and the instruments used, like puppetry. In the ACT project in particular, the use of puppetry was left in the hands of the local artist champions and this was the most appropriate way to share and encourage Applied Puppetry practice.

It is the ecological relationships developed with, between or around the puppets where sensitive developments can be enabled. This is a more holistic approach to the ecologies involved in projects and more appropriate than a one directional information delivery deployment of puppets directed towards the bodies of the people.

Notes

1. M. Smith, 'The Practice of Applied Puppetry: Antecedents and Tropes', *Research in Drama Education* 20, no. 4 (2015): 531–6.
2. Images of Bil Baird on tour in India: https://www.life.com/history/bil-baird-an-american-puppeteer-in-india/.
3. The teaching plays of Brecht are collected in English in this volume: B. Brecht, *Measures Taken and Other Lehrstück* (London: Methuen, 1977).
4. Description of TUPUMUE lung health project: https://www.port.ac.uk/news-events-and-blogs/news/understanding-the-impact-of-air-pollution-on-childrens-lungs-in-kenya.
5. ACT project descriptions: https://www.port.ac.uk/research/research-projects/act-nairobi.
6. Great website that traces the history of Friedman's influential Applied Puppetry: https://www.garyfriedmanproductions.com/archives.html.
7. Mworogo was part of the development of educational puppetry in Kenya as part of CHAPs Community Health Awareness Puppeteers. This was a precursor of what was to become Kenya Institute of Puppet Theatre.
8. Kenya Institute of Puppet Theatre website: https://kiptkenya.org/.
9. Buni Media website: https://www.bunimedia.com/.
10. Article about satirical puppetry in Kenya: https://www.theguardian.com/world/2009/nov/22/xyz-kenya-tv-puppets-satire.

5

Plastics talking about plastics: Marlsite projects and ecological puppetry

Plastic bottle monologue

[I sit in front of a camera shooting a video about plastic waste and hold a plastic bottle cut in half with eyes and nose stuck onto its transparent skin. I articulate the bottle head as a lip sync puppet able to speak about human pollution.]

The bottle speaks:

Hello I am a plastic bottle and I have millions of relatives and we inhabit your world. We are very abundant and numerous and you can find us enjoying our time in some of the most beautiful coastlines on the earth. Today I might tell you something about plastics.

In this chapter I consider trash, garbage and rubbish objects speaking about their own thingness (Brown 2016) when reconsidered as performing objects. I discuss ten years of Applied Puppetry practice called Marlsite inspired by trash, garbage, rubbish, post-industrial sites and their unique environments. Marlsite projects were conducted between 1999 and 2009 in the Northwest of England, supported with Arts Council funding responding to the trash found within these places during unique one-week residencies. Marlsite projects were a 'bricolage' of elements including puppetry, masks, poetry, junk music, site-specific installations, playful irreverence, including immersive and participatory performance. Through this practice objects performed and spoke about the experience of their object status. I explore here my practice towards objects through these performances and workshops, framed first by ecological considerations of trash and the artistic influences that informed this praxis.

Waste, trash, garbage and rubbish

When you start to think about waste it shifts your view of culture, especially in regard to value and ecology. Systems of waste were theorized by Michael Thompson in *Rubbish Theory*, in 1979 (reprinted and updated in 2017) and he argues about how fundamental waste is to our culture. Thompson's thesis surrounds the tripartite relationship between rubbish (which is devoid of value or time), involving transient objects that decrease in value over time and durable objects that increase in value due to being reinvested with new values, like, for example antiques. This system is cyclical for objects and when for example I pick up rubbish to make a puppet, I am involved in changing this value cycle of waste. Liz Parsons in 2007 updated Thompson's points and suggested that rubbish is 'persistent, it never actually completely goes away, we are never completely able to rid ourselves of it' (2007: 391). She also offers ways of thinking about the potentialities of rubbish objects through the important 'find' (2007: 392). By reusing objects, or seeing new potential in trash, she posits that by 'acknowledging the social life of things [we might] explore the career of the object as it traverses a universe of people' (2007: 392). So, objects like junk puppets sit outside and break the cycle of Thompson's *Rubbish Theory* as a rubbish 'find' that is transformed through new narratives, creative remaking, playing and performing.

John Scanlan in *On Garbage* (2005) explores the cultural world of garbage as a fundamental part of the rational project to clean the human world. Waste objects in our ecosystems challenge our notions of perfection as a human process. As well as being a serious environmental calamity, rubbish can be used as a way of thinking about how we separate certain waste objects away from everyday experience. If we adopt this focus on waste, it also challenges performance to understand its practices differently. Scanlan suggests that, like Kershaw (2007), we have to be careful to avoid the paradox of some forms of environmentalism, as part of the rational project of modern perfection by producing even more garbage (Scanlan 2005: 182).

'There is no human-made object so well-travelled, so ambient, as waste' (Thill 2015: 3). Out of the field of OOO, a series of object lesson books have been published recently, including Brian Thill's *Waste* 2015. His description of our current situation is rather bleak as we have reached our peak point of plastic waste, the 'plastisphere' (2015: 22). Thill suggests waste is within a network of desire and time, but also because it is so ultimately ubiquitous this system renders waste an 'ur-object' (2015: 8). We can see the aesthetics in this waste as ur-object in popular culture like in the plastic bag sequence in the film *American Beauty* (1999) (I also explore the plastic bag performatively a few times in this book). Thill reminds us in this exposition of waste that there is no life without residues (2015: 35) and cites Morton's point that there is 'no away' for our human detritus (2015: 50). We literally live within a rubbish tip of our own making. Historically waste is about the abject and removal of objects (2015: 27), but once considered, these waste objects can be emissaries of the chthonic other world we avoid, and waste also signifies cultural artefacts that we like to forget (2015: 28–9). The problem of waste is ultimately for Thill about the human need to have power over things (2015: 68). Thill uses the term the 'cultural logic of trashability' (2015: 109) to understand our interests in scrap and finding value in things outside the value system of consumer objects. For him 'things that have survived the scrap heap are valuable in part because so many objects of its kind found their way to the scrap heap' (2015: 109).

In the processes described in this chapter and in many of my own practice examples, rubbish, found or bound for the scrap heap, is recontextualized through puppetry into something with a new value. It breaks free of the system of Thompson's rubbish theory (2017) where consumer products transfer into valueless timeless entities put away in some other space. Also, the excitement of the find as described by Parsons (2007) is part of the potential joy of working with discarded materials in puppet making.

Figure 5.1 Plastic fish in sea bin, 2017 performance. Photo by Greg Smith.

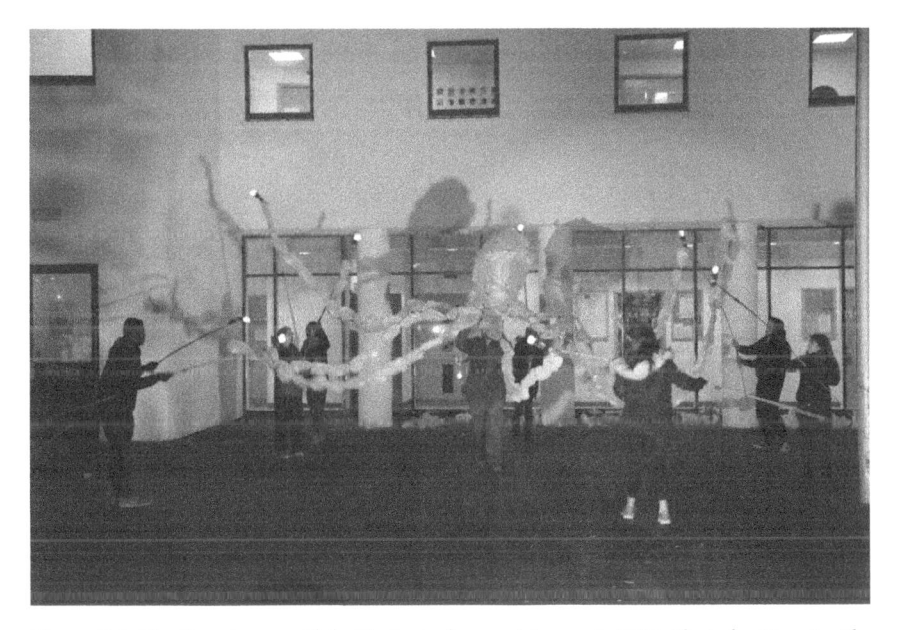

Figure 5.2 Plastic octopus with bottle tentacles, sea bin event, 2017. Photo by Greg Smith.

90　　　　　　　　　　　　　　*Applied Puppetry*

Working with trash feels transgressive, as finding use value in what is usually part of the consumerist system of waste dumping or recycling breaks us from the usual cycles or systems of advanced capitalism. Garbage-based puppets 'speak back' to the system of garbage when their materiality is so obviously present in their form (I am thinking of shoals of ghost fish made from opaque milk bottles that I constructed for a performance about sea bins in 2017, Figures 5.1 and 5.2). I find joy in the way that a plastic milk bottle already has the potential of a fish shape inscribed within its form and its consumer design. I cut out these shapes to accentuate this image of the ghost fish. Puppets and trash are both ur-objects, able to speak back to their material conditions that they are produced within and never escape. Examining waste with objects in this way is a novel way to explore the calamity of the plastisphere. Junk puppets are our guides to this underworld of waste, if we listen to their propensity or the stories they offer.

Through necessity, using waste materials has always been a part of my puppet practice. The abject poverty of my years in Liverpool and London during the 1990s meant I could not afford expensive making materials and this imparted into my practice a talent for finding the potential in trash. The meagre existence of the freelance artist developed in me a very keen eye for skipped and discarded materials from domestic or industrial processes. These bits of trash grew in value through making and animation. This resourceful pareidolia, repurposing waste, also was the main resource of workshops with children, which I have conducted for over thirty years now. The plastic bottle head is a standard part of the making I led using this simple method and I explore this next as it is at the heart of my workshop practice. In these workshops, the waste plastic bottle object enabled the ability of children to create and vocalize narratives of their own choice (Figure 5.3).

Figure 5.3 Workshop for Marlsite project, 2002. Photograph by Jonathon Purcell.

The children's junk puppet workshop

There is great scope for children to gain confidence in expressing themselves publicly through opportunities to present dialogue through a puppet. The attention is diverted from themselves towards the puppet who therefore acts as a support mechanism. (Hogg 2005: 18)

Puppets have powerful and stimulating meanings for children. In all the work I have conducted with children, I have very rarely worked with a child who does not feel excited by the prospect of making their own puppet. In most settings working with children in education, or in less formal settings like festivals, youth centres, playgroups or unusual places like hospitals or shopping malls, the design of the puppet workshop takes a similar format. The children make a rod puppet from recycled materials using quick fixing methods with sticky tape. There is no design process or previous experience of puppetry needed. The children start by assembling objects together and only their intuitive creative energy is required to make a puppet. The activity is open and not reliant on any previous level of craft or technique. The goal of the workshop process towards the end of the workshop is that the child brings the puppet to life in a short performance. The aesthetic value of the puppet as a visual artefact or crafted object is not as relevant or as important as its function as a performing object, as the intention is not to display the puppet on a wall in the workshop frame. The puppet-plays are performances usually spontaneously devised and improvised by the children at the end of the workshop without much structure. The only instruction given to the children with regard to their performance is to make sure the show has an ending, as some children will continuously play until instructed to stop, even when an audience is watching.

So, what value does this children's puppet workshop display in relation to Applied Theatre and community arts? There are three ways the junk puppet workshop offers potential in practice: the vocal possibilities, the visual quality and the way participation is encouraged. When the child speaks lines through the puppet, the displaced 'voice' of the puppet gives the children a chance to vocalize in the performance, even if they are not experienced performers. Even less confident children discover performing with a puppet is possible because the audience's focus is on the object and not the child puppeteer. Giving individuals and groups this chance to find ways of enabling, amplifying their voice has been part of the values, discourse and history of community arts. The puppet is visually more exciting than an actor and engages the participant's imagination enabling and amplifying. This visual dynamic is a key attraction and part of the popularity of puppets in child-based community groups. The puppet workshop offers an inclusive flexible level of participation in which all children achieve success in the art-making process. The making and performing are not coded or introduced by the facilitator as specialized or difficult, instead children are encouraged to enter a free moment of creative expression. Everyone can be a puppeteer in this workshop and this reflects the democratic ethos of the artist Joseph Beuys who proclaimed 'every human being is an artist' (Beuys in Thistlewood 1995:190). Using this ethos and being inclusive produces a sense of equality in the workshop which is evident in puppet making, as all the children involved achieve the same results of making and bringing to life a puppet. Implicit in this practice is that plastics are not evil materials or entities that need to be eradicated. The message in this work is that by approaching this material differently through creative methods the idea of plastics can be rethought and reimagined. Workshops with children making junk puppets, in this experience and style of delivery, do not begin with instructional information on recycling, but instead this message is part of the final reflections of the workshop. A question that is asked by the facilitator at the end of these workshops is, 'What have we done today? A form of recycling?'

Trash fecundity

Through my freelance experience, valuing trash and the aesthetic choices it develops in community practice with collaborators and participants moved me towards practices using repurposing explicitly and this approach became the Marlsite projects. Marl is a fecund fertilizer, as it combines lime and clay, and the first Marlsite performances were created on the rural Alsager Campus of Manchester Metropolitan University, sitting on the site of what was, historically before the campus was built, a marl pit. The idea of two elemental things combining making something new, with the potential to fertilize, seemed an inspiring idea mixed with the process of bringing a site to life by animating its waste. Many of our landscapes sit on top of waste. The aim of Marlsite was to think about how trash, garbage, rubbish or waste of a site could inspire telling stories irreverently or respond playfully to the heritage of the landscape. The 'playful irreverence' towards heritage and site was a key theme discussed when I presented this project at the conference 'Performing Heritage' in Manchester in 2008. This irreverent style of engagement with sites was also an important development of praxis when I reconsidered puppetry through the lens of ecology. Playful irreverence in this way opens up ecologies and their narratives. A key text that informed this development of an ecological practice was the book *The Reenchantment of Art* by Suzi Gablik (1991).

Re-enchanting puppet practice

In a concerted attack on the irresponsible fascination of modernism with the autonomy of art, Gablik counter-argues for a refreshing intersectional approach to art making. Gablik uses phrases like 'making art as if the world really mattered' (1991: 96) and explores listener-centred paradigms arguing for socially responsible and ecologically aware practice that challenges the established markets for art (1991). An influence on Gablik is the practice of Suzanne Lacy whose *Whisper, the Waves, the Wind* (1983–4), is a large-scale installation involving four hundred old women talking on a beach and *The Crystal Quilt* (1986–7) using a similar configuration of women indoors. These iconic feminist works of community-engaged site-specific practice are now well established and documented in major gallery collections like the Tate.[1]

Lacy's work exemplifies Gablik's notions of how the artist can create work that does not valorize, in a masculine way, the human artist as central entity or god in the process. Listening to the waves mixed with old women's voices in Lacy's social artwork presents a clear indication of how participatory art acknowledges the intersectionality of both processes, event and documentation. The other striking artistic narrative in Gablik's text is the story of the artist Dominique Mazeaud who cleans her local river of polluting waste which then becomes a practice (Gablik 1991: 119–22).[2] Gablik's listener-centred critical feminist approach left a lasting impact on my practice in community and Applied Theatre. Listening is a good principal in Applied Theatre and a simple action when approaching groups of participants attempting mutual respect and equanimity. Listening is also a way to think of how to approach practice with forgotten objects and materiality. Listening to objects and then approaching how they might speculatively want to move, sensitively or not, is part of the skill of the puppeteer. Pushing a puppet is like pushing a person around – epitomized thus – 'you will move and you will change' as opposed to 'would you like to move and would you like to change?'. The Marlsite approach aimed to listen to both the people, the site and the trash, then see what narratives appeared in the process. If children spoke of a ghostly flying fox that haunted the site of the Dancing Bridge, it was in the subsequent devised show.

One object central to Gablik's argument against modernism's masculine artistic autonomy is the controversial work *Tilted Arc* by sculptor Richard Serra (1981–9). She explores how its removal was a community act against an arrogant modernist mentality. This sculpture so deeply affected the bodies and minds of the people that they had it removed, which then involved a lawsuit by Serra. What seems relevant here in relation to objects is that the sculptural thing itself had a great impact on the bodies of the community. This impact can still be felt in another of Serra's works, as most of the ground floor of the Guggenheim in Bilbao has a similar monolithic minimalist sculpture *The Matter of Time* (1994–2005). The affect of this sculpture is felt through what it does to your sense of space and movement (It was disconcerting for my partner and too disruptive to her sense of balance when we visited). Serra's macho rusty imposition in space is viscerally felt as part of this object's presence as an entity. It pushes humans around. We are manipulated in the space of this object and the imbalance is overwhelming, through what it is doing to us. This is the object lesson of monolithic sculptures, including giant puppets and art objects like this; we are viscerally and literally moved by their impact.

Welfare State International's influence

Another influence on Marlsite is the work and ideas of Welfare State International (WSI) and their artistic directors Sue Gill and John Fox. I had the great fortune to be a part of their creative collaborators scheme in 1999, and later the company hosted Marlsite projects. WSI has paved the way for art making practices that critically work within the context of community and place. Fox presented their eye-catching and interdisciplinary performances as 'bridges across the void' for communities wishing to celebrate narratives against the mainstream. The work as articulated by Fox intended to provoke joy and wonder in audiences, not through increased participation in the New Labour sense of 'bums on seats' but through the way that events can provoke cartoon-like affective reactions in people as they respond with *Eyes on Stalks* (2002). The publications associated with this company's practices are very useful and engaging, providing a guidebook on how to make community and socially engaged art. One particular manual and guidebook is *Engineers of the Imagination* (Coult and Kershaw 2002), a text which has supplied generations with ways to capture the imagination of people in large or small events. Also more personally affecting, Sue Gill was the celebrant for my daughter's naming celebration and we witnessed how her practice elicits an open method to encourage secular ritual building.

In all of the practices of WSI, performing objects play a central role in capturing and enabling communities. One ubiquitous object from this practice is the paper lantern, seen as part of a multitude of community events in the UK, since WSI popularized this performing object. These simple structures, often in the form of animals or mythic beasts animate the streets and public spaces. Fox emphasizes how things can animate spaces in his practice and has often used small- and large-scale puppetry (Fox 2007).

His encouragement of practice presents making as outside of the established markets of art, a cheap alternative to the postmodern malaise and the crushing of hopes for communities. Consistently, the artists and makers that have made up the WSI history use tools, objects, materials and things in unusual formats to include people in spectacles.

Gill and Fox also encourage freedom of expression for artists, like through their creative collaboration scheme. As part of this scheme, I experienced making art at Lanternhouse, their purpose-built base in Ulverston in 1999. I collaborated with two other artists, Ali Rutherford and Ian Broscombe (we felt we were part of the *Big Brother* house for artists). What was experienced in the space of Lanternouse was that this building's playful architecture encouraged interconnectedness between us as artists in ways we hadn't anticipated. The final outcome of this residency process was not as important as the lesson that physical environments, like Lanternhouse and Ulverston, can do in changing artists. The final event we constructed was a surrealist performance *ShedHead* in which I wore a shed mask that had flapping wings on its roof, with other absurd aspects, including an inflatable granny and a remake of an old Stan Laurel film. A distinguishing feature of this event was its reliance on performing objects to express our practice. This collaboration with WSI subsequently left its mark on the practice of Marlsite and gave me more confidence to see the potential in exploring new networks and ways of making performance away from the inhibiting culture of the small-scale touring of puppet shows. The work model of WSI also influenced the way that my practices using puppetry and performing objects would meaningfully connect with communities.

Joseph Beuys and objects as charged energy batteries

Joseph Beuys was a powerful twentieth-century visual artist and environmental activist. He is an example of an artist creating the total work of eco-art. His objects are highly charged even though usually inert as sculpture. Joseph Beuys is a pioneer in forging art relating to the use of objects within a constructed ecology. His legacy inspired the practice of Marlsite through the way that he imbues objects with a heightened status in his actions, installations and thinking. Critic David Adams emphasizes his powerful contribution to the ecological turn in art: 'An approach to ecology worthy of the epithet "radical" is one that does not limit its concerns to ecological systems within the natural world ... Joseph Beuys was not only a radical ecologist, but also the pioneer investigator of the role of art in forging radical ecological paradigms for the relationship between human beings and the natural environment' (Adams 1992: 26). Adams situates Beuys's thinking and practice as a fully rounded approach to how humans position themselves in the ecology and towards their controversial concepts like nature.

> To encapsulate this overall development in Beuys's conceptions of art and of ecology, we may say that, while his understanding of ecological responsibility moved from scientific interest to public protest and alternative political organisations and then to the need to restructure society itself, based on philosophical analysis, his approach to art developed from traditional objects to installations and performances and then to the idea of 'social sculpture,' involving everyone as an artist. Thus, the two lines of development merged in the conception of the 'ecological *Gesamtkunstwerk*', the social sculpture. (Adams 1992: 28)

Beuys presents an integrated way to think through objects and the social. Works like *The End of the Twentieth Century* (1983–5) comprising human-scale granite slabs with round conical holes lined with felt, personally provoked me to understand mortality at a time when my mother was dying. The hare in *How to Explain Pictures to a Dead Hare* (1965) is puppet-like in its collaboration with Beuys, when they both moved through the gallery. In this action does the dead hare teach Beuys about art and life or is the hare the tutor? *7000 Oaks* (1982 ongoing) by Beuys stands out as his most explicitly ecological work in the way stone and tree remark upon deep time and humanities need to heal the scars of our destructive presence. These objects in Beuys's practice, though relatively still and apparently inanimate, are charged objects like batteries with meaningful presence. As critic Mark Rosenthal suggests, 'whatever his symbolic intent, the characters and objects are given tremendous physical presence and visceral energy' (2004: 57). He gives space for objects to speak to us about ecological time, possibilities and mortality.

In her appraisal of Beuys's approach, Andrea Duncan coined the term 'objectboundaryhood' which she uses to discuss his approach to art making, which includes the use of found objects and his relationship to materiality:

> Beuys' objects remain in transition. They remain in a state of process. They are not finished; Beuys has not STOPPED them. That is, their boundaries are never fully closed but neither are they so without some quality of order that they can be called fully dispersed; they are not 'chaotic'. (Duncan in Thistlewood 1995: 81)

This conception of object status in Beuys's practice suggests a vibrant state that objects inhabit in his performances and installations. This vibrant state in which objects are

Figure 5.4 Crewe Marlsite project puppets, 2002. Photograph by Jonathon Purcell.

transitional, pushing and blurring boundaries within the frame of an event is also at the core of Marlsite performances. Assessing the 'objectboundaryhood' of the puppet characters is part of the reflections offered here. For my practice in Marlsite, this 'charged' approach to objects was an aim, through the way that the vibrant presence of objects was created and felt. In Marsite the total work of ecological art was developed, both as Applied Puppetry and as socially engaged practice. Artistic hierarchies were also disrupted in Marlsite through playing with trash in this inclusive way reconnecting to sites and objects.

Marlsite processes

The process of Marlsite involved connecting to local groups like river charities and countryside rangers in developing the outreach and education potential of the sites they managed. The issue of waste in these sites was ongoing in relation to the ecology and so it was important how local schools or youth groups would connect to the project and sites. The workshops with groups were folded into the one-week residencies and then the work the groups produced was usually presented within the final performance. For example, in the *Dancing Bridge* (2002) event the group of local children brought their puppets and performed their short skits at the end of the performance journey under the Dancing Bridge in Wheelock. Further performance was encouraged as it seemed fitting that within this local space, used historically for dances, it should again be animated with raucous dancing. Finding ways to involve the audience and immerse them in the experience was a continual strategy of Marlsite projects. We used some of the stories from the community workshops retelling these narratives to the audience in the show, like for example, when a strange apparition of a flying fox interrupted proceedings at the Dancing Bridge. This use of local narratives, no matter how fantastical, combined with the playful opportunity of the audience to perform in the heritage or post-industrial site formed an inclusive way to invite participation. The rethinking, remaking and recontextualizing of the junk and waste also played with hierarchies of value in relation to ecologies. Trash was elevated in this process towards a 'magical realist fictional world' where, for example, in the Congleton project giant cardboard butterflies could attack the world of the Clinker Men.

Each of the performances involved a physical journey for the audience after one of the early static versions of this practice was a disappointing event. As we found, the focus of an audience towards an event standing in a static manner did not encourage enough participation, even though the spectacle was large scale. We discovered this as part of an alternative performance during the queen's jubilee celebration weekend when we had created a large-scale event that included a scrap train with beer-can-faced passengers. Unfortunately, this performance was interrupted by the surrounding events. This was a hard lesson as the show celebrated the railway heritage of Crewe, but it failed to sustain audience's attention (Figure 5.4). This lesson informed the development of the audience's interaction in subsequent Marlsite events by exploring a performance 'trail' format. Within the Marlsite process we further explored ways to find rubbish, look for inspiration in its form using pareidolia, find faces or forms in the

Figure 5.5 Headteacher puppet Marlsite, 2002. Photograph by Jonathon Purcell.

98   *Applied Puppetry*

trash seeing objects differently and let those found objects speak, not as a waste thing, but as something revalued and animated within a landscape. To open up reflections on the Marlsite events, next I use some of these performing objects as provocateurs, eliciting reflections, telling some of the tales of the residencies to create a sense of these events.

Suitcase Headteacher, Wheelock

After the disappointment of the performance in Crewe, due to the static audience interactions and inappropriate context, a second performance happened in the semi-rural village of Wheelock in Cheshire sited in and around an old derelict schoolhouse. The audience arrived at the front of the school, greeted by myself, as an old-fashioned schoolmaster, then they were asked to process through the school, which was brought to life with the sounds of children, past hooks for children's bags and coats hauntingly given new presence to the space. In the old playground at the back of the school the audience met other puppets playing. Then I arrived, transformed into a three-metre-high giant rucksack puppet headmaster (Figure 5.5) with its visage in the form of a repurposed leatherette suitcase with buckles for eyes. (This puppet is reminiscent of Gerald Scarfe's monstrous teacher cartoon for Pink Floyd's *The Wall* 1979, which was rendered into a giant puppet for the pop video, feature film and live concerts.) I declared to the audience as the teacher puppet that 'I was somewhat transformed' and clowned about with a cane in the hands of the giant puppet. The audience laughed

Figure 5.6 Whale puppet on beach 2003. Photograph by Jonathon Purcell.

at the grotesque bullishness of the character and the ridiculous transformation (from human-sized headteacher to a giant puppet rendition).

The element of transformation is one of the delights of the potential dramaturgy of puppetry. Many of the popular puppets of the nineteenth century were trick puppets that transformed (McCormick and Pratasik 1998: 137–8). It is also a key point that I impart to students when teaching children's theatre – that transformation is a highlight of puppet narratives and making drama. One of the major transformations in Wheelock was in the active audience moving through the liminal atmospheric disused school building, animated and brought to life in a rather ghostly manner.

During this residency, workshops were conducted before and after the performance with children building puppets made from waste materials. This performance of Marlsite project was the positive turning point in the praxis, when the elements of immersion, engagement and transformation, including activated participants, combined. The old rural derelict schoolhouse became a charged space through which to pass and in which the fictional frame for the audience transformed.

The whale, Ulverston

On a beach near Ulverston, Cumbria, in the northwest of England, we made a whale sized whale from waste car upholstery and steel frames (Figure 5.6). The belly of the beast was full of junk puppets made by local children and an inclusive group of adults with disabilities. The puppets were hung in the guts of the whale, and the audience at the end of the performance walked through the mouth of the whale looking at the colourful creatures inside. This whale was a poetical way we found to 'fold' an audience into a performance space within the week-long Marlsite residency model. The performance became, through the performing object of the whale, an immersive ritual.

Two other companies use the metaphor of the 'belly of the beast' to immerse audiences: Odin Theatre,[3] Denmark, and In the Heart of the Beast Puppet and Mask Theatre from Minnesota. My recollections of Odin's staging were that the audience sat in traverse on either side of the stage and were offered wine and bread by their director Eugenio Barba and the ensemble of actors. The audience were the ribs of a whale. This framing act represented a sense of communion and exchange, beyond the often disciplinary structure of theatre's spectatorship.

In the Heart of the Beast Puppet and Mask Theatre brings together groups to ritually partake in large-scale outdoor events, part of the genealogy of companies inspired by Peter Schumann's Bread and Puppet Theatre, like WSI and Horse and Bamboo Theatre.[4] One of the company members Steven Linsner of In the Heart of the Beast described this approach to communally using theatre thus:

> To be puppeteers in the Heart of the Beast ...
> ... is to find ourselves in the great world Beast made of families, races, ages, sexes, classes, corporations and nations, people, (and creatures!) all different, working out a way to live together.

...is to work puppets. To hold life in our hands, to sense how we are all like puppets – worked by instincts, voices, and forces above us and below us.

...is to carry and protect something very old like a heart within us, a secret, a promise. Like carrying a flickering candle through a dark place. Like carrying a family in a horse-drawn wagon.

...is to travel the roads of history and loss, in search of something like a new heart: new communities, new families, new work, new holidays.

...is to tell the story of people who live in the heart of the beast – as courageous and resourceful as they really are. (hobt.org website)[5]

The bread and wine (echoing religious rites) given out at the start of Odin's theatre, the bread given at the end of Bread and Puppet Theatre shows, the large-scale puppets of In the Heart of the Beast and the literal whale's belly in my company PickleHerring in the Marlsite projects are all examples of objects used to engage audiences and participants together. The objects (bread, wine, puppets, junk, waste) are performing this work of immersive secular communion in collaboration with the human participants.

At the end of the Marlsite show in Ulverston with the whale, the hyperobject (Morton) of a weather front spectacularly arrived changing the performance conditions. The clouds descended with a heavy downpour which closed the performance, like a giant curtain drawn across proceedings. The audience all ran for shelter, mostly to the local pub, and then very rapidly a rainbow perfectly framed the whale and its surrounding

Figure 5.7 Clinkermen puppets in the Hands of Audience. Photograph by Jonathon Purcell.

windsock fish made from old plastic bags. The aesthetic impact of this ecological image on our company was profound and beyond words at the time. It was a moving moment, when the ecological reality entangled and surrounded the belly of the whale, with the humble 'put-together' nature of our performance.

Clinkermen, Congleton

In the post-industrial landscape of Congleton in Cheshire, heavy industries left their marks on the landscape including waste from furnaces called clinker. Clinker is produced from the process of sintering or fusing of coke, slag, grit and coal. Scars in the hillocks around Congleton are full of the volcanic-like forms of clinker left behind and these shapes became the heads for hand-sized puppets. In the narrative of one of the Marlsite residencies in this environment, we built giant cardboard Dingy Skipper butterflies, which inhabited some magical world that had waged war on the Clinkermen, a much smaller species. Children had to collect the little clinker homunculi and protect them in this playful ecological nightmare (Figure 5.7). The children became attached to the Clinkermen and wanted to keep them as playthings.

The Clinkermen were simple puppets with no joints, waste foam bodies and simple eyes and mouths. What they embodied was an irreverent attitude towards human heritage in the changing conditions of landscape, through interactions of humans and materials.

Figure 5.8 The Bunny, Marlsite 2003. Photograph by Jonathon Purcell.

The Clinkermen were celebrated in a song at the beginning of the show using junk instruments (Smith 2008), including waste carpet tube bass tubophones. The Clinkermen were characters that displayed the world of ecological waste and heavy industry in a scale that was approachable, engaging and fun. Taking care of the Clinkermen, when children adopted them as part of the drama as an endangered species, was a form of détournement in the post-industrial context. Many children took these odd puppets home. This ecological narrative was a metaphor for the climate crisis, experienced between generations in this performance. The Clinkermen spoke silently about the environment through their pitted and scarred rock-like faces born from the hellish fires of the Industrial Revolution. Other aspects that were animated in this post-industrial environment were puppets representing invasive species of terrapins in the nearby river (who had thrived after being flushed down the toilet, part of the craze for Teenage Mutant Ninja Turtles). We represented these reptiles by wearing old army helmets with appendages of heads and legs, as a homage to the local terrapins in the river.

The Bunny, Ulverston

Assembled from two wings from a Volkswagen beetle car, a scrap BBQ on wheels, scrap white powder-coated steel and old bath mats, the Bunny was born in Ulverston at the workshop of WSI as part of one of our Marlsite residencies there (Figure 5.8). It appeared like a giant scrapyard magic trick, pushed on top of an earth mound for the audience to see. It was as if a magician had pulled it out of a hat. The Bunny did very little in the performance apart from blankly stare over the proceedings, which included a carousel covered in junk puppets made by participants, a dance macabre of grotesque scrap wooden forms, the skeleton of a bird, the giant skeletons of dead cattle built from scrap foam representing the previous use of the site as a tannery, a giant fat cat with a car grill grinning mouth (taken from a burnt out pick-up truck) with its purring belly made by a drum played by a cordless drill inside, a weird mystical deer that danced along the earth mound and finally a kite flying scrap metal man. The wind that day was very slight and the audience had to blow towards the kite made from plastic bags to enable, what felt like on that windless day, a miraculous flight of scrap kites. The Bunny stared at all of this, stock still, always vibrant in its material reconfiguration on top of a hillock.

The VW beetle is a people's car designed during the Nazi project and in our performance its skull-like form and blank stare produced, because of missing headlights, an image which made this relic rather uncanny. Its blank stillness made it stand out like a talisman in the performance and in photographic documentation by Jonathon Purcell. The ironic image of a 'people's car' reconfigured as another species was both playful and haunting. Also, the giant scale of the Bunny's head rendered it anything but cute. I have used this image of the Bunny as a document numerous times as its simple sculptural form translates performativity so well in photographic documentation. Its blank stare silently speaks beyond the frame of the photograph.

Plastics Talking about Plastics 103

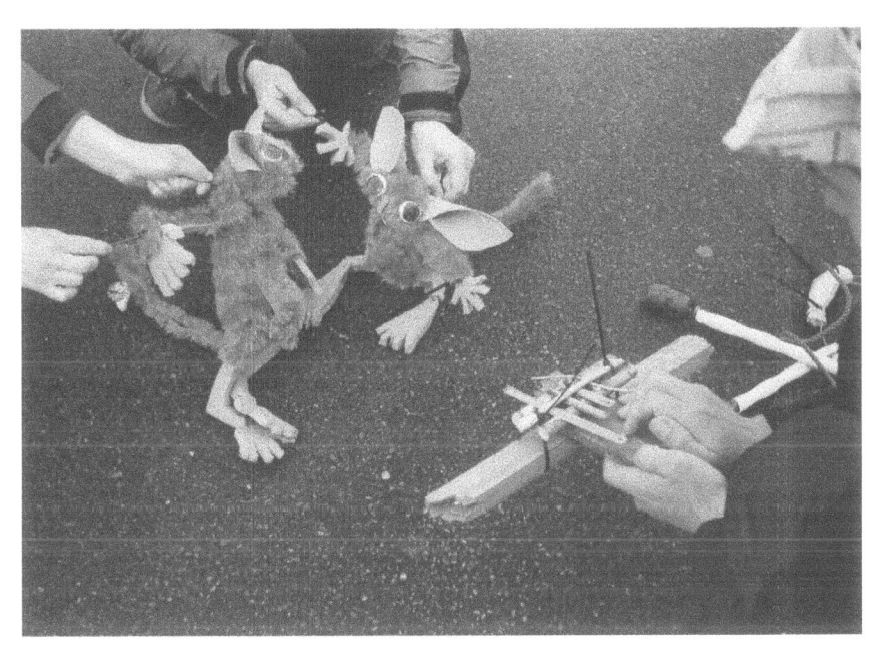

Figure 5.9 Bush Baby puppets, Marlsite, 2004. Photograph by Jonathon Purcell.

Bush babies, Manchester

In the bushes in Platt Fields Park, in inner city Manchester, a group of festival participants follow a trail of puppet animals and are led to a group of puppet bush babies (Figure 5.9) who frolic and dance. They are accompanied by the sound of thumb pianos made from wood scraps and broken hacksaw blades. The instruments make ploppy bass notes and crunchy burrs, as the dissonance of the instrument creates accidental sounds. The bush babies have eyes made from beer bottles and have a simple floppy construction from waste fur material. This event is part of a larger street arts festival held in the park with companies from around the world. The assemblage of the puppets with the junk instruments created an immersive experience for the audience finding puppet creatures in the woods. The sounds of the junk instrument, thumb hacksaw pianos, were amplified using home-made piezo transducer pickups connected to a battery-powered amplifier. The junk instruments gave voices to the scrap puppets better than human character voices and the use of junk instruments was a key development of the Marlsite style of performances (Smith 2008). After using guitars and other tuned instruments it soon became logical to introduce the voice and motifs of the junk puppet characters through the sounds made from junk instruments.

Junk instruments are exciting performing objects that speak clearly to alternative ways of conceptualizing waste and pollution. This practice is influenced by groups like Urban Strawberry Lunch[6] from Liverpool and Einstürzende Neubauten,[7] German pioneering noise makers and users of junk instruments. Like puppets, junk instruments

Figure 5.10 Plastic Bottle Bear, Marlsite, 2003. Photograph by Jonathon Purcell.

appear double-coded, giving them energy, like Beuys's charged objects and they have a vibrancy as performing objects. The bush babies come to life through animation, but they have a unique displaced voice in the use of junk music instruments. This assemblage of sound, image and environment was a 'small-scale attraction', charming to audiences due to scale.

Plastic Bottle Bear, Manchester

Plastic bottles are ubiqruitous and very useful as a resource for puppetry making as they are lightweight, strong and easy to cut. Again, in Manchester's Platt Field Park, I built a full-sized bear who sang the blues and sat in the bushes next to an urban stream. He was covered in waste car upholstery material and was a surprising character to meet on the trail of the Marlsite performance. He could speak and sing in English and this made him slightly uncanny as well as visually impressive. He sung with the voice of Anna Barzotti accompanied by composer Paul Rogers as he played harmonica and they made a dynamic double act (Figure 5.10). The bear was not as obviously revealing about its plastic material form as some junk plastic puppets, due to his upholstery fur, though he was still named Plastic Bottle Bear. What happened to the bear is in some ways the opposite of the story of the artist who cleans the river (Gablik 1991: 119–22) as we had to continually rescue the bear from the stream, as he was kidnapped and drowned by local youths in between shows. As this was inner city Manchester, protection of the performing objects was a constant problem as they

Figure 5.11 Audience with rope, Marlsite 2003. Photograph by Jonathon Purcell.

were often under threat of vandalism or attack. This is one of the issues with close-up immersive street theatre as the performers whether human or puppets are vulnerable. Luckily for us plastic bottles are resilient and float and we would retrieve the bear from the stream for the next performance.

Like the Bunny in Ulverston, this bear became an iconic image of the Marlsite aesthetic in which the musician and the puppet combine in a delightful meshing of material, human animation and imagination. One other object that was important in this show was a long piece of rope which the audience held while they walked through the bushes and around the site (Figure 5.11). The rope became in this performance an enabler for unifying the audience in pacing themselves and sticking together to witness the series of events found at different locations. The rope enabled, disciplined and choreographed the bodies of the audience as they all needed to hold on to the rope to make the performance work in the environment of the bushes.

Pink Spider, Congleton

Often the Marliste performing objects were incongruous with the landscape, including a twenty-metre spider made from bright pink waste plastic, wooden cable drums and with old vinyl records for eyes. This puppet did not move but was more like Beuys's sculptural installation objects. It stood on a hillock made from heavy industry from another time and looked out across to the town of Congleton. At points in the Marlsite

Figure 5.12 Canal barge transformed into a giant fish, 2005, Nantwich. Photograph by Jonathon Purcell.

projects puppet characters did not need to move to animate the environment they inhabited. The pink spider was one of these objects. Its incongruous position was part of the way it temporarily brought to life the landscape for the groups of young people, processing around the nature reserve, situated on top of historical industrial waste. A new mythology was invented there, where a pink spider could inhabit this corner of the earth and watch us. A local special school responded to our irreverent approaches to the site and brought along with them their own giant flying crocodile puppet made from waste plastic. No one questioned why this odd chimaera was made by the school; it just seemed to easily inhabit the odd imagined world of the Marlsite performances. Later the spider's pink plastic was reused to turn a canal barge into a giant fish (Figure 5.12).

Eyes in trees, Ellesmere Port

Along a canal in Ellesmere Port (a heavily industrialized landscape) we placed in trees plastic pizza packaging circles with cartoon-like eyes with pupils roughly drawn onto them. The groups of participants walked past these eyes watching them on the other side of the bank of the canal and again later when they travelled back on a barge to where they started their adventure. For many years, part of my training of potential puppeteers has involved the simple instruction to place eyes on an object, as this action will immediately bring it to life. The object will also become anthropomorphized by the simple placing of eyes. In the example of the trees this process was more about

Figure 5.13 Workshop puppets, Marlsite 2005. Photograph by Jonathon Purcell.

mysterious creatures inside the trees without identifiable forms or bodies than human eyes. When we put an imagined body to disembodied eyes it is not always human, but often reflects the clichéd cartoon world of animated Disney woodlands. It is often animals or maybe the idea of an animal that we imagine behind the eyes looking through the branches. In Ellesmere Port this imagined other in the trees was a way to use plastics to speak to the imaginations of young minds. Adapting trees with cartoon eyes in ecological terms seems to be an abuse of the trees' intelligence as an entity, but one way to look at this example is that the trees collaborated in being part of the drama and the playful narrative of the Marlsite event. This process is not a violence towards the organic life form but a playful interaction within the frame of the post-industrial situation, an organic mixing with the man-made. To attune to environments becomes rethinking, noticing in a ludic way, provoking the mind and opening up sites in this manner. Perceiving entities like trees as sentient and magically alive opens up a possibility of rethinking poetics and was an intrinsic aspect of these processes. In Marlsite, we invigorated these post-industrial spaces through illogical and ridiculous worlds made possible by the disruptive nature of puppetry.

Fly tipping 2008

At the end of the Marlsite process we were commissioned by the Environment Agency to respond to the issue of fly-tipping in a public campaign using our street art performance style, engaging audiences around the UK. This was a departure from the week-long residency model and involved building a one-day performance using trash puppets and junk music. A rat was fashioned from a discarded three-wheel pushchair, a scrap pigeon attacked members of the public and giant figures built from bin bags and plastic shopping bags lumbered into the performance area. Improvised lines were spoken over a megaphone and the whole event felt like agitprop. Mixed in with this was street-based workshops making scrap puppets from waste materials (Figure 5.13). These events were more street theatre than the immersive processual version of Marlsite, and the narrative was slighter, due to the fact that the dramaturgy of narratives in street theatre causes issues in practice.

This issue of narrative in street theatre puppet dramaturgy I also discovered when commissioned to perform a street version of Red Riding Hood as a small-scale suitcase puppet show.[8] Audiences on the streets need to be hooked quickly into street theatre and if they have missed the start of a narrative they will often just walk on. Puppets as street art embody what Schumann has been quoted as saying is the puppets' quality of being 'louder than traffic' particularly his larger-scale puppets used to protest against the Vietnam War (Schumann cited in Bell 2013: 273). Even though these puppets are silent, they speak volumes on the street. Our approach to street puppetry in the commission from the Environment Agency was inspired in this way by the visionary artist Peter Schumann of Bread and Puppet Theatre (Brecht 1988).

Schumann led the pioneering protest puppetry against the Vietnam War and made other performances that used ritual elements. Certainly, the events communicating awareness of fly-tipping were louder than traffic with dissonant junk music and giant puppets, but some of the playful joy and imaginative pleasure was lost in this version. Even so, I was proud that when a member of the Environment Agency looked at our work and commented, he said that we looked like we were 'Greenpeace protesters'. In many ways it was the aim to get the message across loud and clear like activists, but that meant omitting the more explorative versions of our junk puppetry.

Conclusive points about eco-puppetry practice

This practice using waste and rubbish opens perspectives within which to reconsider our materiality and objects' materiality through acts of animating junk, exploring garbage in performance and in this process we 'open up' ecologies. Puppets speak directly about the experience of plastics, like in my use of the plastic bottle telling a plastic story, the shoals of plastic fish in the sea bin event or the Plastic Bottle Bear. To be ecological is not just to immerse ourselves romantically in the soothing rendition of a Gainsborough landscape painting, but instead to confront ourselves with what we discard or bury in the ground of that landscape. The hills around Congleton are full of the heritage of waste like clinker and this seam can be mined creatively to rediscover ecological heritage. Through this listening practice objects like waste plastics begin to speak about the experience of plastic as it is very obviously their skin or their internal skeleton, like the plastic bottle bear. We can explore our relationship with objects like plastic and then understand that we have a much deeper and complex connection to these entities as part of waste ecologies. The methodology of Marlsite developed a pioneering approach to make waste valuable and it also modelled a way to work with communities in its format of residencies and workshops. Changing the system of the production of art, in Pickleherring's sense, was moving away from small-scale touring, developing a novel and liberating shift in the practice, manoeuvring into sites away from the limiting possibilities of venue-based production. This ecological type of practice now at this point in my career (operating within an academic context) has developed into new spaces including looking at how puppetry can describe groundbreaking science in developing how enzymes break down plastic waste (one of my latest projects in 2023). Plastic is not a pejorative word and our approach to plastics can be hopeful, if rethought creatively. As Beuys described his process as 'Plastik' (Rosenthal 2004:24), so Applied Puppetry could also be rethought as a 'plastic' art form. Certainly, Marlsite as a 'plastic' practice elicited an engaging model in creating its sense of a total ecological theatre in specific sites. Plastic means more than a synthetic product, it can mean moulding, shaping and changing into new forms.

Notes

1. Tate webpages about Suzanne Lacy's practice: https://www.tate.org.uk/art/artists/suzanne-lacy-13736/who-is-suzanne-lacy.
2. The important example of environmental practice in Gablik's book is Dominique Mazeaud's work *The Great Cleansing of the Rio Grande River* (1987).
3. Information about the intercultural Odin Theatre Company can be found here: https://odinteatret.org/.
4. The Horse and Bamboo Theatre company has a long history of making visual theatre with masks and puppetry. They have made very effective workshops in shadow puppetry and suitcase puppetry. See https://horseandbamboo.org/.

    Horse and Bamboo was influenced, like WSI, by the important work of Peter Schumann's Bread and Puppet Theatre. They introduced an expressionistic style of puppetry and mask theatre from the early 1980s in the UK. Sometimes they toured using horse-drawn caravans to rural communities.

    'Horse and Bamboo Theatre Company rarely perform in formal venues, tending to tour their shows to the smaller towns and larger villages of Britain and Europe that are distant from theatres, and where an audience may be found which does not want complexly worded plays but will converse through the universal medium of the emotions' (Kemptser 2001: 33).
5. Heart of the Beast website and information about their name: https://hobt.org/about/our-name/.
6. Web-based description of Liverpool Junk music company Urban Strawberry Lunch: https://en.wikipedia.org/wiki/Urban_Strawberry_Lunch.
7. Website of Einstürzende Neubauten: https://neubauten.org/de/.
8. This show was made during a series of workshops on suitcase puppetry with Horse and Bamboo Theatre and I now use this as an example of telling narratives without words for students.

6

Puppetry in HMP Haslar IRC: Working with marginalized and vulnerable participants

This chapter addresses the issues involved with the practice of Applied Puppetry in relation to immigration detention. This scholarly praxis has evolved from ideas drawn from the Practice as Research (PaR) project I conducted in an immigration removal centre in the UK HMP Haslar IRC from 2014 to 2016. The chapter explores making puppets and performing puppet shows in this traumatic detention environment and reflects on the knowledge gained through subsequent lecture performances. The chapter explores personal accounts of practice, experiences of workshops and questions about power and ethics. This experience is an example of how using objects relates to how the bodies of, in this case men's bodies, are othered and dehumanized through the harsh ecology of the UK immigration system. The possibilities of this puppet practice in the IRC I consider in relation to the strange combination of things in this system of biopolitical and object power. This account expresses how through object performance the unspeakable experiences of this space are expressed and how we should consider an idea of a new ethics in relation to these powerful object lessons in traumatic places. Out of this practice an ethics of the 'hand to hand' is proposed drawing from (but also departing from) the intersubjective philosophy of Emanuel Levinas's concept of the 'face to face' (2006).

The puppet workshop borders

At the border of the puppet workshop, when the participant and artist meet for the first time, the event is one that involves uncertain intersubjective relations, power, objects and a negotiation of ethics. The biopower in this situation at the border of the workshop practice can be complicated by the use of puppets. In the specific ecology of HMP Haslar IRC, this biopower was pronounced because of the status of the men as 'marginal others' in UK society. In this space at the workshop border, the acts of hospitality that are usually a necessity for the workshop to proceed were a key part of the early stages. The purposeful hospitality of the puppet workshop was intended as resistant to the in-hospitable spaces of HMP Haslar IRC. This intersubjective border demarcated the beginning of the workshop at HMP Haslar IRC. This was a fluid border – a blurred space that was often hard to distinguish. Viewed in this way, the relatively open space of the puppet workshops at HMP Haslar IRC were uncertain. The practitioner at the beginning stages of applied puppet workshops can either acknowledge or ignore this powerful emotional and haptic information.

Through this practice of breaching the workshop borders in the education department of Haslar, I chose to reflect on this exchange and moment at the beginning of the workshop. I hung a sheet from the institutional ceiling and projected puppet images onto a screen with an overhead projector borrowed from the education department. This activity drew the men into the space, as the door was left open. Then they discussed with me what was occurring, and often we shook hands as part of the introduction.

Sometimes these conversations were difficult because of language barriers. At other points, the men were more engaged as the invitation to 'join in' was understood and appreciated. Often the men saw how the puppets related to their own cultural heritage and made comments about the practice of puppetry. Some would say that the shadow puppetry reminded them of what they had seen in villages back home. As I witnessed, for some men at this stage it was enough for them to participate by just watching the play of puppets on the screen. In smaller groups, the men would become more involved and agree to participate in the workshop further with more engagement after discussion. As a practitioner, I was, at these initial stages, trying to respect the autonomy of the potential participant, as the men were relatively free in the education department to come and join in the workshop or leave at any point. I spent a lot of time waiting for the men to become interested and trust my presence. Once these initial borders between the immigrant detainees and myself were crossed in the practice and space of the workshop, the possibilities for creativity opened up and often allowed a dynamic space for expression. In practice, this shift in the intersubjective border space beyond the state of unfamiliar strangers was often expressed through the human hand in gestures and handshakes because spoken language was not always effective or possible.

Sociologist Richard Sennett presents the workshop as a laboratory in which the individual expresses his or her tacit knowledge through the hands. Sennett emphasizes the importance of the hands in the social space of the workshop. For him, the hands develop a 'repertoire of learned gestures' through experimentation that are 'full of ethical implications' (2008: 178). Literary scholar Kenneth Gross, through his view of the puppeteer's hands, suggests that 'hands are a language and a voice, they are also a body, a face; they provide a passageway for an entire world of relation to be made visible, put in motion, organized, and shaped, means for touching and grasping that world, inviting and doing violence to it' (2011: 52). This view of the hand demonstrates how the puppeteer's hands and hands in general function in the world of workshops and puppets and how the hand engages an ethical space. The puppeteer's hands can manipulate the appearance of objects, but the same hands in Applied Puppetry touch participants' hands directly. I found that an awareness of the power of the puppeteer's hands in workshop practice provokes questions about autonomy and the ethics of this touch. The importance of the hand in creative practice as embodied knowledge is promoted by architect Juhani Pallasmaa in his monograph *The Thinking Hand*. Pallasmaa presents the hand as having a multitude of roles both creative and cultural in arts practice (2009: 25–9). This view of the hand in practice is also evoked by puppeteer Martha Aebes describing her work delivering AIDS awareness programmes in which she describes her practice in *Puppets with a Purpose* as, 'my hands want to tell my people some stories' (Aebes in McIntyre/UNICEF 1998: 19). All of these sources encourage the practitioner to consider the significance of the haptic knowledge the hand produces in arts practice.

The temporal boundaries to the workshop space in the HMP Haslar IRC were relatively fluid and took the form of a 'drop in' session. The sessions were not presented as lessons, and the shape of the workshops were framed by the discipline, timing and daily regime of the prison environment. The micro boundary to the workshop was the moment of the welcome then the initial face-to-face introductions and explanations. The workshop space after this then became a ludic space to inhabit, potentially without imposed rules, filled with the possibility to create and play. During one of the week-long residencies I conducted at Haslar, two men from Nepal became engaged in the process, one became a puppeteer and the other a musician. As well as playing with puppets, we played guitars, and the two activities complemented each other. One of the men described the shadow puppet form as reminiscent of stories from the Ramayana and Arabian Nights they had experienced in Nepal. Reflecting back towards this residency, it felt that the most inspired moment in this workshop was when one of the men took over the control of the puppets and devised a story independently with the shadow figures. He seemed lost in his concentrated devising of the narrative of a king and a kidnapped queen. He improvised scenes while I improvised guitar sounds to support his playing. Later, he wrote down the narrative to remember the story. As workshop 'leader', I was encouraged by this moment, as I was able to step back and let the participant take control of the form of the artistic process. This approach to workshop practice was one of facilitation more than workshop 'leading' and demanded a flexible sensitive approach. This involved listening to the participants knowing when to step in and out of the creative space. Within this strange temporality of the prison workshop space, it was impossible to develop any process with the men without this flexible 'listener-centred' approach (Gablik 1991: 112). The ethical as well as the practical demands of the social space of the workshop meant that this flexible approach was appropriate for the men at HMP Haslar IRC torn away from their everyday social relations outside the prison.

The aim for this practice was to offer creative spaces within the context of incarceration and security. This practice attempted to break down the pressure of the biopolitical situation by offering alternative social networks that temporarily repositioned the relations between participants. To facilitate these changes, the initial issue of the welcome was one of the first hurdles in the workshop space. This welcome was often strange, as the act of hospitality offered was complex in the prison environment due to the detainee's status and circumstances. In the space I usually worked in, I was also a relative stranger to the men in the space. For example, two spaces used in Haslar were the music room in the education block and, during a summer residency, the prison yard. The music room was used twice a week for music activities and the surrounding rooms were used for other learning activities managed through private contract with a company that delivered education activities. My activity was

Figure 6.1 HMP Haslar puppets, 2016. Photograph by Greg Smith.

Figure 6.2 HMP Haslar puppets, 2016. Photograph by Greg Smith.

not part of the contracted work of the education department, and I had to respectfully negotiate my space around other scheduled activities. The hospitality offered to me was usually warm and supportive, but I was in no way 'master of this house' when I was working in the education department. I had to be careful not to disturb this hospitality by disturbing the usual running of the education block. I felt in relation to this hospitality a vulnerable guest at points.

In the prison yard, my vulnerability as a stranger was incredibly pronounced. During a week-long residency in one of the hottest weeks of the year, I made puppets and performed at the end of the week with support from the men and from staff. The men would laze in the sun or shade and come over and play. They would help make or just watch the marionettes built in a style approximating that of Punjabi marionettes inspired by photographs in *Indian Puppets* by Sampa Ghosh and Utpal K. Banerjee (2006). The experience of the prison yard was an embodiment of estrangement. I felt viscerally uncomfortable and fearful of this environment when I first began the workshop in the yard. I felt no direct hostility from the men, but the emotional weight of the surveyed prison space initiated feelings of fear, worry and uncertainty. The bizarre nature of the puppets brought into this space (especially the goat marionette puppet made as a reaction to the goats of HMP Haslar who lived on the perimeter grass) helped to break down my embodied fears and uncertainties. Once I saw the men laughing and joking about the puppets, my worries lessened and I grew in confidence. In this experience, I felt hostility not from the immigrant detainees, but instead as an experience of being enmeshed amongst the power of the carceral space. The act of creativity offered through the puppet workshop in the prison yard was complicated by this enveloping ecology. At the end of the week, after overcoming my feelings of estrangement, I performed with the puppets in the yard for the men, and this proved very popular. This experience of creating a temporary workshop space and performance was certainly one of the strangest in my career in the way I dealt with the issue of spatial hostility mixed with welcome in the space of the yard and the unusual welcome I offered through the puppet workshop. Next, I will explore this conception of hospitality and welcome in relation to my practice.

Hospitality and the welcome in the workshops

A method through which to conceptualize the welcoming of the other is through the way philosopher Jacques Derrida explores the idea of hospitality. Derrida's concept of the welcome is considered in relation to how the stranger is welcomed into the home. The word and act of hospitality for Derrida in his article 'Hospitality' also inhabits 'hostility' for the other (2000: 3). In this sense, the idea of hospitality is not a contradiction, but, for Derrida, impossible. In the act of the welcome towards the other, the host must behave in excess of hospitality and give up their claims to the space. The welcome is a performative act (Derrida 2000: 6) which is enacted without knowing what the outcome could be for the individuals involved. This concept of hospitality connects to the Derridean idea of community which contains in its etymology its opposite, as he described in an interview in *Deconstruction in a Nutshell* (1997: 106–13). This act of welcoming the other as an aim of the practitioner applied to the workshop must account for the problem of its impossibility and hostility in the event of the workshop when part of practice.

In my practice, bringing a puppet to the workshop situation added another level of complexity to the performative act of welcoming the stranger into the creative space. The puppet as object is strange but not a stranger to the space of the workshop, as it is the focus and one of the reasons for the workshop. As a form of distraction to the pressures of the face-to-face 'nakedness' of the situation of the welcome, the puppet also potentially offers a humorous focal point and distraction for the opening stages of the workshop. The experience of the puppet also became a form of creative gift, in relation to the famous anthropologist and sociologist Marcel Mauss's influential ideas about gift exchange and modern society (2004: 83). Through the acts of hospitality and exchange at the beginning of the workshop, the puppet was exchanged between hands. This exchange in relation to applied drama as political gift is a key element in practice as presented by applied drama authority Helen Nicholson (2005: 160–1), and, in my project, politics of exchange and reciprocity were focused around the puppet. The reciprocity in this exchange was filled with uncertainty because of the potential for deportation or other dehumanizing actions of immigration framing this exchange and events. At HMP Haslar IRC, the puppets opened up possibilities through this exchange of puppet as gift as part of the event of the welcome. The participants were not pressurized or as embarrassed with the puppet as they might be in actor-centred drama activities. The awkwardness of the face to face was apparent in these early exchanges, but, with puppets, the point of focus moved away from the face towards the hand-to-hand exchange of the puppet. In this way, the puppet lessened awkwardness in the moment of welcome. The puppets also enticed the participants into the workshop as surrogates opposed to me directly welcoming them into the space of the creative acts. This enticement was a key factor in the development of an effective practice, as the docility and awkwardness of the men was pronounced and their involvement in activities difficult to enable. The puppets as vibrant objects provided through displacement and enticement a form to disrupt issues of awkwardness of the welcome and face to face, and this enabled creative exchanges to occur but ultimately did not remove the problems of intersubjective demands.

From face to shoulder to hand

Applied Theatre scholar Alison Jeffers explores the issues of performance, ethics and identity in relation to asylum seekers' bodies in her conclusion to *Refugees, Theatre and Crisis* (2011). She presents the problem face to face with the asylum identity in shows by actors or real asylum identities. For Jeffers, the audience confronting the face of the other is unresolved when the performance concludes (2011: 161). Jeffers suggests in her book the ideal notion of standing not face to face but shoulder to shoulder with asylum identities. At HMP Haslar IRC, I stood shoulder to shoulder in the workshops with people caught within border politics, but, through this attempt at solidarity, I recognized the contradictory pressures of powerful forces outside these *othered* bodies. The puppets enabled, as objects within this political ecology, a shift in the hegemonic processes and contextual objects that separated the incarcerated men from outsiders like me. The puppets, compared with other entities in the space, did not conform to the same rules and acted like clowns breaking down the social norms between 'us and them'. The clown-like status of the puppet in regard to power is described by puppet scholar Eileen Blumenthal as the trickster puppets 'court jester-like licence' (2005: 189). This 'licence' in regard to power, when performing puppet work with exilic identities, meant that power and ethical demands were changed but usually left unresolved. This uncertainty in relationships between things often made the ideal of standing 'shoulder to shoulder' with exiled identities posited by Jeffers difficult to enact between participants. The puppets did not promote equality through shoulder-to-shoulder relations; instead, through hand-to-hand relations new social relations occurred through the welcome when the puppet was exchanged as a creative gift. In relation to the workshop's aim of being ethical and inclusive, there were three recognizable levels of engagement: at the moment of the welcome with initial face-to-face relations, the performative acts in the workshop with their representation of identities and, finally, after the workshop in the contradictory awkward moment of congratulatory farewell. In this moment of congratulatory farewell, I found this situation difficult, as it was important to offer thanks to the men who participated, but also a desire was expressed to never see the immigrant detained again in the context of pain at HMP Haslar IRC. As such, in this farewell, there was both the need to celebrate the relationship formed, as well as to effectively say, 'I hope to never see you again in this place'. After the moment of farewell between us, the identities faded into a shadow, then their visibility provoked questions of uncertainty and doubt. This incomplete event of farewell produced a sense of grief and frustration towards the men surrounded by biopolitical power. Throughout all of these performative acts, the hands of the participants played a key function in the practice through border objects, puppet play, awkward handshakes and everyday gestures. To develop a viewpoint of this space of ethical moments, through my research I applied the philosophy of Levinas as a reflective method.

Within the complex painful mosaic of the Haslar prison, I negotiated the very difficult, complex and demanding moment: the face to face. This happens fleetingly in corridors and more intensely in the space of the workshop. Emanuel Levinas brought attention to the ethical demand of the face-to-face encounter, through his conception of this way subjectivity operates. This conception helps the practitioner to consider these embodied ethical acts in practice. Levinas, in *Entre Nous* (2006), challenges us to feel a profound sense of responsibility towards the other through the face to face and, in doing so, we might improve our intersubjective and spiritual life beyond everyday experience (2006: 9). For Levinas, the relationship between the subject and the other is one in which the 'interhuman is thus an interface: a double axis where what is "of the world" qua phenomenological intelligibility is juxtapose with what is "not of the world" qua ethical responsibility' (2006: 56). Through the 'interhuman' exchange with the other, the subject can become ethical in responsibility to the other's demand on the subject. The face of the other demands the subject takes responsibility in an ethics in which the autonomy of the individual subject is brought into question. Levinas emphasizes, in the same interview, the primacy of the relationship to the other in the way he suggests that 'man's ethical relation to the other is ultimately prior to his ontological relation to himself (egology) or to the totality of things which we call the world (cosmology)' (2006: 57). In the temporal moment of the face to face, both the love for the other and the context of the world collide into a 'heady mix' of ethical demands for the subject. This relation between self and other also in relation to puppetry raises questions about the relation and respect for the non-human. Does this ethics relate to the artificial puppet as an *inter-face*?

In the practice of HMP Haslar IRC, the ethical demands of the other were so pronounced that it was often the case that the puppet's ethical role was unrecognized until after the workshops. The puppets as interfaces were a part of this ecology of ethics in the workshops, but the puppet as an active object complicated the ethical relations in the space. This was disrupted by taking the focus away from the human face to the space of the hand and the face of the puppet as artificial life. According to communications scholar Johanna Hartelius, the ethical situation of immigration involves being 'faced' by immigration (2013: 330). The puppet in this context defers this 'facing' and disrupts the ethical encounter. In the context of Haslar, through meetings, greetings, farewells and thanks for positive experiences, the embodiment of this ethical exchange often shifted. This shift was beyond the intersubjective because of the pressure of the contextual position, the vibrancy of objects, the power and the authority of the state, as well as the ethical responsibility of the workshop leader. Often in this ecology, this ethical exchange between individuals was experienced in the ways our hands touched, using objects and stories. This grounding of experience in the bodily exchange mixed with objects creates issues when considered in relation to Levinas's ethical philosophy and his spiritual transcendental ideas of the face.

As expressed by performance scholar Nicholas Ridout in *Theatre and Ethics*, Levinas's thought has been used to open up contemporary discussions of theatre as ethical practice (2009: 56). Ridout is careful to assert that, though Levinas's ethics is a method through which to perceive the issues in performance acts, the artificial nature of theatre presents a major difficulty (2009: 55). Performance does not resolve the problems of the face and relationship with the other. In the work of Julie Salverson, theatre scholar, the way that ideas drawn from Levinas can be applied to working with groups has influenced her view that 'this encounter with the "Other" is a surprise, a deformalisation of what is assured, an infinite of the Other that requires attentiveness to hear beyond one's conceptions' (Salverson 2008: 248). This 'breaking open' of experience for Salverson means that, when practitioners confront the other, especially when dealing with trauma, they become a form of 'foolish witness' (2008: 252). The puppets operated in my practice as co-collaborators also became fellow foolish witnesses.

The performance critic Tom Burvill explores performance ethics and this witnessing of the other through his writing about theatre and asylum in Australia. Drawing on Levinas to understand the way the asylum seeker is represented in performance, Burvill concludes that 'we are always already "hostage" to the other, for whom we have an infinite and therefore "unassumable" responsibility, which we must nevertheless strive to assume' (Burvill 2008: 241). The weight of this responsibility and sense of feeling 'hostage' to the other was experienced at HMP Haslar IRC through the practice of workshops. Another point made by Burvill is that the 'Levinasian encounter can only occur fleetingly, in powerfully affecting moments' (2008: 241). These encounters were recognizable at Haslar but felt even more ephemeral than the performances. Burvill acknowledges the problems associated with Levinas's ethics when mixed with performance practice in regard to the face. He also acknowledges the response needed to the face through the performance encounter and how that can 'facilitate' or 'embody' an ethical process. The ephemeral temporality of the ethical moment or event recognized by Burvill was a feature of the practice at HMP Haslar IRC.

In the context of the workshop practice at HMP Haslar IRC, two puppets illustrate relevant points about the relation of creativity with the concept of the other through the face to face. One such puppet is the faceless shadow of an abstract female figure (Figure 6.1). This figure was drawn by one of the men in a workshop and, although it shows the female form using curves, it clearly has no facial features. This objectification of the female form in this shadow puppet relates to the fact that, at HMP Haslar IRC, female prison staff and visitors were in a different network of power to the men. Some men expressed frustration at the way they missed the company of women. My experience was that the men in workshops displayed anguish and frustration especially around female puppets. In the performing object that is the faceless female shadow figure, this gender relationship is represented as disturbed and uncertain. The otherness of this faceless puppet was a reminder of the difference of female faces in relation to the men's lives in detention. This mysterious face also indicates the impossibility of capturing and truly representing the face of the other. According to Levinas' ethics (Levinas 1990: 202), it is impossible to represent the other's face. The making of the puppets did not reduce the detainee to just a 'countenance' which is seen as an evil act by the moral philosopher Roger Burggraeve through his reading of Levinas (Burggraeve 1999: 35). Alternatively, in Haslar the puppet became a reminder of the symbolic identity of the immigrant detainee and not a simple substitute for the other's face.

The second example of a puppet face that raised issues of representation of faces was one drawn on a simple papier-mâché marionette by one of the detainees during a very hot summer's day in the prison yard (Figure 6.2). This puppet face, with simple cartoon-like features, also contained, within their hand-drawn lines, a representation of the anguish and trauma of the man who drew them. This puppet was part of a performance of puppets in the yard using an approximation of Punjabi Street marionette performances at the end of a week-long residence. This performance was comic in style, but the strange grimace on the face of the puppet drawn by the detainee was in opposition to this humorous mode of performance. When reflecting on and interpreting this puppet, its face is a reminder of the face of the 'other' fixed in puppet form. This puppet face also captured my relationship to the representation of the other towards whom I felt responsibility. Confronting this puppet's face provoked questions about agency. My relation with the other in this process becomes a form of 'disrupted agency' when applying philosopher Benda Hofmeyr's (2007: 156) view of Levinas and the face to my practice. My personal intervention into the space of the immigrant detainee's life felt questioned in this puppet's gaze. The disruptive puppet in this specific workshop process did not obscure the appearance of alterity; it actually made the processes of otherness visible. Additionally, this puppet, through the connection of hands, shared the traces of our hands in the space of the strange workshop in the prison yard. The puppet's face inscribed by the detainee was also a trace, a representation of the other, but not the face of the other according to Levinas, as it was an interlocutor and artificial. Reflecting in this way about the possibilities of ethical encounters with puppetry through the practice at HMP Haslar IRC, it appears that the puppets as fellow 'foolish witnesses' enabled me to take ethical risks in the way I related to the men. The puppets were part of our shift from relative strangers to collaborators in a workshop. This process occurred through the way the puppet drew the focus from the face to the hand, which then could lead into the development of performances.

The puppets in this process of welcome were transgressive objects in the prison, crossing the borders of the prison not directly coerced by the rules of institutional bureaucracy and discipline. The puppets and puppetry in the workshop provided a limited form of creative anarchy in the way the objects operated outside forms of normalized everyday power networks. This form of anarchism relates to contemporary philosopher Simon Critchley's conception of contemporary ethics and politics in his book *Infinitely Demanding*. In the book, he describes a hopeful view of how to approach the global malaise by employing ethical approaches. Critchley presents this conception of ethics in action as 'anarchic meta-politics', and he goes on to suggest that 'It is the anarchic moment of democratic dissensus articulated around the experience of the ethical demand, the exorbitant demand at the heart of subjectivity by dividing it and opening it to otherness. This demand is not some theoretical abstraction' (2008: 130). Through actions, Critchley presents the ethical demand as the potential space for philosopher Jacques Rancière's resistant political and cultural dissensus (2010: 88–9), an alternative political artistic state. The anarchic puppets in Haslar as performing objects enabled a space to open up between the subjectivities of the participants that contained a limited form of dissensus. The puppets occupied a space between subjectivities and divided the experience of the workshop space into interstitial events. In the workshop, these liminal moments of action were visible, ephemeral but also rare in practice. The puppets in these moments did not comment on the situation directly; instead, they provided an entertaining 'gap' or alternative to the trauma.

In the case of HMP Haslar, the way these 'alternative relations' operated was present when I crossed the threshold of the prison to meet the exiled individual and work beyond the normal biopolitical situation for social 'cast-offs' in immigrant detention. The puppets in this unique situation as objects playfully divided and re-inscribed the issues of subjectivity between participants. The puppet was a strange representation of otherness that was uncertain, and these puppets encouraged new social spaces to emerge, with the potential for dissensus. The puppet introduced a new imagined world of relations. Unfortunately, this was a temporary change to the institutional space quickly forgotten in the institutional memory.

The demands of the face to face in the context of the current contemporary climate of fear are debated and explored by Simon Critchley. Influenced by Levinas and contemporary moral philosopher Knud Ejler Løgstrup, Critchley proposes that political commitment cannot be separated from ethical demands. Critchley, in his polemical book, offers an inspiring justification for artistic social practice for engaged art and creative interventions. For Critchley, this 'is the continual questioning from below of any attempt to impose order from above' (2008: 13). In relation to the other, the subject's experience 'is the experience of an exorbitant demand which heteronomously determines the ethical subject' (2008: 57). This relation to the other is an infinite responsibility and relates to trauma. Ultimately, in this engaged practice, Critchley demands that 'ethics is the experience of an infinite demand at the heart of my subjectivity, a demand that undoes me and requires me to do more, not in the name of some sovereign authority, but in the namelessness of a powerful exposure, a vulnerability, a responsive responsibility' (2008: 132). In the experience at HMP Haslar IRC, I felt throughout the practice the pull of the infinite demand of the other and attempted to enact this 'responsive responsibility' through the creative workshop. This awareness of the infinite was also in relation to an awareness of the biopolitical process involved around my practice. Critchley's approach and reaction to the 'tragic paradigm' in Western thought proposes a committed form of ethical practice and the potential of humour (2008: 78). The potential of humour offers an alternative to the melancholia of life, and this humour can be used as a positive practice (2008: 85). This use of humour, provoked by puppets as disruptive objects, was employed at HMP Haslar IRC as a positive approach in the practice.

Looking at the workshop practice at Haslar, I intended to produce with the help of the puppets this form of interstice or playful gap brought about through action. Viewed in this way, drawing on Critchley's thought, this encouragement of momentary gaps was resistant to controlling forces. In the momentary interstices or gaps, an event that can offer a space for the face to face or even hand to hand to connect in the workshop is a complex ecology that involves power and networks of objects. Workshops can form these gaps and interstices in the prison environment, but they are temporary fragile spaces.

Spontaneity, control and the limits of the puppet workshop

During the experience of the residencies at HMP Haslar IRC, there was a very exciting but risky moment in the workshop space that was indicative of a type of interstitial space. Relating back to how Critchley explains how there is the possibility for gaps and interstices opposed to the control of the authority, there were points in the next example where this occurred. This occurred when, for seemingly unknown reasons, spurts of creativity and performance would appear in the space without prompting or structure.

These moments occurred when the situation was out of my creative control. In these moments, I was no longer taking the artistic lead, and the men in the space were 'running the show'. This involved both puppets and improvised music, including playing drums in the space. The events were ironically (because of the context of the prison setting) autonomous and creatively free in the educational space. This lack of control was a positive state or 'interstice' in the lengthy experience of encouraging creativity in the project. An artistic and social change within the confines of the workshop was encapsulated in these moments of anarchy with creative autonomy, as the usual everyday relations were disrupted or blurred through unstructured performances – for example, men would sing in their own first language, songs relating to their heritage; play drums; and improvise bawdy silly tales with the puppets without any structure. These moments of play involving creative free expression happened in forms that were recognizable as collective and embodied – a sense of what influential anthropologist Victor Turner calls 'communitas' (2008: 96–7). I witnessed that, once the men trusted the space of the workshop and my role as relative stranger combined with puppets, we could enable spontaneous responses as moments out of the time of the prison regime. This included a sense of 'flow', a state of joyful immersion in creative experience as defined by psychologist Mihaly Csikszentmihalyi (2002: xi). This created a place of release for the men in which they were diverted from and actively forgetting, through performance, their carceral predicament. The benefit of humour and stress relief through creativity cannot be underestimated for men traumatized by the uncertainty of their incarceration. The puppets were a point of focus for the acts of forgetting and represented another imagined humorous world beyond the prison. As a practitioner, I was pleased with the apparent lack of control that I encouraged in the workshop space through these moments of laughter and flow. At the end of the week, the workshop material was usually shared in one of the classrooms to small audiences of around ten to fifteen staff and detainees. These performances were positive celebrations of the process, though they did not embody the powerful sense of creative freedom as in the shapeless creative energy of the uncontrolled workshop events.

These events in the gap space of the workshop were shapeless because there was no explicit form encouraged by me as workshop leader. Instead, the group or individual was lost in the flow of doing, playing and sense of communitas. The flexible boundary of the puppet workshop allowed space for this process and performances to emerge, and this was a positive aspect of the workshops and project.

The creative freedom, flow and communitas acknowledged in the workshop setting were limited by the temporality of the carceral context. The otherness of the participants to the workshop leader changes in these moments of relative freedom, but, in Levinas's ethics, the participants and the workshop leader and facilitator do not become equal due to the impossibility of this state of being. Through transgression in relation to the social norms and the usual rules of the prison, the puppet workshop did shift intersubjective relations through the performance of objects in creative acts, but the alterity of the immigrant detainee was only blurred or deferred. The participants appeared safe in sharing a space and being playful in the act of puppetry against the biopolitical situation. Through the process of the welcome, the face-to-face and the hand to hand playful acts of creative freedom in the space or interstices of the workshop temporarily resisted the coercive forces of detention. The practice of ethics in the workshop space encouraged limited autonomy against the controls of the sovereign power. During the 'downtime', when I was conversing with the men in the workshop, the opportunity to express their situation during the sessions emerged. After the creative improvisations and makings, during these conversations towards the end of the residency weeks, I cherished points where the inequalities of social barriers between us shifted. Therefore, through my own embodied tacit knowledge of these workshop spaces at Haslar as an Applied Theatre maker, I was also changed by these exchanges. This knowledge was experienced through the touch of hands, the playing of puppets and instruments, as well as through the demand of the face in this unusual ecology of objects and forces.

In my experience as artist and researcher in the practice of workshops, there did often arouse a feeling of personal pain. I share with the poet Andrew Jordan his view of his experience, as artist in residence at HMP Haslar IRC in 2005–6, when he found that 'to create in there is to hurt'.[1] This experience of residual pain is from the pronounced demand of the face-to-face and hand-to-hand exchanges occurring between the practitioner and the imprisoned in this space. In relation to these challenges of working with traumatized migrant identities Applied Theatre scholars Michael Balfour et al. (2015) advocate the application of resilience in regard to the oppressive context of this type of practice (18). In my experience the application of resilience in the context of Haslar was vital to continue the emotionally demanding process.

Through the practice at HMP Haslar IRC, an awareness and reflection on the role of practitioners and participants developed with particular regard to hands. This awareness combined with consideration of the ethical issues of the face in relation to Levinas's philosophy led to my invocation of the phrase 'hand to hand'. This phrase relates to both proximity and violence but can be invoked to describe a positive bodily connection between people in the context of arts practice. The violence of the face-to-face that Levinas explores in *Totality and Infinity* (1990) can also relate to the potential for violence of the hand-to-hand. This conflict can move beyond the associations with the violence of combat to the possibility of communication and responsibility towards the other. This haptic physical connection, though, moves the ethical from the ideal space to the dirty space of the bodily and, with puppets, the uncertainty of objects. In this way, this hand-to-hand interaction complicates the ethics of the face to face. For the applied puppeteer, this ethics is an intersubjective problem to address because this practice between objects and bodies emphasizes the hand as a key interface. Hands become 'dirty' in puppet workshops through handshakes, making and performing. Playwright and philosopher Jean-Paul Sartre dramatized the problems of violence, politics and ethics as 'dirty hands' in his 1948 resistance war play *Les Mains Sale*. This issue of dirty hands is also a point made by the political and applied philosopher Cecil Anthony John Coady (1996: 423) to describe the issues of ethics, politics and life. In the Applied Puppetry workshop, the shifting of the ethical from the face to the hand makes the practice both dirty and political. In Applied Puppetry practice, it is usual to engage with the other with hands when making and performing with puppets. The applied puppeteer has to get their hands dirty, and this means they are engaged in ethical or political problems between or beyond bodies and objects. This physical interaction when hands interact disrupts the ideal status implied by Levinas for the other through face-to-face and transcendental thought. Responsibility and sensitivity for the other are felt through the hand-to-hand, but the applied puppeteer who uses their hands irresponsibly could manipulate or even coerce if not careful or aware of the power they have in practice.

In relation to hands as powerful aspects of practice, the logo for Haslar symbolizes a relevant narrative. Two hands of different skin colours joined under the crown are represented in the logo for HMP Haslar IRC. One meaning connoted by this image is hands shaking in some form of mutual equality; though, when compared to the everyday realities of HMP Haslar IRC, this logo symbolizes other relations. The hands in the logo are locked perpetually together under the symbol of the sovereign instead of being free to let go. Under the crown and associated with this prison, the hands are not equal in this image. This logo and the handshakes that I experienced through the moment of touch and release at HMP Haslar IRC had different meanings. The release from the handshake in the workshop was as important as the connection made between bodies. Hands were also connected with objects and enabled the opening of alternative spaces between participants. This unusual space and way of relating between objects and others can develop for the subjectivity's consciousness through what Levinas describes as the 'powers of welcome, of gift, of full hands, of hospitality' (1990: 205). The political force of the hand is balanced by the ethical responsibility to the other through the face. In the workshop space, this physical and political interaction is a complex mix of allowing space and crossing boundaries between the people affected by the objects involved. Reflection about this important dynamic for the practitioner does involve a greater degree of understanding of the ecological space of objects, biopolitical context of actions and intersubjective relations. This reflection is especially important when using artificial others like puppets. The applied puppeteer gets their hands dirty and must acknowledge this in their practice.

This chapter has mostly explored the problems faced in the laboratory of the workshop. This practice is ethical through the way the welcome, the face-to-face and, particularly with puppets, the hand-to-hand are engaged. This practice is possible within traumatic geographies, as the workshops at Haslar evidenced. The process of puppetry can further develop creative ways to negotiate the ethical demand of the other in workshop space and temporarily change the relationship between entities. Unfortunately, these possibilities are provisional and often lost inside the ecology of institutional memories and forgetting, sovereign power and powerful national border forces in places like Haslar.

The workshop's boundaries are closer to the everyday in terms of face to face and hand to hand than the divided act of audience and spectacle. This potential for participation in workshops indicates Applied Puppetry's radical potential. The flexible applied puppet workshop at Haslar valorized spontaneous improvisations where divisions between participants were bridged by using puppetry and the workshops contained these resistant acts through dissensus. The radical potential for the workshop was discovered when I challenged the physical boundaries of subjects and others both inside and outside the domain of the creative space, using puppets. By encouraging this creative process, I encouraged temporary interstices or gaps within the frames of fear. Puppets as transgressive performing objects in this project were employed in this process as uncanny and radical others that opened up collaborative possibilities in breaking down estrangement, through hand-to-hand relations.

Note

1. This line is in Andrew Jordan's poem 'HMP Haslar an Etymology' in his collection *Boneheads Utopia*. The poem can be found on the webpage: 'Bonehead Utopia', http://smokestack-books.co.uk/book.php?book=8 (accessed 7 April 2013).

7

Toy Theatres, Kamishibai and Puppet City: Participatory ecologies

[Meanwhile] the philosophy of toy theatres is worth any one's consideration. All the essential morals which modern [men] need to learn could be deduced from this toy. Artistically considered, it reminds us of the main principle of art, the principle which is in most danger of being forgotten in our time. I mean the fact that art consists of limitation; the fact that art is limitation. Art does not consist in expanding things. Art consists of cutting things down, as I cut down with a pair of scissors my very ugly figures of St. George and the Dragon. Plato, who liked definite ideas, would like my cardboard dragon; for though the creature has few other artistic merits he is at least dragonish. The modern philosopher, who likes infinity, is quite welcome to a sheet of the plain cardboard. (*The Toy Theatre* (1909) by G. K. Chesterton (2007: 121))

The case is made throughout this chapter that artists and practitioners think by playing with objects, as part of engaged practice. This ludic space decentres the human subject through play with objects, helping participants in reconsidering ecologies, like imaginariums and cities. The proposition considered here is that by attempting to allow play with objects using performance practices new dialogues or narratives are unlocked about experiences, culture and ecology. Objects are more than just consumer products or instrumental tools within playful practices, if their ontological status is redefined and foregrounded in these ludic process. The practice that illustrates this proposition indicates that 'scaled performing objects' educate humans about immediate and imagined ecologies. This process is described here through examples, including my practice in Redsands Children's Care Home, Aya Nakamura's online Kamishibai performance *The Spiders Thread* (2020) and the project Puppet City (2018).

Toy theatres

Model theatre, with its cunning collapses and reversals of scale, reawakens the mimetic faculty, reminding us to be educated by child's play, to play again with models and toys at moments of crisis in the world of adults. (Sussman 2014: 277)

There is a list of famous artists who played with toy theatres in their early years, including Alfred Jarry, Frederico Lorca (Polansky 2014: 101) and luminaries like Hans Christian Andersen, Jane Austen, Edmund Bacon, Ingmar Bergman, James Burke, Edward Gordon Craig, Lewis Carroll, Charles Dickens, Johann Wolfgang von Goethe, Edward Gorey, Filippo Tommaso Marinetti, Laurence Olivier, Pablo Picasso, Oscar Wilde and Jack Butler Yeats. There is an even bigger list of cultural figures who used doll houses as a site of play and performance (Fell 2013; Sheriko 2017: 25). The word puppet in the English language has long been disarticulated from its etymological roots in relation to doll or *poppet*. This disentangling in language is not the case in other cultures, including Poland (*Lalak* means both puppet and doll). In 2014, I was part of a network and conference in Poland, led by Kamil Kopania, that looked at both dolls and puppets together.[1] The discussions of puppetry and dolls is a rich vein of knowledge that taps into the uncanny and the material social histories of objects both in play and performance. Dolls are as animated, loved and vibrant as their cousins and kin in the world of puppetry.

Many ritual performances use dolls as animated figures[2] and the distinguishing marks between puppet or doll are hard to recognize in many cultural forms or social spaces outside of the matrix of 'artistic puppetry'. In performances puppets can exploit their doll-like qualities, for example, Iranian company the Yas-e-Tamam Theater Group presented Lorca's *The House of Barnada Alba* (2011) at the London Suspense festival using around a hundred doll figures dressed in nuns' garments to explore the oppressive world of religion and gender in Lorca's melodrama.[3] The three puppeteers who animated the doll figures were dressed in identical garb with their faces obscured with a plain white cotton full mask, mirroring the doll/puppets' faces. This staging developed the text beyond its naturalist dialogue and towards a magic-realist-expressionistic rendition of the play. The doll-like scale of the puppets, exploited in this production, enhanced the audience's sense of empathy for the 'little other' of the puppet or doll.

It is ironic that the worst insult on the British stage for a puppeteer is 'dolly waggler' as this insult seems to contain a semblance of truth to the role, because of this close relationship of dolls and puppets. This pejorative use of dolls is connected to playing as a generally silly and childish pursuit. This negative association of working with doll-like others is less childish or silly when one considers how this playing within another scale is used in the development of military robots capable of autonomous movement programmed by the hand of the engineer.

A form of theatre, similar to the traditional toy theatre popular in nineteenth-century Britain, and which is now a new form of popular puppet theatre reaching Western audiences, is the Brazilian form of Lambe Lambe. Lambe Lambe is a style of puppetry invented in 1989 by Brazilian puppeteers Denise di Santos and Ismine Lima (Parsons 2022). In this theatre, born from street theatre practice, the audience of one peep into a box and watch a short personal immersive show wearing headphones. PuppetSoup[4] in 2021 ran a workshop in this practice led by puppeteer Fagner Gastaldon which explored the way that pleasure can be found in building personal narratives inside the Lambe Lambe miniature box. I found this experience of the workshop, in reflection, mirrored my personal journey into miniature worlds during the pandemic.

This kind of practice is like a memory theatre similar to the boxes of American modern artist Joseph Cornell. Inside the box of Lambe Lambe the puppeteer's hands are clearly visible and part of the narrative during performances. In Lambe Lambe the assemblage of box, objects, puppets, puppeteer's hands and recorded sound on headphones produces a unique miniature scale of performance ecology. Artist Nina Vogel from Concordis Theatre produced a novel version of this Lambe Lambe practice, *The Heart*[5] in 2021, using, instead of a separate box, a wearable oversized heart on her chest to express a series of scenes in the hearts' ventricles. This heart piece literally allowed us to cross bodily boundaries and explore the heart of the puppeteer, performed either in person or online. The poetic conceit in this show is that the audience and puppeteer share heartbeats through the mediation within the artificial heart. This performance produces a safe intimacy between the participants exploring the bodily and the haptic.

Play boxes with youth at Redsands Care Home

On the screen a fast car cut from a magazine moves into the collage box of bronzed models and celebrities cut from magazines.

In puppetry practice in community settings, I have utilised the use of cardboard boxes to create intimate spaces for performances in a few settings. These projects take the flat two-dimensional simplicity of toy theatres and doll houses as their inspiration. In Cheshire, while I was a freelance artist, I was commissioned to work with teenagers in the youth service and in the social care system. Working in this context as an artist stretched my abilities as the children's care sector in the UK in the early 2000s was volatile and violent. I taught drama at Redsands Care Home and at points would bring puppetry into this environment. At the centre I worked on both what was known as the open and closed sites. The closed site was similar to detention facilities as the children were locked in rooms for their own protection with the shouts and screams of locked-up youth as a constant part of the soundscape of that space. In this secure environment there were educational spaces that were very secure, used frequently by myself and other education staff. In this environment I encouraged a workshop using animated boxes, which turned into safe imaginative spaces for the participants and worked well in this volatile space. The workshop process at Redsands involved filling cardboard boxes with images drawn, but usually they were found images in magazines and these were then incorporated by lining the inside of the box with these cut-outs in the form of collage.

Other images, again often from magazines, could be constructed into flat puppets simply animated in the space and frame of the box. These would often reflect interests and aspirations of the young people, like fast cars or glamorous famous bodies. These elements would be simply animated and then filmed using basic video 'in camera' effects like fuzzy chrome colour mixing or the negative switching of colours. These effects added to the vibrancy of the recording of the box when played back on a TV monitor. The imagery was accompanied by a dance or trance music track of the young person's choice. This way of working directly borrowed from the heritage of toy theatre and tapped into the imaginative pleasure of building a personalixed boxed space for these moving images. The remediation using video further developed this 'imagined landscape' within the context of the care home. Reflecting back now at this practice born from the aim and desire to distract young minds towards a play space, it seems ironically contextualized, when considered within the 'boxed in' space of incarceration. Three important aspects were part of this work which included eliciting a playful environment, using performing objects and the workshop developing creative imagining. This combined to produce pleasure in these individual self-contained places which displaced the participants' minds from the trauma of life and personal pain through this form. Theatre and puppetry like this are a conduit, through which these imaginative spaces are invoked by individuals in workshops. The simple cardboard box taken from a supermarket enables this process within the wider network of objects. This flat ontology of cardboard and magazine paper facilitated the young traumatized people in this context, creating spaces beyond their daily circumstances of boredom, trauma and frustrations.

Rouge 28 Theatre's *The Spider's Thread*

A piece of card with the image of clouds crosses the screen. First in linear fashion and then off kilter.

The above is a description of one of the opening images from Aya Nakamura's online puppet work, *The Spider's Thread*[6] created for her company Rouge 28 Theatre. This online piece was made during the pandemic for a paper theatre presentation at the Japan Foundation.[7] This event was a cultural highlight of the pandemic during what was a bleak time for audiences and artists alike. Against the context of fear and apocalyptic miasma artists like Nakamura made and performed in virtual spaces performing objects and puppet shows in the online format exploiting these screen-based digital formats in new ways.

In *The Spider's Thread* Nakamura presents an epic tale of gods and villains in the micro world of flat card performance. Nakamura was inspired by the Japanese tradition of Kamishibai, or paper theatre. This tradition was popular in the Japanese street culture of the 1930s, with performers selling sweets to audiences then performing this comic book format. Carrying their shows on bicycles, performers would tell simple fables and stories written on the back of picture cards. This compact way of animating stories is an antecedent to other forms of educational drama and it was also a very important weapon (like the Spanish Civil War mentioned in Chapter 4) employed to promote propaganda during the Fifteen Years War in Japan (Orbaugh 2017). Nakamura exploits the bold graphic simplicity of Kamishibai in her performance of *The Spiders Thread*. Overall, the performance celebrates the dynamic invention of using flatness inventively in object performance.

The exegesis of *The Spiders Thread* is an adaptation of the short story by poet Ryūnosuke Akutagawa (1918), which involves the main character trying to escape hell by climbing the spider's thread, towards Buddha, an attempt which is thwarted by the spider, wittily evoked through vertical action and cut outs animated 'live' by the hands of Nakamura. This show is an updating of the traditional Kamishibai for a contemporary audience, combining music, the world of flat cardboard and transporting the audience into a mythic ecology. The climb away from humanity on the spider's thread towards the sublime or nirvana space encapsulates the absurdity of human's plight in these imagined spaces.

Nakamura in her discussion of puppetry describes its duality and its representation of an 'open magic'. She suggests that to enter the puppet world the audience must enter into the consequences of puppet 'logic'. This logic involves a dynamic animism in which the puppets are often cast as tricksters, fools or cartoons representing humanity. This space for Nakamura is full of tricks and masks. Puppet and object theatre for her is a veritable underworld of revealing the strange and uncanny. Nakamura cites as her influences the powerful practice of Ilka Schönbein's autobiographical explorations of identity and her magic realist space of doubles (the idea of the double is a recurring trope in puppetry).[8] In an email discussion Nakamura explained to me that Alain Lecucq's paper puppet world[9] of existential storytelling and dynamic experimentation have had an influence on her practice. Lecucq's practice shares a common spirit with Kamishibai which Nakamura calls 'a tool for storytelling'.

During the pandemic, visual storytelling using paper was a very practicable alternative, when studios and theatres were closed. The flat cut-out was a novel way to fill the box (clearly framed like a toy theatre) that was Zoom video calls and online video events. The flattened plane of paper theatre comments about how the screen experience is emotionally flattening, in the daily experiences of meetings and social distance control measures. In my own work with students, making use of Nakamura's work of flat puppetry as inspiration presented me with an imaginative space through which it was possible to teach, inspire, play and interact during lockdown. This small world of paper theatre is both immersive and playful like Toy Theatres and the Puppet City example explored next. There is a form of 'open magic' in this type of online hybrid experience. Kamishibai is now a global style of storytelling medium found in many schools (Castillo-Rodríguez, Cremades and López-Fernández 2022). This flat otherworld of ludic performance is also used to promote environmental learning combined with new media techniques like holograms in Indonesia (Hernawan et al. 2022). The relatively simple graphic style of Kamishibai inspires innovative practice using new technologies in this way.

Souls of puppets

John Gray, the popular British philosopher, appropriates the metaphor of the puppet, the golem and the Übermarionette to discuss issues of human freedom and consciousness in his book *The Soul of the Marionette* (2015). Gray begins his journey in this text with the 1810 Henrik von Kleist's essay 'On the Marionette Theatre' where Kleist provokes the reader to consider human grace and freedom through the soulless object of the puppet. In Kleist's philosophical dialogue, one of the men considering the

Figure 7.1 Puppet City, Journeys Festival, 2018. Photograph by Greg Smith.

marionette theatre suggests: 'Grace appears most purely in that human form which either has no consciousness or an infinite consciousness. That is, in the puppet or in the god' (Baudelaire, Kleist and Rilke 1994: 12). Gray and Kleist are some of the many important literary philosophical voices who have taken the puppet as a heuristic in relation to ideas about what it is to be human, by reflecting their philosophizing through the puppet. Puppets in this way provoke the deepest thinkers in society, discussing subjects difficult to comprehend using these dynamic objects, but puppets also want to play. The absurdity of the puppets' 'life' as an object imbued with agency troubles our daily assumptions about the centrality of humanity and the status of material existence. The paradox of the puppet is attractive to philosophers and critical thinkers as tools to unlock thinking. This use of the puppet as metaphor and heuristic does not even have to involve the physical presence of the puppet. The idea of the puppet is enough to provoke powerful metaphorical thoughts about power, freedom and control applied to human follies and circumstances. Marionettes adorn the cover of paperback political thrillers, are applied to dictatorships and represent dystopias. This use of the idea of the puppet by philosophers is not in decline and is as relevant as it was since Kleist's important essay at the beginning of the nineteenth century. In my own research looking at the ontological problems of puppetry these tricky figures represent ideas but also disrupt assumed notions about human ecological problems, like our cities.

Puppet City: Ludic space through puppetry

The city is not just a place but an object like the puppet. It lives and moves, but never totally on its own. The city and puppet both depend on human animation, but they are a particular kind of object that dictates and controls its movements. Cities and puppets interact with humans to generate meanings and to negotiate identities. (Goodlander 2019: 8)

In the above quote Goodlander discusses her exploration of the puppet and city intertwined in her studies of South Asian puppetry. Many of the projects and performances Goodlander explores were community arts events, including looking at ecological narratives (2019: 90) in relation to people's identities, enmeshed in urban geographies. Her assessment of the use of puppetry within specific locales impressed upon her that puppetry intersects in the city with heritage, development and urban planning agendas (2019: 7). In 2018 I explored this potential of playing at a smaller scale in the imagined ecologies of the city. Next, I describe and reflect upon a project that looks at the specific way that puppets can (similarly and in relation to Goodlander) intersect with the urban space through play. In the multitudinous number of settings explored in my practice, it is apparent that the puppet provokes play often involving some surprising events and experiences.

I embarked on a project initially called Puppet Psychogeography in 2017 exploring how three academics approached playful geographies through a commissioned play 'kit'. I worked with a geographer Tara Woodyer and Architect Guido Robazza developing what was to become a very powerful vehicle for play. Woodyer's research explores the ludic space of young people with toys and in particular military figures. She explores the intersection of human geography and childhood studies. Her work interrogates the production, exhibition and consumption of toys in both historical and contemporary contexts. She theorizes the relations between materiality, bodies and space in play (Woodyer and Carter 2020). Robazza explores co-design and creation in urban architecture. His research focuses on public spaces, mobility in contemporary cities through the lens of design and democracy. He has a deep interest in urban transformation processes through a multidisciplinary approach. His research projects and research contributions are focused on cities and socio-economic dynamics and urban environmental studies (Robazza and Smith 2022). This was my first collaboration with Woodyer and the third collaboration with Robazza. The first project with Robazza I conducted was providing junk music for Robazza's heart installation on Winston Churchill Avenue, Portsmouth, and then the much more involved junk music structure *Sound Garden* (2017).[10] Once we were awarded funding for *Puppet City*, we brought in the local arts companies the Makers Guild, Portsmouth (a local organization that facilitates making of all kinds, a business that provides a space to inspire the next generation of design innovators, a space to grow and incubate making and ideas),[11] to fabricate the kit, and Hush Nation theatre company, the performance. This kit and installation eventually called *Puppet City* was inspired by and relates to the haptic pleasure that toy theatres bring to audiences.

The idea for the Puppet City kit evolved from conversations about developing a set of objects that could enable puppets to move around urban spaces as urban actors challenging participants to think differently about the built environment. As vibrant objects able to inhabit different scales, puppets already have an advantage over humans in this endeavour. The original design concept was to make the figures and the objects to a scale of 1:6 as this was suggested by Robazza as it roughly mirrors the scale of toys like Barbie dolls. This use of scale and its relation to toys links to the work of Woodyer and the ways she has engaged groups and geographers in considering playful geographies. So, in this way we envisioned a playable architect's model in which the identities of the figures were given more agency, character and animation through shifting geographies.

The project started exploring ideas of new geographies as it evoked the history and practice of psychogeography as a concept or practice that linked the collaborators. The notion that a puppet has anything like an internal psychology is absurd but is also a witty way to rethink object and human separateness. A loose question considered in this collaboration was what would it be like for a puppet to move through the streets, inspired by psychogeography, in the guise of the *flâneur* on a *dérive* through the contemporary metropolis? How would the puppets and, by extension, participants find the streets and infrastructure that is in a city model? How can you make a city for puppets? To answer these questions, we commissioned the Makers Guild, Portsmouth, to make a space and kit to build this city for puppets. This was a four-metre square set of playmats brightly and abstractly painted by Gavin Hodson in a style reminiscent of artist Patrick Heron combined with a complementing kit of cardboard shapes including laser-cut triangles, rectangles and squares that could be slotted into each other to build structures. For more advanced making the kit used commercially available MakeDo©[12] tools to fix cardboard with plastic bolts. The instructions on how to use this kit for the participants was simply 'make a city for puppets'. In practice, with random participants joining the play, this instruction was not really needed, as the puppet city was incredibly popular with the public who continually explored it, building and rebuilding.

Throughout the day the public, particularly, although not exclusively, families and children, were invited to use the bespoke 'city design toolkit' imagining what a future cityscape may look like. Playful construction was punctuated by improvised performances where puppet surrogates explored the imagined city provoking questions about the built environment and urban living. The initial aims of the project were to capture the public's questions, concerns and thoughts about urban living; critically question the use of a play as a participatory tool for researching urban living; and create an experimental space where disciplinary knowledge or practices around urban living are opened up to critical examination. Working in this participatory, interdisciplinary manner enabled critical questions about the 'playful turn' across urban planning, policymaking and design involving the extent to which participatory approaches can function as democratic tools, including the current direction of urban futures research.

> Contemporary Western society undervalues play, assigning to it a frivolity, a time – wasting quality (or lack of quality). Children play; adults may play, but only in their spare or free time; the words spare and free indicating the extent to which play sits outside the main serious business of making one's way in the world. (Peacock 2009: 9)

Play is recognized as a powerful tool for communication and creative thinking, providing an experimental space for playing with roles, materials and ideas (Peacock 2009: 11–13). *Puppet City* pilots a participatory 'toolkit' developed through collaboration with the specific brief of using cross-disciplinary conversations to raise and address critiques of extant disciplinary practice. By combining puppetry from a performance perspective with a block-based construction kit from architectural practice, the toolkit embeds empathy within the participatory process, provoking additional questions about the built environment and urban living than might otherwise be the case. Furthermore, the event was designed not only to create an experimental space in which to engage the local community with questions of (future) urban living, but also to ask critical questions of the participatory process itself. By encouraging participants to become active citizens in a knowledge-making activity relating to their own local and global concerns about the built environment relates to contemporary concerns with democratic citizenship. In advancing play as a participatory approach to urban planning, this project fits with the wider field of play as a creative force.

The most salient finding in *Puppet City* is that it was a great way to elicit play in a public site between young people and families. The puppets became the focus when they inhabited the structures built for them, and this puppet focus lessened the awkward interactions between people. The puppets helped people feel less conscious of playing in public space. Our initial intention was that we would provoke questions about urban futures in this project but in fact what we really developed more fully was intensive play. This play was certainly ludic in the sense that the play explored the urban world in the form of the toy theatre city space. In devising the kit, I noted that commercial children's city toys had a general lack of humanoid figures and often automobiles were the main protagonist or characters in these city play toys. Conversely, in the *Puppet City* space there were no cars, only wheelchairs and scooters. This conscious choice to erase automobiles from *Puppet City* was rather utopic and idealistic, but it did leave a lot of room to play with the scale of humanoids inhabiting space. This seems to be an outcome of this practice research, finding joy in modelling cities through play.

We found that this play once it began was hard to systematically contain. Much of the play with puppets and structures in *Puppet City* mimetically reproduced scenes and structures as part of cityscapes like hospitals, shops, malls, police, dog houses and the like.

These reproductions were also strange critiques about what is important or relevant to include in a city for puppets. The first performances as part of this project were within Journeys Festival and this meant it was surrounded by the context of this festival that promotes positive stories and images of migrant experience. The image of puppets coming out of a suitcase and carrying luggage into a new and strange city is framed by this context of a festival about migration and belonging. This rendering of playful objects further disrupts concepts of what a city's ecology can be, or is not, in practice, though this message or reading was not explicitly made in *Puppet City*. When puppets are employed to explore the possibilities of urban culture, they seemingly mess things up and this makes us reflect on city life. This project found itself as part of the movement and burgeoning area of play as a serious academic and social force in conferences about play.[13]

Figure 7.2 Puppet City, Journeys Festival, 2018. Photograph by Greg Smith.

The puppets built for *Puppet City* were seven humanoids and a cat and a dog puppet. The animal puppets drew a lot of attention and a lot of the play centred around building the pets a home. At some points these dog and cat puppets met real dogs (as this project was often set outside) and this intersection between puppets with 'real' canines produced confusion in the 'real' dogs, plus subsequent merriment in the public. The puppets had no obvious clear markers of race or gender and this was a conscious decision to give the puppets a universal appeal. It did not stop participants from ascribing identities onto the puppets like 'bad neighbours' or 'police', and this ascribing seemed based on their previous contextual experiences of cities and urban life. Within the wider context of Journey's Festival, the loose notion of the puppets looking for somewhere to live did also reflect the migrant experience and ideas of displacement. It was clear that overall, the use of the puppet's inclusion drew together the kit of the building block cardboard shapes and playmats. Similarly, to how a doll brings to life a space, a doll's house or a toy theatre needs the figures for this completion of meaning, and the puppets in puppet city gave the play kit a purpose through the exploration of making models representing urban settings. Two other puppet types in the kit did draw attention; a very simple cardboard aeroplane animated on the end of a two-metre bamboo cane and a paper seagull who left paper droppings on buildings. *Puppet City*, in this way, through puppets acting in its invented ecology, became a powerful 'engine' for play. When I reflected on the events that lasted usually for over four hours watching the city kit built and rebuilt, serving the needs of rather clumsy puppets, playful children, adults and families, I was impressed by the continually shifting process of play. It provoked thoughts about how playful approaches to cities are formed or can be remade in the future.

Psychogeography is a playful post-Marxist reclaiming of the streets rooted in freedom to wander and roam. The attitude of purposely losing oneself is embedded at the heart of this practice. Situationist pioneer Guy Debord[14] amongst others in this movement were attacking the stultifying status quo of disciplinary city experiences through playfully reimagining the city (Coverley 2006). The use of the term 'psychogeography' in our project was a playful way to think about how a puppet figure can be lost amongst an imagined city or landscape and through its transgressions and dérives explore an imaginary space. Psychogeography was and still is a practice that provokes individuals to reclaim the built environment through purposeful meanderings and remapping of space. According to Merlin Coverley, psychogeography 'demonstrates a playful sense of provocation and trickery' as well as a 'search for new ways of apprehending our urban environment' that seeks to 'overcome the processes of 'banalisation' by which the everyday experience of our surroundings becomes one of drab monotony' (2006: 13).

The witty idea of using puppets to engage in this type of psychogeography shifts the practice towards the odd idea that puppets have a form of agency. In the puppet city project this irreverent stance towards human geographies of space and place inspired the making of the strange cityscape with its performances. Puppets gave people the opportunity to disrupt and play around with the assumed ideas of urban living because puppets instigate and encourage play so effectively for them. Puppets' affinity with toys, dolls and childhood gives them a powerful potential to explore in this idealized ludic space. Puppets cast as psychogeographic travellers in this way challenge us to rethink our positions in urban spaces.

One particular performing object that seemed to offer a moment of *détournement* was a small wheelchair for one of the puppets, inspired by my own experience of my mother-in-law's disability and our struggles to navigate urban spaces. In the playful world of Puppet City this puppet wheelchair was not a negative image or part of the kit that represented victimhood from disability. This puppet wheelchair was an exciting kinetic plaything that opened up potential new imaginative landscapes for the performances. Displacing the wheelchair into a puppet use did not humourize disability but instead offered the potential to explore how wheelchairs have kinetic potential in a different cityscape and are exciting in this kind of play. This valorizing of the wheelchair is not reflected in the way that real city spaces generally disable wheelchair users. Also, in *Puppet City* the city had to be built and rebuilt in relation to the needs and form of the wheelchair-using puppet. This flipping of conventional ableist systems for the wheelchair is one outcome that was not assumed, but discovered through playing, in this project.

In the practice we observed in *Puppet City* we found that the puppet augments the participant's playful exploration of space at the smaller scale. As theatre scholar Eleanor Margolies suggests, scale works well in puppetry: 'Puppetry, celebrated for its capacity to play with scale, offers one way to help audiences visualise interactions at scales beyond ordinary human perception' (Margolies in Posner, Orenstein and Bell 2014: 325). This playing with scale encourages an engagement with the idea of urban space challenging and questioning the way we view the city. The puppet reflects our world in its *dérive* or drifting journey, but also at times takes this into an imaginative space that is surprising and bizarre. In the way we set up the *Puppet City* the encouragement to participate involved suggesting to the public that we needed to build a city for the puppets to live in. During the event, it was apparent that there was not much more encouragement needed to enable participation after this simple invitation.

It was part of the development of the project that the kit we built would be a thinking space as well as a playable space, and the context of already culturally entrenched ideology would have to be considered and to some extent countered in the objects constructed. This in itself was quite a difficult challenge. No object, especially those made by people, is neutral within the relational space between human and object encounters. Even abstractions of forms come from an ideologically tainted space or context. Even so, in our attempts we used abstraction in the approach to the forms of the puppet city as an attempt to construct relatively 'open' objects and forms that provided a playful object with ludic possibilities. This was in reaction to already established issues within our cities where people are alienated from their environment amongst the dangers, pollution of vehicles and faulty infrastructure.

Once we had the base and the cardboard shapes built, we set up a testing event at a local primary school, Ark Ayrton, in Portsmouth. We used some unfinished puppets and puppets from previous performances roughly to the scale intended. The children were very excited to play with the kit and they were given the invitation to build a city for the puppets, then they vigorously slotted forms together and created odd structures including buildings with the prepared cardboard. One surprising activity that came about from this short testing was the children's desire to put labels on the forms, mostly from brands like ASDA or the name of the city shopping mall in Portsmouth, Cascades. Once the children had created structures, we asked them to sit outside of the space and see how the puppets moved through the city – one of the puppets used the wheelchair to enable this exploration. This play with puppets elicited laughter and mirth at the strange group of figures exploring this new constructed city. What was particularly funny was when the puppets inhabited a structure that was fragile and it failed to hold its form. These accidental breaks or collapses were both entertaining and ridiculous. The children were then asked to reflect on how they felt the figures were 'feeling' in their new environment. To make this easier we asked them to decide which puppet was happier than others. This was quite a strange part of the event as some of the test puppets had fairly grotesque expressions. Once we finished this reflective phase the children were asked to play with the puppets and this was by far the most exciting and joyful part of the testing. With such an engaging vehicle for play it felt awkward to interrupt, stop and ask for reflection or conversation about the meaning of that play.

Freely making and playing in this mode is hard to mix with a mode of reflection with young people in this school environment. This said, it was clearly apparent that the kit and use of puppetry elicited, with ease, very inclusive joyful playing which resulted in the idea of an imagined city.

Cardboard

You can smell the burn of the laser cutter around my edges. I am cut with crevices so as to allow me to integrate. I am cardboard. I am everywhere.

After initially devising a performance format that was 'led' by artist facilitators through which we thought play with Puppet City would be encouraged, these ideas were quickly scrapped when we worked directly with the public. The initial idea similar to the school testing was for the structures to be built, then followed by our performance with puppets, with time to stop and reflect; then there was the chance for the participants to play with the puppets again. The improvised journeys were framed and underscored by a composition created by composer Ben Macpherson which was partly improvised on Kaoss pads.[15] Leading the puppet performances did not seem necessary as the puppets when played with by families did not really need any encouragement after the space was set up and people were using the space. The use of the puppet city was continual, once it was set up. It was clear that the puppets and play objects elicited play without boundaries and these silly figures and making kit were actually doing most of the work. Some of the most joyful moments were when the puppets enabled play between adults including the artists, children and family members who were relatively strangers. The puppets made playing in this way less embarrassing as the figure was the focus and was the one mostly engaged in the space. Short improvisations with the puppets quickly evolved and for some became quite complex with mimetic social issues played out.

Quite a lot of this play reflected already established notions of what urban spaces are and less about what they could be. When the puppets intersected and through this play interacted, this was where some of the most interesting comments about urban living ensued. For example, conflicts and arguments between puppets were not resolved, they became contained by the improvised environment. In fact, the city had to adapt to contain these conflicts, sometimes punitively through the building of prison cells. So, the puppets' psychogeography became one that involved not purposeful dérives but the containment of the puppets' potential to cross urban space. Without the limitations of the city structures the puppets had nowhere to play out their études which involved finding a space or getting into trouble within a chaotic urban malaise.

Overall, the improvised play elicited by the puppets, facilitators and researchers in practice created a set of activities that commented upon urbanity and the experience of the city. This was framed by the wider context, for example, the festival promoting positive views of immigration and asylum within a wider ecology of an increasingly hostile national situation for migrants. Comments about urban issues and mobility were not overt or explicit in the way the performance event was facilitated. The comments through play were implicit, with the objects as catalysts for this emancipated play with objects. It was an initial aim to see if these playful interactions could develop a dialogue about what is a good city or good environment, but playing seemed to be the positive outcome at this phase of the project. Provoking this form of discussion instead of playing seemed an imposition as the interactions were so intense, joyful and vibrant.

Was it enough to just play? Is this really an exploration of ideas? Enabling people to play within an imaginary urban space in miniature does suggest more than just an indulgence, thinking back to Gilbert K. Chesterton's point at the start of this chapter: 'The modern philosopher, who likes infinity, is quite welcome to a sheet of the plain cardboard' (Chesterton in Rahn 2013: 23).

Puppet City puppet

Cork. Polystyrene balls. Copydex glue. Red webbing. Staples. Brown paper. Wooden slats. Dowel to control my head. Name me. En-gender me. Play with me.

The humanoid puppets that I constructed were developed initially not displaying any markers of gender or obviously sexed. The aim of this was to present a relatively neutral object, but the idea of any object being neutral within a system or culture is incorrect. Making the puppets in the style of an 'every-person' meant that the puppets attempted to provide an open figure with which to ascribe meaning for the participant. Soon within the process of making these figures the puppets seemed to present the qualities and characteristic markers of gender types. The issue was that these figures without obvious genitals became masculine due to dominant patriarchal ideologies and the dominance of male figures within certain cultures. So, during the making I wanted to address the male dominance of the figures with difference. This change from androgyny to difference did inevitably mean that these puppets could reinforce some stereotypes when they are played with. For example, the female figures became parents or carers displaying these qualities in relation to the smaller childlike puppets when observed in the improvised play conducted by families. The androgyny or not of the puppets was a problem to solve through play and not absent from the participation. Play displays ideas of gender and the puppets did not exist outside of this context. Puppets were named, given gendered identities and given clear jobs within the puppet city by participants.

These were placed onto the bodies of the figure, sometimes literally with children making badges for cops or drawing designs for clothing onto the puppet. It could be speculated that this would have happened even if the puppets had a strictly androgynous appearance. The puppet city shapes and cityscapes had a less clear sense of gendered spaces until it was inhabited by the puppets. These puppets could play, perform and also change the way gender is performed or displayed. This development of identities for the puppets in turn changed the improvised unfixed shapes of the urban puppet city space. This interplay with encultured types and ideas was left unresolved in the puppet city.

To summarize *Puppet City* as a research project, I recognized a number of points. It is challenging when trying to make playful objects that can elicit ideas about urban spaces. Puppets give meaning to spaces in ways that are surprising and improvised. Issues of gender and disability can be explored through puppetry and objects, but often both puppets and toys display and mirror dominant contextual ideologies. Puppet City as a playful kit for families to engage in creativity and unstructured play is efficacious in attracting participation. Through the powerful documentation by Greg Smith in video and photographs it is clear that puppetry in this format was a bridging mechanism between relative strangers. This methodology can encourage playfulness with scaled models of urban spaces.

Puppets represent metaphorical meanings for audiences and they are often employed to represent or comment upon human freedom. John Gray's reading of Kleist's views of the puppet, where he suggests that 'compared with that of humans, the life of the marionette looks more like an enviable state of freedom' (2015: 5) makes this point about freedom explicit. In the puppet city imaginarium and play space the puppets commented on the freedom cities deny or encourage. A city's ecology can be a free space for the psychogeography of an individual or a prison-like disciplinary maze that restricts the mind of the individual.

Recently in 2022 I led a session with the Puppet City kit with primary schoolchildren and the issue of caring for the city emerged after a rather rough testing of the structures built by the young people. I asked for a more 'careful' approach to the way the city could be rebuilt and then inhabited by the puppets. Afterwards one of the teaching staff thanked me for highlighting my concern with 'care' as she wished that this value could be imparted more often in schools.

Puppet City as a research tool provided a set of outcomes around how scale modelling can be playful and exciting. Epstein et al. (2008) make clear claims that puppetry is a legitimate research tool that can effectively elicit talk with children. The researchers in Epstein's project found that 'despite the many challenges of using puppetry with children, this technique can render rich data, as it allows children to further verbalize and express their views' (2008: 53). The puppet in this way disrupts power relations between adults and children and Epstein et al. found that 'this switching [of] roles between the child and the puppet rendered richer data and helped children further identify, clarify and verbalize their feelings' (2008: 52). The puppets mobilize children to discuss and enact what is often awkward in adult projects.

This enabling quality was also a continually recognizable outcome of the play in Puppet City. Once the families were playing with the objects, whether the cardboard shapes for building dwellings or the puppets or their props, the playing was free and open-ended. This then changed the intersectional relations around the performing objects during the sessions the *Puppet City* installation was used within. In this way puppets enabled participants to explore the very human ecology of cities. As highlighted at the beginning of this chapter, *Puppet City* is inspired by the seriousness of the Toy Theatre as a play space. Historical figures like Chesterton remind us of the seriousness of play, and puppets are playfellows in these small-scale spaces. As puppet scholar Mark Sussman suggests, 'perhaps contemporary model theatre, instead of reinforcing the commodified or disempowered subject position of childhood in a liberal economic marketplace, can, in fact, reimagine how we conceive of children (and, by extension, adults) in the first place- as experts in play with scale' (Sussman in Posner, Orenstein and Bell 2014: 270).

In this chapter I have made a case for play as a serious way to move beyond the usual bodily and contextual boundaries that we are often moving within. The toy theatre, Kamishibai, Lambe Lambe show or the meagre cardboard box can open up a new imaginative world in miniature. This remodelling of our experience is also expressed, in a larger scale, in the Puppet City project. To rethink our current ecologies and boundaries, this practice can be conducted with these imaginative figures and smaller-scale versions of spaces representing our experiences or problems. Puppets as agents, can adapt to any scale, as good fellow travellers that can guide us or help us become purposely lost within these spaces, imaginariums or theatres of marvels. The scale of the doll is also often the scale of the puppet and it is important to remember this when both are dismissed as mere playthings. This play is a skill for living, not exclusively left behind as the domain of the child. Objects and especially puppets play with us and affect us and our development of relationships between each other and this is beyond our bodies in the material world. What was striking was how the puppets in *Puppet City* changed the participants in the contained zone of the colourful playmats into 'players' and through this play created a new design for living as the city was explored. Our need for play was exemplified in Puppet City and it suggested to us that we need playful city ecologies more than ever.

Notes

1. K. Kopania (ed.), *Dolls and Puppets as Artistic and Cultural Phenomena*, Białystok, 23–5 June 2014. Information about this conference including the papers can be found here: https://www.academia.edu/37973848/Dolls_and_Puppets_Contemporaneity_and_Tradit ion&nav_from=e5f482f4-6aab-4b82-97dd-fd7263fab0e5&rw_pos=0.

2. C. Orenstein and T. Cusak, *Puppet and Spirit: Ritual, Religion, and Performing Objects: Volume I. Sacred Roots: Material Entities, Consecrating Acts, Priestly Puppeteers* (London: Routledge, 2023).
3. Director of this important show was Zahra Sabri.
4. Puppet Soup company based in Wales make community-based practice as well as pioneering Lambe Lambe in the UK: https://www.puppetsoup.com/.
5. Images and description of Vogel's *Heart Piece* can be found here: https://www.facebook.com/OpenEyeTheatreMN/videos/396111128360117/.
6. Link to video of the performance can be found here: https://www.youtube.com/watch?v=GT4UJihRwQM.
7. Resources that contain *The Spiders Thread* can be found here: https://www.japansociety.org.uk/resource?resource=96.
8. Images and description of Schönbein's haunting puppet theatre found here: https://www.marekwaszkiel.pl/2022/06/27/puppeteers-of-the-world-ilka-schonbein/.
9. Lecucq's paper puppet theatre work is part of this companies' website: http://www.papiertheatre.com/English.
10. Details of the Soundgarden installation project here: https://researchportal.port.ac.uk/en/publications/sound-garden-temporary-urban-installation.
11. Website of Makers guild: https://www.makers-guild.com/.
12. These kits are very good at making with cardboard. They are a series of fixings that can join cardboard to make structures quickly (https://www.make.do/).
13. UK-based organizations promoting play and hosting conferences: https://www.playfulplanet.org.uk/play2021programme and https://www.playfulplanet.org.uk/bristol-session.
14. The influence of Debord is found within the following culturally challenging book: G. Debord, *The Society of the Spectacle* (New York: Zone Books, 1994).
15. Kaoss Pad is an audio sampling instrument and multi-effects processor originally launched by Korg in 1999.

8

Talking to objects: Kinship with the more-than-human and envoi – sharing spaces with objects: Listening, caves, ephemera, popularity, reciprocity and chimaeras

As part of the development of practice with performing objects, the final chapter of this book discusses why I am talking to a deformed and displaced root and a blob of expanding foam. A multi-modal text form is employed in this chapter evoking this organic world of animated objects or 'vibrant others' through performance texts and interpretations. Connected to this is the rhizomatic way that arts practice operates with the identities of participants, communities and assemblages of objects. This chapter addresses the following questions: Can we (re)consider performing objects as part of practice with the 'more-than-human' when imagining shared futures? How can we (re)consider practice in relation to the vibrancy (Bennett 2009) of objects like puppets, plastic waste and natural forms in practice? This shifting positionality responds to Hughes and Nicholson's framing of Applied Theatre's 'ecology of practices' involving both the material and the human (2016: 9). This chapter also connects to themes of materiality and applied performance within the context of the Anthropocene. The provocations in this chapter and its performance texts offer a ludic space within which to explore our relation to often-ignored objects.

My argument throughout this book has been that performance has the ability to explore new thinking in light of the shifts in eco-theatre and materialism as part of wider cultural paradigm shifts. To explore this shift, I present next a performance document, first shown to Applied Theatre colleagues at TAPRA in 2019[1] and subsequently presented as part of research events at other universities and conferences. In 2019 I was responding to possible futures, exploring the ecological malaise and climate crisis as an academic and practitioner. The script is interconnected or entangled with practices using objects and puppets, exploring 'embodied materiality'. The root script explores the imagined experience of the object. This performance presents objects as part of a 'non-human ensemble' with the root in the script cast as an actor with more significance than me, the human counterpart. I demonstrate this presence and significance through my intensive playful interaction with the root and discuss 'with' the root its unique relationality (Figure 8.1).

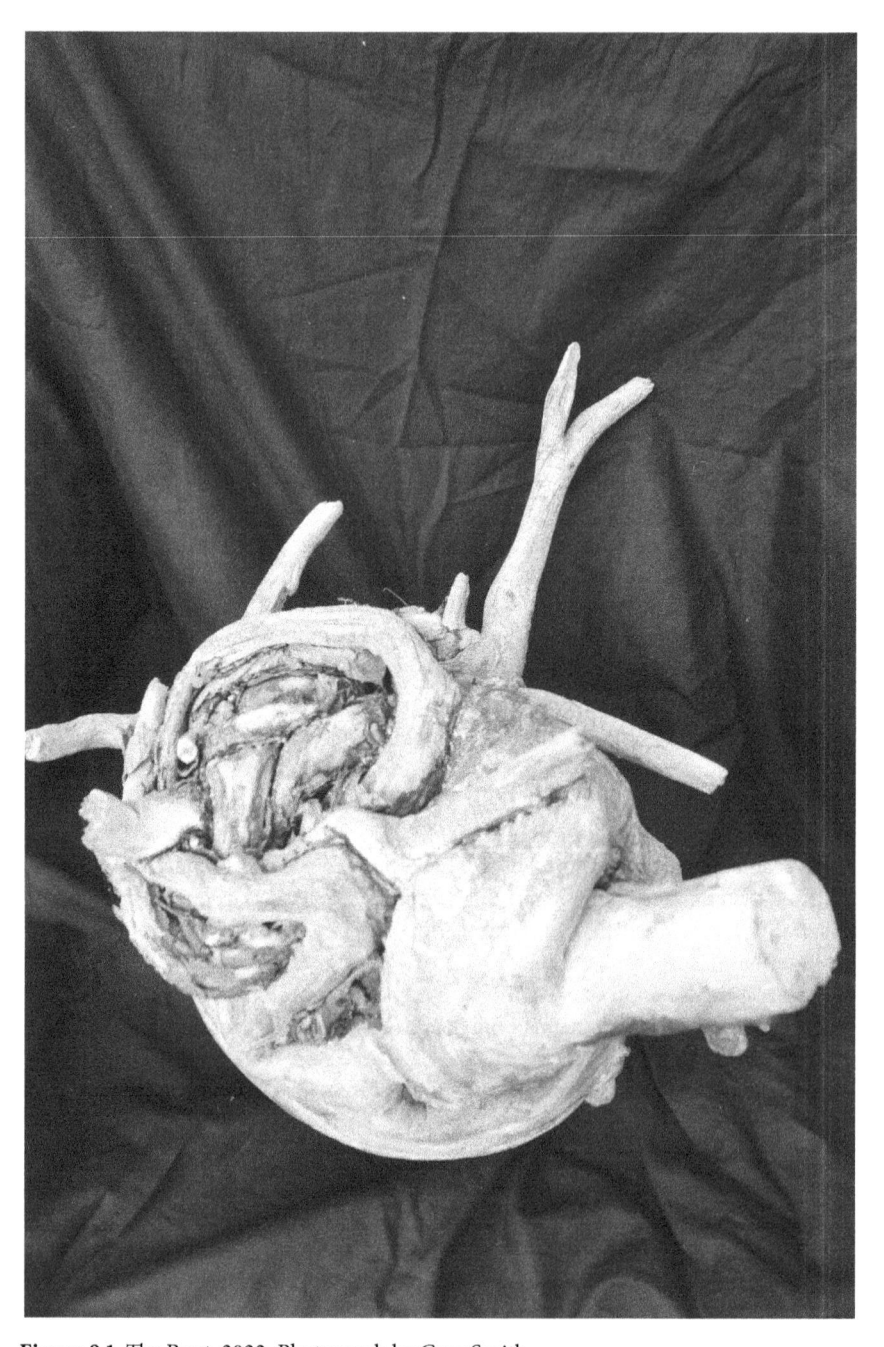

Figure 8.1 The Root, 2022. Photograph by Greg Smith.

Performance text: Explaining the future to a dead root

[A mutated root sits atop a stepladder. Smith sets up a small battery-powered Marshall Amplifier on one of the rungs of the ladder with a looper pedal.[2] An oyster pick-up[3] is placed on the flat bottom of the root. The root has a flat bottom because it grew next to concrete architecture or it was cut that way by a saw. The nature of the root mutation is unknown. Smith touches and minutely moves the root and this touch creates a sonic loop of clicks and plops. This sound is manipulated and adjusted throughout the presentation.
The text is spoken directly to the root that was discovered on the street. The list of words can be read in any order.]

Tangled[4]	Dysfunctional	Nomad
Heave	Bulbs	Observe
Rhizosphere	Decentred	Fecundity
Adventitious[5]	Tubers[6]	Unbounded
Flare[7]	Multiplicity	Animacy
Girdling[8]	In-between	Bridges
Unstoppable	Interbeing	Haptic
Gall[9]	Intermezzo	Absurd
Morphogenesis	Deterritorialized	Ludic
Mitosis	Assemblages	Flattening
Neoplasmic	Flows	Meta-object
Tumorous	Strata	
Hypertrophies[10]	Molar	

You resist my attempts to define you. You contradict knowledge formed about you. You confound my attempts to rationalize your existence.
You laugh at my meagre language that confuses the experience of you …
You sit there stock still, knowing I do not fully understand you. You are material and you are metaphor.
You can help me if you like. Looking at you, I can begin to understand what it is to be human, though I will never understand how it feels to be a root. Your otherness is uncanny and playful. Welcome to the future.
My gaze animates you. You are given the appearance of an autonomous object. Try and make this process work with a human being and not a root and it is impossible.

My active gaze animates your presence and you seemingly come to life.
You remind me of how complicated it is to relate to each other.
You are an enigmatic problem for me to solve.
You welcome me through your body without organs tainted by the polluted air, concrete and my hands.
Are you a false idol? Are you a dysfunctional root heaving between architecture?
Are you an adventitious root transformed through stress?
Are you a gall born from the interaction of insects?

I am not attempting to know you. I look at you and then look away. I do not want to remake you in my image. I do not want to penetrate your surface. Is this about desire? Neurobiologists describe you as the brain of the plant[11] observing and navigating. Your form can be mutated, through human husbandry or plant shaping.[12]

I found you on the street and you spoke to me. You said, 'Take me home with you as I am lost.' And 'I don't want to be left and discarded anymore ...' Well, that is what I thought I heard in my head. I picked you up and took you home in my bicycle basket. My relationship to my bicycle makes me think of *The Third Policeman* by Flann O'Brien, a comic novel which explores the magic realist world where human and object entities mesh.

The behaviour of a bicycle that has a high content of humanity ... is very cunning and entirely remarkable. You never see them moving by themselves, but you meet them in the least accountable places unexpectedly. ... If you let it go too far, it would be the end of everything. You would have bicycles wanting votes, and they would get seats on the county council and make the roads far worse than they are for their own ulterior motivation. But against that and on the other hand, a good bicycle is a great companion; there is a great charm about it. (O'Brien 1999: 65)

You weighed heavier than I imagined and sat in my kitchen until all your bugs started to vacate, so I then lay you in the garden. You came from Somerstown, an urban area of Portsmouth. Near the fire station and the mosque. It is also near the roundabout within which I made the semi-permanent *Sound Garden* installation for people to play with.[13] This sonic object was an attempt to co-create and make playful architecture in a space that was a hive for drug dealing and drunken violence.

The *Sound Garden* was vandalized within days of completion, but much of it still stood years after and functioned as a playful intervention in a bleak urban space. Making something as seemingly permanent as the *Sound Garden* makes me nervous as a maker of theatre and performance events. I like the illusion of endings and I like ephemeral experiences. Objects do not really stop performing. Puppets are often kept after shows and, in my case, clog up university spaces with their inherent object oddity.

Lacrimae rerum ... Lacrimae rerum [14] ... Lacrimae rerum ... object, abject ... abject, object ... I object ... I object.[15]

Contextual discussion of root text

The schools of OOO and New Materialism reconsider the material existence and experience of art with a non-anthropocentric bias. Harman presents OOO as a method of thinking that considers how things do not hang together and that the associations between objects involves autonomy, despite interrelations. For Harman the aesthetic object is inwardness – 'it is each thing as an I ... everything from within itself is an I' (2018: 71). OOO as a study of things in themselves involves this exploration of the executant inwardness of things (2018: 82). Harman presents the object as a bundle of mysteries (2018: 165) in an environment in which things act as a chain of differences (2018: 206). His view of art is that art does not produce knowledge but things in themselves and theatre produces directly, by the mystery of the artwork (2018: 100).

OOO draws from the ideas of Latour and Actor Network Theory (ANT) in which a flat ontology creates actors out of objects. These objects act because they exist rather than existing because they act (Harman 2018: 260).

The inner language of the object remains a mystery, absence and lacuna in practice, but speculations about this imaginative space of the mise-en-abyme, or world within a world, offer potential creative sources for dialogue as demonstrated by the root script. It is an old idea in Western thought, like William Blake's romantic call 'to see a World in a Grain of Sand. And a Heaven in a Wild Flower' (Blake 2002: 88). In the ludic space with the root, I actively and theatrically imagine consciousness and voices, and then offer speculations about materiality. This contemplation (influenced from years of puppetry practice) about the inner life of objects as participants, is a method to appreciate the autonomy of the object as thing, which Jane Bennett describes as 'vibrant matter' (2009). This viewpoint creates what political philosopher Bennett in *Vibrant Matter* describes as a powerful 'assemblage of things' (2009: 23–4) related to the politics of the situation. Considered from Bennett's perspective, each aspect in this assemblage is of equal importance, with my human perspective not privileged – over and above, the performance of other objects and connections to other species, puppets or objects. Analysing puppets as objects perceived with more agency relates to Bennett and what she calls the 'vibrant matter' of objects. Speculating about what is represented within the puppet through this method is a means to make sense of the way 'being' is expressed in these objects within unique spaces filled with other assembled objects like, in my practice, the classrooms, prisons, post-industrial landscapes, the plastisphere, medical spaces or drama studios.

The relations of objects within networks are considered by Bennett through her concept of 'thing power' (2004: 348), which operates in the networks of vibrant matter, a viewpoint developed in her article 'The Force of Things' from 2004 that predates her influential book *Vibrant Matter*. In this article, she suggests a shift from body materialism towards 'thing power materialism' and a naive speculation and horizontal plane of the network of objects as a way to approach a new ecology of matter. In this new perspective, the 'ontological imaginary of things and their powers' (2004: 349) can be appreciated in a new form of realism. As well as acknowledging the body as a site of resistance, Bennett suggests that 'cultural forms are themselves material assemblages that resist' (2004: 348). Bennett's description of thing power appears clearly analogous to the life of the puppet when she writes, 'Thing Power: the curious ability of inanimate things to animate, to act, to produce effects dramatic and subtle' (2004: 351). Through this shifting in perspective towards a kinship between things, objects and people it flattens hierarchical systems of thinking about relations. As well as valorizing the object, Bennett warns against the problem of reducing subjects to 'mere objects' and the dead object to the live human subject. For Bennett 'Thing power materialism, in contrast, figures things as being more than mere objects, emphasising their powers of life, resistance, and even a kind of will; these are powers that, in a tightly knit world, we ignore at our peril' (2004: 360). This materialist conception of politics applied to practice can use objects as part of its networks in workshops and performances, and this was a method applied to the performance with the root.

Bennett considers the waste object in *Vibrant Matter* and objects in general as appearing to have 'recalcitrance' in relation to human relations (2009: 3). She wants us as we reconsider the ecology to see its patterns as a speculative ontological story through which we can reconsider vibrant materialism through our bodies. In this process we must be surprised by what we see and look at the ecology as distributed with variable power systems that are on a horizontal plane. These ideas are ghosted by the 'taint' of animism (2009: 18) when we consider objects and things as a swarm of vitalities at play in practices and networks of assemblages (2009: 32). Throughout her argument Bennett uses Latour and his concepts, now known as ANT, including his concept of networks as a Parliament of Things (2009: 104). She questions the idea that humans are active and things are passive in her view of ecologies (2009: 119).

Generally, she sees our subjective experience as possible only through the agentic assemblage of stuff (2009: 121) and that we can see experience as a form of common materiality that exposes the distribution of agency amongst things (2009: 122). By shifting our position in this way, we can reshape our senses of self without hubris or arrogance and begin to reshape ourselves and our interest towards the ecology.

Through considering the intense network or assemblage of objects, things or actants, we can understand this rhizome-like root system of self-ordering effects of heterogeneous materials when they mesh together. The root performance for me is an experiment in this type of bodily shift towards the more present object in practice.

Throughout Bennett's *Vibrant Matter* she cites and is influenced by Deleuze and his consideration of the multiplicity of things. She draws our attention to Deleuze's point that for him nature is a 'plane of morphogenesis' (Bennett 2009: 145). When we encounter the material world, we can allow ourselves to be 'overcome' by the experience of the object in our practice. We become open to these effects on us emanating from the vibrancy of the materials which can also be seen in puppet making and performing objects. The artist in this experience allows the materials to determine their effect on the artist's body and then beyond that towards the bodies of the audience. Often in puppetry the experience is that the performing object seems to be doing things that surprise the puppeteer and audience as if the volition of the object is beyond the human performer. Blame can then be ascribed to the performing object instead of the human accomplice in actions, like violence in children's puppet shows or erotic acts when adults improvise with puppets. It is as if the objects 'decentre' the performer allowing them less responsibility for their actions because of the powerful object. The 'body' of the performing object produces complex somatic affects towards the body of the human in practice.

For the practitioner, materialism that considers the object as vibrant focuses not just on the bodily materialism of events like performances and workshops but also on the significance of objects in time and space. Bennett's ecology is a paradigm through which to conceive of the vagaries of these experiences in social spaces. Within this network of bodies and objects, 'for a thing-power materialist, humans are always in composition with nonhumanity, never outside of the sticky web of connections or an ecology' (Bennett 2009: 365). In this new paradigm of thing power, the project of the critical discourse of biopower is extended beyond its body materialism by Bennett. This awareness of the way objects affect and produce effects on bodies is a key speculation of the puppeteer as researcher and an important theme of this book. Bennett's arguments encourage us to think about the distribution of power in a complex way that does not simplify objects within their ecologies and connotations in audiences. Her project is political, but her materialism is also a gift to the researcher of Applied Puppetry framing how we reconsider networks of things. The performing object is part of these networks becoming a form of disruptive 'interstitial fissure' in the sticky web of materialism in social practice within complex ecologies. Through this speculative and embodied practice in places like post-industrial landscapes or prisons explored in this book, I attempted the navigation of this inner poetry and imagined experience of objects.

A vision for the future role of the artist was one of the inspirations for my creation of the root performance. The root opened up new ways of thinking about concepts of being and otherness and these concepts and ideas are in flux, around the contours of the root, opening a space of new surprising knowledge about materiality. This viewpoint, about the propensities of objects like the root, has led me to reconsider materiality in practice. By exploring this method, I think *with* the object in practice. The vibrant object, reconsidered through practice, in this way troubles the practitioner's role and the participant's location as positioned within networks of actants (Latour 1993). The root in the dialogue and performance is the tutor in this particular object lesson.

Harman, through his controversial reading of Heidegger's tool theory and Latour's ANT, adopts a position in which the post-human subject is considered within an 'equality' of forms (2010: 24–36). Harman's philosophical project asks the question: 'Is there any possibility of a fresh and concrete research into the secret contours of objects?'

(2010: 66). Through practice with the root as collaborator, I am attempting this research. The performing object appears as autonomous and is also imbued by the puppeteer with a sense of agency, when combining their presence with the object.

Harman presents the object 'other' using the metaphor of the puppet when he presents it as 'reversed from a natural object, a sort of puppet under unceasing causal coercion, into a vulnerable actor in the world' (2010: 16). This use of the puppet metaphor by Harman relates to the concept of the puppet under the human master, the 'other' as a strung marionette, operating within the forces of a wider network of objects. Compared with this view in my practice with objects they are less 'controlled'. Using a speculative approach demonstrated within the root performance, I project myself towards the imagined consciousness of the object and explore what is there. Understanding this dynamic is enacted through appreciation of the way objects, space and time interact.

This temporality is in continual process as the puppet or performing object never fully gives up their 'secrets'.

The surprising experience of the object in performances is mysterious, poetic, unknowable, odd and uncanny. Objects considered as collaborators in practice means that when we play with them, we give them more attention through acts of cathexis and this changes us and them. Viewed in this way the possible futures for Applied Theatre involves a closer awareness of non-human objects expanding the field of practice. This expanded field could be a world where we imagine a respect for objects through a positive non-violent companionship with the object world with a deep understanding of things and their networks. We often look at objects as signs, surfaces for the past or ways to understand temporalities. Drama scholar Alice Rayner suggests we can view objects as able to 'fold time into their surfaces' and it is possible to see how objects 'then appear to shelter both past and future' (2006: 197). Collaborating with objects we can think of these objects as divining rods for future experiences or connections to the past.

Understanding our object world has become even more prescient as objects affect our lives more and more. Through digital virtual objects, we make or undo ourselves through augmentation, digital shifts and extending our realities. A focus on materiality in multiple networks makes us reconsider our positionality and by doing this we rethink our relationship to the world instead of just towards each other. According to Theatre scholars Marlis Schweitzer and Joanne Zerdy, 'though often consigned to history's metaphorical dustbin, the object that remains allows performance scholars to "touch time" to experience the past in the present and to imagine new futures' (2014: 1).

Reconsidered in this way in the network and space of performance, potentially everything becomes an actor. Being onstage is not necessarily being conscious in the human sense. If we respect the object as an actor, potentially more of the mise-en-scène becomes vibrant through this shift in attention. In this way props have a stage 'life' like all stage objects – we are just used to the habit of ignoring this animacy. The non-human ensemble is a space full of unconscious players, like the light that illuminates the scene. When practice moves out of the stage space and into the wider environment, this attention to the materiality of surfaces and the inner poetry of objects is extended. It is also a route towards a form of ecological performance.

Sustainable puppetry?

A possible sustainable future involves challenging the idea of capitalist consumer economic growth in an anthropocentric culture. By attunement and consideration of 'more-than-human' entities, either on the giant scale, as in a river or in the smaller scales of non-human species, or (for me) a malformed root, or even a blob of foam, we can form new perspectives. Puppetry as an art form is about collaborating with objects and non-human entities and so is placed at an interstice between things enabling dialogues with the more-than-human. Puppetry in this liminal space has the potential to playfully imagine how we share the planet with other entities. Practice with puppets can also interact with other technological objects like phones, computers, YouTube and Zoom software (as in the ACT example in Chapter 4). Objects appear to 'break the frame' of screen technologies with their punctum and artificial presences, inhabiting the mediated space in a lively and entertaining manner. Puppets are enablers in this 'in-between' context telling community narratives like in Marlsite or sharing concerns like puppetry with a purpose explored in this book. Puppets also engage with issues and have the potential to speak about how we rethink our human-centred idea of the environment and sustainability from the object's viewpoint. Objects in performance potentially speak not just about human concerns, but the concerns of the 'more-than-human' world.

Applied Theatre is engaging with materiality and its impact on the ecology and this is part of engagements across the globe. In this ecology of practices, the 'non-human' or 'more-than-human' are included within this expansion of the field of socially engaged practice. If the current and future plural landscape of Applied Theatre is an ecology following Hughes and Nicholson, then questioning this ecology speaks to the wider climate crisis issues. These issues are not anthropocentric and based on the service model of the planet as subservient towards people's needs. Objects and things reconsidered in this expanded field are paid more attention to by attuning our focus towards these entities. This can be explored in relation to wider ecological issues as explored next.

In the realm of the performing arts, puppet interlocutors are collaborators in exploring this potential of speaking to ecological justice for objects and hyperobjects in the current unsustainable crisis. Puppets sit at the 'interstitial junction' between humans and our object kin. They also help us to think differently about the waste culture and plastisphere, like in the Marlsite projects. It is now a key point of the field of eco-drama, as a growing field, to make performance work that accounts for this shift in non-human focus as suggested by eco-drama scholars Carl Lavery and Clare Finburgh Delijani:

> Faced with theatre's long anthropocentric history, it is little wonder that scholars in Theatre and Performance Studies have been slow in developing a robust, critical language for engaging with the presence of the 'more-than-human world' in key dramatic texts. While this situation is slowly being rectified by critics interested in animals, cyborgs and objects, the fact remains that the majority of publications

in the field continue to pay little or no attention to anything beyond the human realm. (Lavery and Delijani 2015: 7)

Applied Theatre, like theatre in general, centralizes the human identity in practice, which is socially engaged. This centrality of the participant – and their wishes and concerns in workshops and projects and community stories – is a very important practicable way of conducting Applied Theatre, especially when marginalized people are often not given room for expression. Early in my experience of person-centred practice as a puppeteer in communities, the puppet was an instrumental tool used simply to capture the imagination of groups in making or performing. Now, as a much more reflective practitioner and scholar, the instrumental use of the puppet has shifted and the performing object is much more central to my concerns, entangled within my practice of Applied Puppetry. Since reconsidering ecological thinking with its anti-anthropocentric position combined with ideas from OOO and New Materialism like Bennett, Harman and Morton's, this approach moves towards a position where objects have gained more status. In this less anthropocentric frame the performing object, for example the chairs sitting in a drama circle, enable the discussion (a whole set of my games that I use in practice to facilitate a group are predicated on the use of chairs – 'chair games'). So, it is not just about considering objects that are framed by performance like puppets but, potentially, all objects that enable the possibility of the performance or workshop. These objects could be the pizza used to coax the participants to join in the project, drawings used for devising or digital technologies that interact with processes. Learning from these objects, whether in the physical space or virtually enacted, gives us a new perspective on applied performance spaces and ecologies.

The vibrant ecologies of objects

Performance scholar Aline Wiame valorizes performing objects based on her reading of Deleuze and she concludes that 'automata and marionettes are not only mere dark faces of a lost humanity, they mainly are invitations to create and compose new possibilities of being, sensing, thinking and resisting in a world made of human and non- human elements which constantly mix' (Wiame 2016: 5). Being within the ecology of objects in practice is an enriching experience if overwhelming at times. It also involves being open, to finding the voices playfully in the environment, which the next performance text explores, a development of the root dialogues. This was performed virtually at the 2022 earth.art conference Sentient Performativities. This event was a hub of academics and practitioners which proposed its purpose thus:

> This symposium seeks delicate antidotes to an increasing dis-embodiment and apathy towards the aliveness of the more-than-human world and wishes to revoke the prevailing operating system based on dead matter. We propose that eco-somatic practices can contribute towards the cultivation of sensorial capacities that assist our awareness of how we co-evolve within expressive ecologies and that

Talking to Objects and Envoi

what happens to our environments is inevitably and inexorably happening to us. (Performativity's website)[16]

There is a general shift in thinking due to the urgency of ecological thinking and actions like the messages found in this statement. Reconsidering the more-than-human and non-human during this conference by Earth Arts indicates the diverse approaches to eco-practice. The inclusion of a 'man-made' object for me is a sisterly act between the root and expanding foam blob texts. This act compliments the way we follow the diversity of assembled matter, inspired by Bennett in our application of ecological performance practices. Through the use of the litany and personal ethnography in the performance text I next explore the expanding foam and focus my attention towards its being.

Expanding foam dialogue

[The blob of expanding foam sits atop a desk and is captured on an old video camera lens and live fed through a projector onto a screen above the blob. The camera also captures ghost-like shifts of figures around the blob because its old circuitry cannot capture movement effectively like current digital technologies. This text is spoken towards the assemblage of blob, desk, camera and screen]

Expanding Foam:

Polyurethane…isocyanates…polyols…amine catalysts…tack free…methylene diphenyl diisocyanate…asthma…amine catalysts…halos…ethylene glycol…hexabromocyclododecane…tris phosphate… halogenated compounds…synthetic…bioaccumulative…thermal resistance…biopower…polyisocyanurate…closed cell…medium density…hydrofluorocarbon…

Ken Campbell gave the front row of his solo performance, *Mystery Bruises* (1994), protective goggles and hard hats as he placed a can of expanding foam in front of them. He then hammered a six-inch nail into the can. The can exploded and Ken declaimed 'instant art' in his weasel-like nasal voice.

Little bits of foam that have bled out of a cavity in buildings are called 'snots'. Don't wipe the snot clean as the dust can be carcinogenic. Expanding foam is full of very dynamic compounds and chemicals which means it is very vibrant.

I found you little frog-like friend on my street next to a car exhaust and you spoke to me.
Put me in your collection. Don't put me in the bin.
You have presence like the root but are man-made. Like a blob in a B-movie. The green tinge you wear so well makes you look almost organic.
Created wrought … fabricated … constructed …made … to make … artificially produced … formed independently of 'natural' development.
[Matt Stops talking to the blob. End of performance cycle.]

Throughout this chapter, I adopt the decentred practitioner as a position and model for future practices. Decentring in relation to the ecology is a fecund and productive activity. Puppets are 'man-made' objects with human intentionality built into their fabricated joints and surfaces. Part of the joy and wonder of them as entities is to imagine and explore beyond a human-centred myth into the expansive field of thinking of them as autonomous performing objects. Also, things like the discarded root or foam blob can open up new forms of performance narrative when reconsidered in this object-oriented way. These objects shepherd me towards finding something anew, like how human participants or artists have helped me find things out about myself through the possibilities of creative collaboration in workshops and performances. Next, I draw towards an endpoint to my discussions of a materialist view of performance practice.

Envoi

Sharing spaces with objects

Listening, Caves, Ephemera, Popularity, Reciprocity and Chimaeras

Throughout this book I have explored how to listen to objects in performance with people in communities. This decentred view of objects with agency has been the guiding principle of this book. Objects move us, as they shift our positionality and affect our daily or extra daily practice in areas like performance. This experience can be joyous, sublime, unsettling or uncanny, when objects like puppets have the power to move or disturb our position. When puppets are mobilized towards the bodies of participants in communities this power to move or this 'unsettling disturbance' needs careful framing and attention. Puppets and performing objects are popular and generate a lot of pleasure, as haptic somatic effects, or as emotionally charged objects in motion through performance, or even in their stillness. Through contemporary shifts in human attitudes towards objects, and by extension, the ecology, there is the possibility to move away from prevailing centrist anthropocentric cultural mindsets.

At the start of my journey using puppetry, I took for granted the puppets as a tool within the process of making shows, running workshops and teaching with young people and specialized groups in the community. Back then I had developed a non-judgemental person-centred practice based on training in Applied Theatre techniques like Augusto Boal's *Theatre of the Oppressed* (2008) and the work of Geese Theatre, a company known for their important prison and probation practice (Baim et al. 2002). I would often reflect that when the puppets were put away, interesting conversations or events would happen amongst participants and now, I realize they were enabled by the puppets and objects. I have since discovered that over-instrumentalizing things like puppets as just serving a task as a tool leads towards a rather empty experience of practice with objects. I now emphasize in workshops or projects that the power between the human subject and objects continually shifts due to the contextual dynamics and the intersectional interplay of the entities involved. This assemblage of power is never fixed, neutral or distributed equally.

As an approach, I encourage taking the position of 'being ecological' as set out by Morton, through shifting practice, towards a new materialist conception of the object in performance. By 'attuning' to entities, then the wider environment, in fresh and embodied ways, art objects become reinvigorated or reimagined in practices. This vibrant space enables what seems impossible, like making collaborations across continents, for example in the ACT project. In this book I explored the strange litany of objects in the carceral environment of Haslar prison which enabled an opportunity to make puppetry in that traumatic and challenging space. I also explored the space of waste objects within the landscapes of the post-industrial north-west of England where I was able with teams of artists to find narratives then invigorating and exciting groups in their journeys with performing objects. This practice with vibrant objects morphed into ways to reconceive the urban, through playful puppets and cardboard structure making in Puppet City. The objects within the *Puppet City* kit are a microcosm of an imagined ecology in which participants played out fantasies exploring their contextual influences and urban behaviours. All of this practice with puppets and performing objects leads towards the malformed root/foam blob collaboration, which speculatively speaks towards the essential and ecological relationship I have to object others. Reflecting back and within all of this stuff, where objects become things, objects are always mixed with my subjectivity and with the powerful intersubjective relationships amongst people in communities.

Listening ... again

Throughout this book I argue that the 'object turn' in philosophy and critical thinking impacts the field of Applied Puppetry and the wider fields of performing arts.

Technological developments, climate crisis and disruptions of Western rationality about the 'shape of things' has pushed ecologies towards a position where humans are decentred, off-kilter, shifted away from a central unifying position. To think our way out of the waste bin or plastisphere, we could start to reconsider positions in networks by listening to the material world. Objects guide us through this confusing and disturbing labyrinth, if we listen to objects carefully. Hope, if that is possible, is found in the way that we discover new things about our object kin, like listening to trees and discovering their enclosed 'voices'.

Artist Alex Metcalf, founder of the Tree Listening Project,[17] opened up this internal space of trees in 2021 at Kew Gardens where he enabled a space for audiences to wonder at the internal sounds trees make. As part of the same set of commissions sound artist Jason Singh created *Extinction Songs*,[18] a specially created sound experience that uses naturally occurring 'biodata' from plants to form a musical score. I encourage in any puppeteer or facilitator of eco-art this intensive listening or cathexis in relation to objects. To animate a puppet, this intensive listening, experiencing and feeling of the object other, is part of the process of 'moving' with puppet figures. We learn so much from objects, even trash objects with no consumer cultural value by being creative or inspiring imaginations through this intertwining in workshops or performances.

The 'trick' is to listen haptically to the objects first, then respond by making these imaginative landscapes in theatre or in site-specific playful environments through embodied awareness.

The RSC in 2019 'listened' to the pressure and concern of its public when it broke its sponsorship ties with British Petroleum (BP). This public event of political change was enacted so the RSC could align with the 'eco zeitgeist' and appear in tune with current ecological concerns. This break with the sponsor was after public outrage and the departure of a famous leading actor, Mark Rylance.[19] The artistic director of the RSC, Gregory Doran, announced: 'Amidst the climate emergency, which we recognise, young people are now saying clearly to us that the BP sponsorship is putting a barrier between them and their wish to engage with the RSC. We cannot ignore that message' (RSC website 2019). Part of this issue was the development of a consultation with young people who were the focus of BP sponsorship, which led to the RSC making the decision and this report was titled *A Time to Listen*.

Applied Theatre practice is always fundamentally about creating a space for listening. This listening is not just about the ears but the whole body attuned to the environment of practice. Work with groups in the community is about listening as a practice, as encouraged by Gablik, when she argues that listening is an antidote to the destructive drive and speed of modernism. This listening paradigm can be extended beyond the human within our immediate ecologies and beyond that towards the hyperobjects of the macro environment. This leads to actions like the RSC dropping its oil-based sponsorship, or a movement of a puppet, or even the stillness of a sculpture made from a tree. Puppets, movable or still, say a great deal in their performance or inertia as powerful vibrant material beings.

Back to the cave

> Humankind lingers unregenerately in Plato's cave, still revelling, its age-old habit, in mere images of the truth. (Sontag 2008: 3)

One ecological way of looking at Plato's cave allegory, about truth and enlightenment, is that the chained prisoners who watch the shadow puppetry find themselves in the unique position, set *within* the earth in the dark, as opposed to being placed *upon* the earth. The chained prisoners watch the shadow puppet show on the wall of the cave until one escapee leaves and returns with the truth of the enlightenment discovered outside. The prisoners in Plato's cave are immersed in the earth when they watch the puppet show affecting them and their constructed reality. These imagined platonic beings are affected by their surrounding ecology. In the allegory the escapee sees an alternate reality outside the cave, but this outside space is just the wider ecology. Does enlightenment come from seeing that we are always enmeshed within the ecology?

One key factor of ecological thinking is that the negative human attitude towards the earth is one in which the earth just serves and supports us in our endeavours. Freeing humans from the cave does not free them from the earth or the surrounding ecology. As communications scholar Valerie Peterson suggests, all of these roles in the allegory of the cave are partial and an ecological viewpoint does not emancipate us from our surroundings:

> Because Plato's story is an allegory, however, there is no guarantee which role a person is playing at any particular time. We may be the prisoners in the chains, or we may see ourselves as enlightened. We may be puppeteers for 'the good' (leading the unenlightened in the cave) or partially enlightened puppeteers who intentionally or unintentionally manipulate. We may all be partially enlightened. We may all be each of these things at different times. (Peterson 2017: 284)

A point I have pondered is that the puppet show in Plato's cave must be pretty good to keep the chained audience entertained. Another way to think about the roles in Plato's allegory is to be critically aware of our ability to manipulate using puppetry, both using objects and human participants. Also, playing the role of the applied puppeteer in a world that is ignoring the truth of the climate crisis is a problem. This role of puppeteer might involve new ways of narrating the way we see the world in the hope the puppeteer is part of what Plato calls 'the good'. In this book I hope you can see that engaged puppetry is enlightening about some things in a very murky and confusing world.

Ephemera and waste

Increased awareness of the object world developed in puppetry, encouraged by a pronounced sense of materiality in practice, opens horizons of thinking about performance. Waste and the focus on the object world make us reconsider many assumptions about performance. The performance event does not disappear into some other realm and this disrupts ideas of the ephemeral. During the one-week model of the Marlsite projects, assumptions about ephemerality were valued as every show was unique and usually lasted just one day. The site was cleared and we moved onto the next location. There was joy in this process of not having a lasting run or repetition of the shows. This temporary style did not mean that the performances just disappeared, because the performance remains in documentation, minds and other material leftovers. Every year I use the same set of plastic drums originally used in Marlsite projects to teach junk drumming. None of this stuff ever goes away.

The ephemeral is no longer valid when considered in relation to objects and appears like a myth around the experience of performing arts. The waste and the 'remain' of performance (Schneider 2003) contain ephemera and because of these things the act of performance in the 'imagined magical ephemeral state' does not make things disappear. Sometimes these ephemera have a special life in other spaces, like the work of William Kentridge. His ephemera and experiments often a part of his internationally lauded exhibitions of stuff. His animated screens in the Whitechapel Exhibition Thick Time (2015)[20] made for a production of the opera by Berg's *Lulu* (2015) are examples of the life of things designed as part of a theatrical process having another life outside of the original production. The presence of Kentridge's animated screens as performing objects and ephemera is mesmerizing.

Drawing from materiality we can think differently about the concept of the ephemeral not as disappearance in performance. We live in an ecology where performance never disappears. Puppets are a reminder of this 'material problem' of performance. Puppets do not conveniently go away after a show. I have accumulated a lot of stuff, like a performance hoarder with cupboards full of puppets and associated ephemera. It gets used and reused in performances with some puppets like Humphrey given lots of work.

Puppetry reminds us that performance materially has its leftovers, as the puppets outlive the performances (I have seen stores full of redundant puppets in Poland due to the forms' popularity and state sponsorship since the Second World War). Puppets problematize our affection for the 'disappearing acts' of performance. Some puppetry has its own recyclability built into its process, so the problem of storage is lessened. For example, a recent puppet I built quickly out of cardboard (as this is an easier material to recycle) of a four-metre-high giant robot puppet was constructed specifically to be temporary. Also reusing puppets encourages a lessened impact in terms of resources and waste. As explored in Chapter 5 looking at waste, the ecological way to explore this issue is through a very clear choice about using waste or everyday litter to make a 'new' life. The wonder of seeing a puppet clearly articulated from detritus is a successful détournement of the usual use value of stuff in our cultures of consumption.

Assembling a kit for a workshop, in my experience, is usually mostly made from waste materials from either domestic or commercial spaces. I would encourage anyone considering running a puppetry workshop to assemble their kit this way, lessening the need for costly specialist art materials. Plastic waste is a great structural basis for puppet forms. Usually, the stick for operation and the fixing method are what is purchased beforehand in this kind of workshops. I am convinced after years of experience of this form of making, that exploring materiality gives joy to individuals.

Objects give us so much back in workshops. One hope of this book is that it could give you the encouragement to make puppets for yourself or in communities.

'There is a New Show in London ... Surely it will have Puppets.'

Since the phenomenon of *War Horse*, a show that changed the fortunes of the National Theatre,[21] London's West End theatre ecology has seen the popularizing of puppetry in the UK. When I share this story of economic impact with colleagues in the east of Europe (where the infrastructure of puppetry is established under the influence and legacy of communist cultural planning) they are astonished at this relation of puppetry to the National Theatre. Puppetry has often been connected to the scholarly field of popular theatre but as an unusual marginalized art form. This is no longer the case in

UK culture, and since the puppet horse from *War Horse* visited the queen in 2013 the status of puppetry is definitely part of mainstream culture in the UK.

As I write this book the RSC are selling very popular expensive tickets for a production of *My Neighbour Totoro* (2022), which is as much a celebration of puppetry as a celebration of Japanese culture including the animistic Shinto perspective, in a Western context.[22] This mainstream practice for a wide audience could be seen as part of the 'popular materialism' of our current era where puppet figures share their presence with famous actors in London's West End. Since my first endeavours to explore the praxis of puppetry in the early 1990s the form has now definitely established itself into the mainstream of the UKs popular culture. Objects are as much the stars in this newly established UK theatre scene where the giant puppet is part of large-scale spectacle, for example Royal de Luxe's *Sultan's Elephant* (2006), *Le Princes Spider* (2008), Golden Tree's *Giant Miner* (2016) or The Walk Productions and Good Chance's *Little Amal* (2021).

Cultural studies scholars Anna Malinowska and Karolina Lebek (2016) describe and advocate for the meshing of popular and material in a new approach to reading culture. This materiality involves the relation of materiality through the quality of things, their presences, functions in society and their 'performative volume'. This relation can be approached as a 'praxis of matter' that is received as an 'enchanting vitalism' (Malinowska and Lebek 2016: 2). This approach to the object world can involve appreciating the reciprocal relationship between subject and object which constitutes a popular materialism (2016: 4). As well as a way to approach popular culture, these scholars advise that there is a possibility to look at the 'subversive rereading of things as a way to see some popular cultural systems as transgressive acts against the hegemonic positions usually ascribed to cultural exchange' (2016: 4). Within their edited volume on the 'popular life of things' there is a chapter about a historical community arts practice that leads the author journalism scholar Lucia Vodanovic to suggest a 'fluid materiality' (Vodanovic in Malinowska and Lebek 2016: 140). This fluid materiality is part and parcel of the way that my company PickleHerring operated within sites and social spaces using objects to disturb and subvert the hegemonic system of how objects and things are presented. This fluid materiality is also a way to read the popularity of puppetry in the West End. Also, Applied Puppetry can be assessed as a form which applies an aesthetics of popular materialism approaching praxis, transgressively looking for ways to experience or ways of thinking about our environment. Throughout this book I have explored this popular materialism that disrupts positionality and plays with objects, affecting subjects, in a cosmology where all things potentially have agency.

Reciprocity

One of our responsibilities as human people is to find ways to enter into reciprocity with the more-than-human world. We can do it through gratitude, through ceremony, through land stewardship, science, art, and in everyday acts of practical reverence. (Robin Wall Kimmerer 2020: 190)[23]

At the heart of Applied Theatre and Applied Puppetry is the belief that there is a possibility for reciprocal exchanges between practitioners with participants in community or educational settings. In Applied Puppetry this exchange can involve an appreciation of how objects like puppets open up this possibility between agents in the complex environment of practice. The fluid materiality that a puppet enables is often funny, surprising and outside of the everyday. If a secure sense of reciprocity is developed amongst these three spaces of puppet, community and practitioner, new knowledge about what all the stuff means in an ecology can be opened up. It can also reveal the unbalanced power that needs to be challenged in our current ecology and Anthropocene. This performance can take the form of puppet effigies on the streets as political puppet theatre. Many examples of this form exist, such as the Vietnam War protests of the 1960s populated by Bread and Puppet Theatres' giant puppets (Brecht 1988) mutely being 'louder than traffic', or Little Amal in 2021 crossing contested borders and stoned by the xenophobic, or even, Occupy puppets destroyed by the police. David Graeber eloquently describes this disturbing clash of forces during the Occupy protests during 2009–12:

> As many activists have observed, the forces of order in the United States seem to have a profound aversion to giant puppets. Often police strategies aim to destroy or capture them before they can even appear on the streets. As a result, a major concern for those planning actions soon became how to hide the puppets so they will not be destroyed in pre-emptive attacks. What's more, for many individual officers at least, the objection to puppets appeared to be not merely strategic, but personal, even visceral. Cops hate puppets. Activists are puzzled as to why. (Graeber 2009: 1)

Puppetry as a popular art form has historically had a strong relationship with the street as in Polish propaganda shows, Kamishibai, Punch, Kasparl and Guignol shows, to name a few examples. Puppetry is a people's form embedded in communities. The way the community assembles from dusk till dawn around the shadow screen in Wayang Kulit is now a protected example of heritage since 2003 (UNESCO).[24] Often coming from the streets and not the stage, puppetry has this coding of the popular through which to enact its fluid materiality. A major part of the practitioners' labour and skill is developing this reciprocity with communities. Spectacle with no engagement is a rather empty and hollow experience. A task for future Applied Puppetry is to develop meaningful spectacles and not just produce more empty images.

Puppets enable large- and small-scale spectacles and are used to enhance miniature theatre (Lambe Lambe) to small-scale (children's workshops) to mid-scale (the shows of Puppet Rites[25]) to giant-scale events (Royal de Luxe's Sultan's Elephant). In my practice the puppet does more than just enhance the spectacular possibilities, as it has defined me and my practice since I started playing with this form. Puppets define me in the way that they enable me to voice concerns about the world, extending my body as a performer. They also impact the way that I consider the idea of performance as a material practice affecting bodies in spaces. My material impact is extended out into the world with the collaboration of puppets continually looped back towards me, changing me. Being enmeshed with the material realities of my practice is at the heart of what I do with puppets, participants and projects. It is also at the heart of the practice of Applied Puppetry. The puppet collaborates with me, the clothes I wear define me, the floor supports me, the walls contain me, the air I breathe keeps me alive, and the food I eat chemically enhances me within this vibrant materiality of assemblages – like in Bennett's political ecology of things (Bennett 2009).

The pre-expressive (Eugenio Barba 1995) material definitions and objects, centres my practice away from hubristic anthropocentric heroism. Being a meek entity in the space of practice does not diminish my ability to perform or facilitate performance. In community practice I am always happier to be a less visible facilitator turning the focus on the community group, like a puppeteer lessening their presence through a focus on the puppet other. Applied Theatre, like puppetry animation involves creating an explorative space created betwixt and between a group, a facilitator, allowing others to flourish. This is a nuanced intersubjective/inter-object-lived complex space and network of actants.

Throughout the book I have explored the interstitial zone somewhere between or on the outside of this list of binaries:

…animate/inanimate … active/passive … object/subject … life/death … known/unknown … organic/manmade … authentic/false … body/entity … waste/value … explicit/implicit … direct/multi-directional … inside/outside … performance/stillness … distance/attachment … emotions/concepts … agency/connection … puppet/actor … character/object … chthonic/quotidian … resistance/manipulable … hollow/embodied … life/residues … matter/transcendence … control/freedom … ephemeral/permanent … social/individual … alienated/enmeshed …

This list is evoked here due to my attraction to litanies, since reading materialist philosopher Ian Bogost's use of Latour Litanies where he explores OOO (2012). Listing the litanies of objects within a network allows us to reconsider the ecology of practice when we reflect as critical artists. The puppet never settles anywhere in between or next to any of these words and instead occupies some other space of materiality in regard to binaries. Even so, I would encourage this method for others in practice as it has allowed me a way into the poetic spaces of things.

Chimaera performers

Before visionary feminist Donna Haraway famously proclaimed we are all cyborgs in 1985 (because of our augmentation by technologies), she suggested a chimaera as an analogy for the post-human identities we are shaping in the advanced technoscapes (Haraway 2012). We are shaped by advanced technologies and affected by these objects in performance cultures as well as everyday life experiences. Understanding the way advanced technologies affect experiences is part of material awareness of applied practices. The potential of puppetry to make meme-sized culturally replicating images is part of the continued popularity of puppetry in embodied and virtual spaces. Objects and puppetry work well in our contained hybrid zoom spaces for both communities and educational groups. In these spaces the objects break up the monotony of human faces in Zoom squares. Mobile phones can be used to capture puppet skits and performances, in addition to having the ability to shine a very focused beam of light for shadow performances (as I found in collaboration with artists in Nairobi). Puppetry is also a cousin of robotics and is similarly an interface between humans and objects in technological practice.

As I am finishing this book, I am conducting a project with scientists in the Centre for Enzyme Innovation looking at how puppetry can enhance engagement activities with communities and cutting-edge science explaining how enzymes can break down plastic waste.[26] As well as furthering knowledge of how puppetry can be used to develop narratives between science and technology this project uses the character of the chimaera enzyme as a theme. In the breaking down of plastic the enzymes join to make new enzymes with better plastic munching capabilities. In the mythic creature of the chimaera there are also some analogies to arts practice. I have always felt that the fecund combination of more than one thing together in a new configuration encapsulates the artistic process for me. Often these combined things can be incongruous or very different and produce exciting juxtapositions.

This figure of the chimaera is also a useful analogy for the puppet and puppeteer becoming something new through combinations in performance. The puppeteer and the puppet combine into a new configuration that is conjoined in performance. This new performance creature, mixing human with object can be both monstrous or charming or even a focus of empathy. Putting together a plastic bottle and a piece of scrap fabric in the hands of a community group member and seeing them surprised, excited or playful with this new configuration is an experience at the heart of the Applied Puppetry experience.

I hope some of the ideas covered in this book will add to your next experience with puppets or performing objects. At the end of this book if you have not already made a puppet or surprising figure made from combinations of stuff you could put down the book and get your hands dirty.

Notes

1. Theatre and Performance Research Association (TAPRA) in September 2019 at Exeter University, I first presented this performance with the root and for this event and it was titled; 'Sharing the Future with Objects: Applied Theatre, New Materialism and Horizontal Ontologies.
2. Boss guitar loop pedal.
3. These are also called piezo transducer pick-ups – it is a type of microphone that picks up vibrations from objects and turns these into voltage. I have used this on other objects like a plastic bag that was animated by a former inmate of an immigration removal centre as part of my PaR in 2016. The plastic bag represented an object witness of the immigration jail.

4. This litany is influenced by OOO theorist Ian Bogost in *Alien phenomenology*, and he creates what he calls Latour litanies in a computer http://bogost.com/writing/blog/latour_litanizer/.
5. Roots that try and grow in unusual places. This can be called root heave. Great images of this can be seen here: https://www.theguardian.com/cities/gallery/2015/dec/10/root-force-unstoppable-urban-trees-in-pictures.
6. Enlarged structures in plants.
7. Exposed roots above the ground.
8. Lateral root systems that choke the plant and can cause ill health.
9. Another root disease that is a knobbly growth and can be caused by parasites.
10. Deleuze uses this word a lot in regard to growth. The words here are influenced by Deleuzian and Guattari's language in *Thousand Plateaus*. They also make an interesting philosophical use of puppetry in their text: 'Puppet strings, as a rhizome or multiplicity, are tied not to the supposed will of an artist or puppeteer but to a multiplicity of nerve fibres, which form another puppet in other dimensions connected to the first' (Deleuze and Guattari 2000: 8).
11. Charles Darwin suggested this – it is still an idea that plant intelligence, and cognition, exists.
12. David Nash and Diana Scherer are artists who slowly manipulate plants in this way. These are artistic exercises in plant domestication.
13. Description of *Sound Garden*. installation: https://creativespace.cci.port.ac.uk/2017/07/the-sound-garden-giant-musical-installation-brings-life-to-somerstown-public-space/.
14. Reference to P. Schwenger, *The Tears of Things: Melancholy and Physical Objects* (Minnesota: University of Minnesota Press, 2006). Lacrimae Rerum is a phrase from Virgil's *Aeneid*.
15. This text – M. Miodownik, *Stuff Matters: Exploring the Marvellous Materials That Shape Our Man-Made World* (London: Penguin, 2014) – influenced the performance text.
16. Sentient Performativity's website: https://performativities.info/.
17. Tree Listening Project information here: https://www.kcw.org/rcad-and-watch/the-tree-listener.
18. Jason Singh created *Extinction Song video* – https://www.reecestraw.co.uk/journal/2021/4/5/kew-gardens-extinction-songs-jason-singh.
19. An account of the controversy of Rylance's departure from the RSC can be found here: https://www.theguardian.com/stage/2019/jun/21/mark-rylance-resigns-from-royal-shakespeare-company-rsc-over-bp-sponsorship.
20. Whitechapel Exhibition Thick Time details here: https://www.whitechapelgallery.org/exhibitions/william-kentridge/.
21. The fortunes of the *War Horse* phenomena are discussed in this article: https://www.theguardian.com/stage/2013/oct/04/national-theatre-record-87-million-war-horse.
22. 2022 Review by Akbar of *My Neighbour Totoro*: https://www.theguardian.com/stage/2022/oct/19/my-neighbour-totoro-review-barbican-london.
23. Robin Wall Kimmerer's book *Brading the Sweetgrass* is a beautiful memoir of how she learns from the teaching of plants based on both science and her heritage in Native American folklore.
24. Description of the status of Wayang as a world cultural heritage: https://ich.unesco.org/en/RL/wayang-puppet-theatre-00063.

25. Discussion of Theatre Rites company and their work can be found in Jarvis and Buckmaster (2021).
26. Details of this project here: https://raeng.org.uk/programmes-and-prizes/programmes/uk-grants-and-prizes/ingenious-public-engagement-awards/awardees/awardees-2022/puppets-as-enzyme-engineers-of-the-imagination.

Exercises

These exercises extend the knowledge of this book and can be conducted individually or in groups. They are points of departure that should be adapted to your needs and situation.

Chapter 1

1. Think of a new application for puppetry with a particular community group or individual.
2. Consider a game or exercise you know and think about how you could adapt this by using a puppet or performing object.
3. Make a simple puppet from just one kind of material; for example, paper, plastic or cloth.

Chapter 2

1. Think of your position within the ecology and draw this relationship within a set of interconnected circles. Where do you find yourself within this network?
2. Think through how you are affected by objects in your daily and extra daily practices. Who is affecting who in this relationship?
3. Find an object to perform with – explore how that object seems to want to present its presence (either with you animating it or not). Try not to mask or hide the materiality of the objects you use.

Chapter 3

1. Play a game and think about how objects enabled you to achieve this activity.
2. Explore how objects could allow you to safely explore violence. Does this make you feel good?
3. Find an object that has some form of historical significance. Think about how you can animate this history of the object. Does this say anything about the object's or human life?

Chapter 4

1. Think about how objects could help you connect with someone from another country.
2. Make a puppet skit for use on Zoom. What does the puppet do to the viewing experience?
3. Consider the issues involved in using objects to represent specific identities.
4. Discuss how objects affect the biopolitics of people in different social contexts.

Chapter 5

1. Consider a site you know and explore how you could perform in relation to that site as a text. What narratives emerge from considering that site?
2. Think of an ecological issue and decide how a puppet could communicate that message. What can the puppet say that a human being might not be able to say as well?
3. Find an object from a landscape and reflect upon what that thing says about the space it was found within. Imagine dialogue emanating from that object. What would that object like to say?

Chapter 6

1. Make a list of benefits of theatre practice in a prison setting. Do they seem appropriate?
2. Reflect upon how objects could be considered ethical.
3. Consider the way that immigration is presented culturally. How are the people involved 'othered' in this set of presentations?
4. Think about objects that could represent narratives about migration and use that object to tell that narrative or account. Does this seem an appropriate way to represent migration?
5. Consider how you use your hands in both daily life and in performance practice.

Chapter 7

1. Make a small toy theatre or box of delights and fill it with collaged elements or figures. How could you animate this box?
2. Tell a story using the flat two-dimensional style of Kamishibai with five different story cards. How could you adapt this form for an online performance?
3. Think of an object in a cityscape and write the narrative of this object's experiences as though it has a voice. What does this story tell you about urban life?
4. Consider how integral play is to your life and practices. Then consider this in relation to performing arts and puppetry.

Chapter 8 and Envoi

1. Find an organic form that is not part of a living entity like a branch, stone or leaf, for example. Concentrate on this thing and consider its complexity.
2. Speak towards your chosen object. First about your experience of this object then secondly about the object's point of view. What new poetics comes from voicing the object in this way?
3. Using your hands and touch concentrate on understanding an object in much more detail. Explore the weight of the object and then animate this form trying not to just push it around the space. How has this performing object changed in regard to its presence?
4. If you could have a dialogue with any entity, what would it be? Write down the questions or words you could speak.
5. Focus really intensely on an object and think about how that makes you feel.
6. Think about a new application for puppetry and how it can enable, give pleasure and engage a specific community group.

References

Abed, H., and R. Deák (2020), 'Breaking Out of Time: Dafa Puppet Theatre', *Applied Theatre Research*, 8(1): 135–42.
Adams, D. (1992), 'Joseph Beuys: Pioneer of a Radical Ecology', *Art Journal*, 51(2): 26–34.
Abram, D. (2012), *The Spell of the Sensuous: Perception and Language in a More-Than-Human World*, New York: Pantheon Books.
African Research and Educational Puppetry Programme (AREPP) (2022), https://esat.sun.ac.za/index.php/AREPP#arepp:Theatre_for_Life (accessed 29 November).
Agamben, G. (2005), *State of Exception*, Chicago: University of Chicago Press.
Akbar, A. (2022), '*My Neighbour Totoro* Review – Dazzling Staging of the Studio Ghibli Classic', *The Guardian*, https://www.theguardian.com/stage/2022/oct/19/my-neighbour-totoro-review-barbican-london (accessed 4 November 2022).
Allen, K., and P. Shaw (1992), *On the Brink of Belonging: A National Enquiry into Puppetry*, London: Calouste Gulbenkian Foundation.
Arons, W., and T. J. May (2012), *Readings in Performance and Ecology*, New York: Palgrave Macmillan.
Astles, C., E. Fisher, Laura Purcell-G. and P. Sextou (2020), 'Broken Puppet Symposia', *Journal of Applied Arts and Health* 11(1 and 2): 200–7.
Azaria, T. (2015), 'Trickster: Archetype of Changing Times', *Depth Insights*, 8: 29–33.
Baird, B. (1971), *Puppets and Population*, New York: World Education.
Baird, B., and A. Zanger (1965), *The Art of the Puppet*, New York: Macmillan.
Baim, C., S. Brookes and A. Mountford (2002), *The Geese Theatre Handbook: Drama with Offenders and People at Risk*, Winchester: Waterside Press.
Balfour, M., P. Bundy, B. Burton, J. Dunn and N. Woodrow (2015), *Applied Theatre: Resettlement: Drama, Refugees and Resilience*, London: Bloomsbury Methuen.
Barba, E. (1995), *The Paper Canoe: A Guide to Theatre Anthropology*, London: Routledge.
Barthes, R. (1971), 'On Bunraku', *The Drama Review*, TDR, 15(2):76–80.
Barthes, R. (2000), *Camera Lucida: Reflections on Photography*, London: Vintage.
Barthes, R., and S. Heath (1977), *Image, Music, Text*, London: Fontana.
Bass, E. (2014), 'The Myths of Puppet Theater', *Howlround*. https://howlround.com/myths-puppet-theater (accessed 24 March 2016).
Baudelaire, C., H. V. Kleist and R. M. Rilke (1994), *Essays On Dolls*, London: Penguin Syrens.
Bell, J. (1997), 'Puppets and Performing Objects in the Twentieth Century', *Performing Arts Journal*, 19(2): 29–46.
Bell, J. (1999), 'The End of Our Domestic Resurrection Circus: Bread and Puppet Theater and Counterculture Performance in the 1990s'. *TDR/The Drama Review*, 43(3): 62–80.
Bell, J. (2013), 'Louder Than Traffic: Bread and Puppet Parades', in *Radical Street Performance: An International Anthology*, 272–80, edited by J. Cohen-Cruz, London: Routledge.
Bell, J. (2016), *American Puppet Modernism: Essays on the Material World in Performance*, London: Palgrave.

Benjamin, W., and H. Arendt. (1999), *Illuminations*, London: Pimlico.
Bennett, J. (2004), 'The Force of Things: Steps Toward an Ecology of Matter', *Political Theory*, 32(3): 347–72.
Bennett, J. (2005), *Empathic Vision: Affect, Trauma, and Contemporary Art*, Stanford: Stanford University Press.
Bennett, J. (2009), *Vibrant Matter: A Political Ecology of Things*, Durham: Duke University Press.
Berrada, O. (2015), 'The Bare Scene of Re-telling: Wael Shawky on the Thresholds of History', in *Wael Shawky Cabinet Crusades Drawings*, 29–34, edited by T. D. Trummer, Bregenz: Kunsthaus Bregenz.
Bidgood, J. (2014), 'The Problem of Bunraku: A Practice-Led Investigation into Contemporary Uses and Misuses of Ningyo Joruri', doctoral dissertation, Royal Holloway, University of London.
Blake, W. (2002), *Collected Poems*, London: Routledge.
Bleeker, M., A. Kear, J. Kelleher and H. Roms (2019), *Thinking Through Theatre and Performance*, London: Bloomsbury Methuen Drama.
Blum, D. (2002), *Love at Goon Park: Harry Harlow and the Science of Affection*, New York: Merloyd Lawrence Books.
Blumenthal, E. (2005), *Puppetry and Puppets: An Illustrated World Survey*, London: Thames and Hudson.
Boal, A. (2008), *Theatre of the Oppressed* (new edn), London: Pluto.
Boal, A. (2013), *The Rainbow of Desire: The Boal Method of Theatre and Therapy*, London: Routledge.
Bogost, I. (2012), *Alien Phenomenology or, What It's Like to Be a Thing*, London: University of Minnesota Press.
Brecht, B. (1977), *The Measures Taken and other Lehrstück*, London: Methuen.
Brown, B. (2001), 'Thing Theory', *Critical Inquiry*, 28(1): 1–22.
Brown, B. (2016), *Other Things*, London: University of Chicago Press.
Brecht, S. (1988), *The Bread and Puppet Theatre* (two volumes), London: Methuen.
Burggraeve, R. (1999), 'Violence and the Vulnerable Face of the Other: The Vision of Emmanuel Levinas on Moral Evil and Our Responsibility', *Journal of Social Philosophy* 30(1): 29–45.
Burvill, T. (2008), ' "Politics Begins as Ethics": Levinasian Ethics and Australian Performance Concerning Refugees', *Research in Drama Education*, 13(2): 233–43.
Candlin, F., and R. Guins (2009), *The Object Reader*, London: Routledge.
Cappelletto, C. (2011), 'The Puppet's Paradox: An Organic Prosthesis', *Anthropology and Aesthetics*, 59(60): 325–36.
Castillo-Rodríguez, C., R. Cremades and I. López-Fernández (2022), 'Storytelling and Teamwork in the Bilingual Classroom at University: Impressions and Satisfaction from Pre-service Teachers in the Kamishibai Project', *Thinking Skills and Creativity*, 45, https://doi.org/10.1016/j.tsc.2022.101098 (accessed 10 November 2022).
Chesterton, G. K. (2007), 'The Toy Theater', in *Tremendous Trifles*, 117–22, New York: Dover.
Coady, C. A. J. (1996), 'Dirty Hands', in *A Companion to Contemporary Political Philosophy*, 422–31, edited by R. E. Goodin and P. Pettit, Oxford: Blackwell.
Cohen, M. I. (2007), 'Puppetry and the Destruction of the Object', *Performance Research*, 12(4): 123–31.
Connelly, M. (2006), 'Population Control in India: Prologue to the Emergency Period', *Population and Development Review*, 32(4): 629–67.

Connor, S. (2000), *Dumbstruck: A Cultural History of Ventriloquism*, Oxford: Oxford University Press.
Contractor, Meher R. (2001), *Creative Drama and Puppetry in Education*, NBT: India.
Coult, T., and B. Kershaw (2002), *Engineers of the Imagination: The Welfare State Handbook* (revised and updated edition), London: Methuen.
Coverley, M. (2006), *Psychogeography*, Harpenden: Pocket Essentials.
Critchley, S. (2008), *Infinitely Demanding: Ethics of Commitment, Politics of Resistance*, London: Verso.
Critchley, S. (2012), *Impossible Objects: Interviews*, Cambridge: Polity Press.
Crone, R. (2006), 'Mr and Mrs Punch in Nineteenth-Century England', *Historical Journal*, 49(4): 1055–82.
Crothers, J. F. (1983), *The Puppeteer's Library Guide: The Bibliographic Index to the Literature of the World Puppet Theatre, Volume 2: The Puppet as an Educator*, London: Scarecrow.
Csikszentmihalyi, M. (2002), *Flow: The Classic Work on How to Achieve Happiness*, London: Rider.
Dakroub, K. (2020), 'Puppetry for Building Bridges: Psychosocial Intervention in Emergency Settings in the Middle East', *Applied Theatre Research*, 8(1): 57–71.
Debord, G. (1994), *The Society of the Spectacle*, New York: Zone Books.
Derrida, J. (2000), 'Hospitality', *Angelaki: Journal of Theoretical Humanities*, 5.3: 3–18.
Derrida, J. (1997), *Deconstruction in a Nutshell: A Conversation with Jacques Derrida*, New York: Fordham University Press.
Duffy-Syedi, K. (2022), 'Refugee as Spectacle: Good Chance Theatre's The Walk and the Politics of Performing "Unaccompanied Minor"', *Contemporary Theatre Review*, 32(2): 221–6.
Earth Art (2022), 'Conference Sentient Performativities', https://performativities.info/ (accesssed 12 June 2022).
Educational Puppetry Association (EPA) (1945), 'Puppet Year Book, 1944–1945'. London: EPA.
EPA, Wall, L. V. (ed.) (1953), *The Puppet Book: A Book on Educational Puppetry, 1944– 1945*, London: Faber and Faber.
Epstein, I., B. Stevens, P. McKeever, S. Baruchel and H. Jones (2008), 'Using Puppetry to Elicit Children's Talk for Research', *Nursing inquiry*, 15(1): 49–56.
Fell, J. (2013), 'Paul Ranson, Alfred Jarry and the Nabi Puppet Theatres', in *The Art of Theatre*,113–34, edited by C. Moran and P. Jeannerod, Oxford: Peter Lang.
Foucault, M. (1991), *Discipline and Punish: The Birth of the Prison*, London: Penguin.
Foucault, M. (1998), *The History of Sexuality*, London: Penguin.
Foucault, M. (2006), *History of Madness,* Abingdon: Routledge.
Fox, J. (2002), *Eyes on Stalks*, London: Methuen.
Fox, J. (2007), 'Welfare State International – Our Puppet Story', in *Animated Encounters: A Review of Puppetry and Related Arts*, 21–5, edited by D. M. Prior, London: Puppet Centre Trust.
Gablik, S. (1991), *The Reenchantment of Art*, London: Thames and Hudson.
Gentleman, G. (2021), '"People Felt Threatened Even by a Puppet Refugee": Little Amal's Epic Walk through Love and Fear', *The Guardian*, https://www.theguardian.com/stage/2021/oct/18/threatened-puppet-refugee-little-amals-epic-walk (accessed 22 August 2022).
Ghosh, S., and U. K. Banerjee (2006), *Indian Puppets,* New Delhi: Abhinav Publications.

Goodlander J. (2019), *Puppets and Cities: Articulating Identities in Southeast Asia*, London: Methuen Drama.

Graeber D. (2009), 'On the Phenomenology of Giant Puppets: Broken Windows, Imaginary Jars of Urine, and the Cosmological Role of the Police in American Culture', in *Possibilities: Essays on Hierarchy, Rebellion, and Desire*, 375–418, https://files.libcom.org/files/puppets.pdf (accessed 22 August 2022).

Grant, D. (2020), '"Objects with Objectives": Applied Puppetry from Practice into Theory', *Applied Theatre Research*, 8(1): 13–29.

Gray, J. (2015), *The Soul of the Marionette: A Short Inquiry into Human Freedom*, London: Macmillan.

Gross, J. (2001), *Speaking in Other Voices: An Ethnography of Walloon Puppet Theaters*, Amsterdam: John Benjamins.

Gross, K. (1997), 'Love among the Puppets', *Raritan*, 17(1): 67–82.

Gross, K. (2011), *The Puppet: An Uncanny Life*, Chicago: University of Chicago Press.

Guattari, F., and G. Deleuze (2000), *A Thousand Plateaus: Capitalism and Schizophrenia*, London: Athlone Press.

Hall, S. (ed.) (1997), *Representation: Cultural Representations and Signifying Practices* (vol. 2), London: Sage.

Haraway, D. (2012), 'A Manifesto for Cyborgs: Science, Technology, and Socialist Feminism in the 1980s', in *Coming to Term: Feminism, Theory, Politics*, 173–204, edited by E. Weed, London: Taylor and Francis.

Harman, G. (2010), *Towards Speculative Realism: Essays and Lectures*, Winchester: John Hunt.

Harman, G. (2018), *Object-Oriented Ontology: A New Theory of Everything*, London: Penguin.

Hartelius, J. (2013), '"Face-ing Immigration: Prosopopeia and the "Muslim-Arab-Middle Eastern Other"', *Rhetoric Society Quarterly*, 43(4): 311–34.

Heidegger, M. (1995), *Being and Time*, London: Blackwell.

Hernawan, A. H., D. Darmawan, A. I. Septiana, I. Rachman and Y. Kodama (2022), 'Environmental Education in Elementary School with Kamiholo: Kamishibai and Hologram as Teaching Multimedia', *Journal Pendidikan IPA* Indonesia, 11(2): 229–36.

Hogg, A. (2005), *The Potential of Puppetry: A Review of the Sector in Scotland*. Edinburgh: Scottish Arts Council.

Hofmeyr, B. (2007), 'Radical Passivity: Ethical Problem of Solution? A Preliminary Investigation', *South African Journal of Philosophy*, 26(20): 150–62.

Hughes, T. (1968), *The Iron Man*, London: Faber and Faber.

Hughes, T. (1969) *Seneca's Oedipus*, London: Faber and Faber.

Hughes, J., and H. Nicholson (2016), *Critical Perspectives on Applied Theatre*, Cambridge: Cambridge University Press.

Hyde, L. (2008), *Trickster Makes This World: How Disruptive Imagination Creates Culture*. London: Canongate Books.

Juntunen, J. (2020), 'Human/Object/Thing: Tadeusz Kantor's Puppets and Bio-Objects', in *Theatremachine: Tadeusz Kantor in Context*, 29–40, edited by Magda Romańska and Kathleen Cioff, Illinois: Northwestern University Press.

Jarvis, L., and S. Buckmaster (2021), *Theatre-Rites: Animating Puppets, Objects and Sites*, London: Routledge.

Jeffers, A. (2011), *Refugees, Theatre and Crisis: Performing Global Identities*, London: Palgrave Macmillan.

Jennings, H. (1987), *Pandemonium. The Coming of the Machine as Seen by Contemporary Observers 1660–1886*, London: Picador.
Jordan, A. (2013), 'HMP Haslar an Etymology', in *Bonehead's Utopia* by Andrew Jordan, http://smokestack-books.co.uk/book.php?book=8 (accessed 7 April 2013).
Jurkowski, H. (1988), *Aspects of Puppet Theatre*, London: Puppet Centre Trust.
Jurkowski, H. (1996), *A History of European Puppetry from Its Origins to the End of the 19th Century*, Lewiston: Edwin Mellen Press.
Kamenetsky, C. (2019), *Children's Literature in Hitler's Germany: The Cultural Policy of National Socialism*, Ohio: Ohio University Press.
Kang, H. (2015), *The Vegetarian*, London: Portobello Books.
Kantor, T. (1993), *A Journey through Other Spaces: Essays and Manifestos, 1944–1990*, Berkely: University of California Press.
Kei, R. M. (2012), 'Health Education for Primary Health Care Development in Kenya', *Journal of Emerging Trends in Educational Research and Policy Studies*, 3(1): 39–45.
Kempster, H. (2001), 'The Girl Who Cut Flowers', *Dramatherapy*, 23(1): 33.
Kent, L. (2022), 'Performing Objects: Working in between Materiality and the Imagination', *Academia*, https://www.academia.edu/27405876/Performing_Objects_working_in_between_materiality_and_the_imagination (accessed 4 June 2023).
Kershaw, B. (2007), *Theatre Ecology: Environments and Performance Events*, Cambridge: Cambridge University Press.
Kimmerer, R. W. (2020), *Braiding Sweetgrass: Indigenous Wisdom, Scientific Knowledge and the Teachings of Plants*, London: Penguin.
Kohler, A. (2009), 'Thinking through Puppets', in *Handspring Puppet Company*, New York: David Kurt.
Kopania, K. (ed.) (2014), *Dolls and Puppets as Artistic and Cultural Phenomena (19th–21st Centuries)*, Białystok, Poland: Aleksander Zelwerowicz National Academy of Dramatic Art in Warsaw, The Department of Puppetry Art in Białystok.
Kruger, M. (2010), 'Social Dynamics in African Puppetry', *Contemporary Theatre Review*, 20(3): 316–28.
Laakkonen, R. (2020), 'The Art of Expressive Objects Supporting Agency in Palliative Care', *Applied Theatre Research*, 8(1): 107–16.
Latour, B. (1993), *We Have Never Been Modern*, London: Harvester Wheatsheaf.
Lavery, C., and C. F. Delijani (2015), *Rethinking the Theatre of the Absurd: Ecology, the Environment and the Greening of the Modern Stage*, London: Bloomsbury.
Levinas, E. (1990), *Totality and Infinity*, Pittsburgh: Duquesne University Press.
Levinas, E. (2006), *Entre Nous: Thinking-of-the-Other*, London: Continuum.
Linn, S. (2020), 'It's Not Me! It's Him! Interactive Puppet Play to Help Children Cope', *Journal of Applied Arts & Health*, 11(1–2): 103–8.
Malinowska, A., and K. Lebek (2016), *Materiality and Popular Culture*, London: Routledge.
Margolies, E. (2014), 'Return to the Mound: Animating Infinite Potential in Food and Compost', in *The Routledge Companion to Puppetry and Material Performance*, 322–35, edited by D. N. Posner, C. Orenstein and J. Bell, London: Routledge.
Marneweck, A. (2020), 'On the 10-Year Anniversary of the Barrydale Giant Puppet Parade South Africa: A Conversation between Parade Creative Directors Aja Marneweck and Sudonia Kouter', *Applied Theatre Research* 8(1): 31–44.
Martin, R., and E. O'Malley (2018), 'Eco-Shakespeare in Performance: Introduction', *Shakespeare Bulletin*, 36(3): 377–90.

Maubert, O. (2019), 'Puppet and Dancer, Choreography of Object-Body: Meeting, Control and Vertigo', in *Puppetry in the 21st Century: Reflections and Challenges*, 38–54, edited by M. Wiśniewska and K. Suszczyński, Warsaw: Aleksander Zelwerowicz National Academy of Dramatic Art in Warsaw.

Mauss, M. (2004), *The Gift*, London: Routledge.

Mbugua, T. (2004), 'Responding to the Special Needs of Children Educating HIV/AIDS Orphans in Kenya', *Childhood Education*, 80(6): 304–9.

McCormick, J., and B. Pratasik (1998), *Popular Puppet Theatre in Europe, 1800–1914*, Cambridge: Cambridge University Press.

McIntyre/UNICEF (1998), *Puppets with a Purpose – Using Puppetry for Social Change*, Penang: Southbound.

McPherson, C. (2021), 'On The Horrifying, Hilarious Violence of a Punch & Judy Puppet Show – Who Doesn't Love a Puppet, with a Wriggling, Uneasy Love That Might Be Terror?', *CrimeReads*, https://crimereads.com/punch-and-judy-puppet-show-violence/ (accessed 10 January 2023).

McCarthy, J. (1998), 'Militant Marionettes: Two "Lost Puppet Plays of the Spanish Civil War, 1936–39', *Theatre Research International*, 23: 44–50.

Miller, D. (2008), *The Comfort of Things*, London: Polity.

Millar, M. (2018), *Puppetry: How to Do It*, London: Nick Hern.

Miodownik, M. (2014), *Stuff Matters: Exploring the Marvellous Materials That Shape Our Man-Made World*, London: Penguin.

Mori, M., K. F. MacDorman and N. Kageki (2012), 'The Uncanny Valley [from the Field]', *IEEE Robotics & Automation Magazine*, 19(2): 98–100.

Morton, T. (2018), *Being Ecological*, London: Pelican.

Mothers Union (2023), 'Using Puppets to Teach about Gender Based Violence in South Africa'. https://www.mothersunion.org/news/using-puppets-teach-about-gender-based-violence-southern-africa (accessed 20 August 2022).

Mworogo, P. (1996), 'Initiatives: Kenya. Puppets Say It Better', *Africa Link: A Publication of the Africa Region*, 15–16. https://pubmed.ncbi.nlm.nih.gov/12292576/ (accessed 23 March 2022).

Nainar, N. (2021), 'Pushed Out of Kathputli Colony, Its Magicians, Puppeteers and Acrobats Wait Endlessly for a New Home', *The Hindu*, https://www.thehindu.com/society/pushed-out-of-kathputli-colony-its-magicians- puppeteers-and-acrobats-wait-endlessly-for-a-new-home/article34664575.ece (accessed 28 November 2022).

Nelson, V. (2001), *The Secret Life of Puppets*, London: Harvard University Press.

Ngunjiri, P. (1995), 'Puppetry: Handy Tool for Mobilising Communities', *Option (Nairobi, Kenya)*, 36–8.

Nicholson, H. (2005), *Applied Drama: The Gift of Theatre*, London: Palgrave Macmillan.

Nugroho, K. A., and L. Sunarti (2019), 'The New Order Play: Wayang as a Medium for Development Messages, 1969–84', *Pertanika Journal of Social Sciences & Humanities*, 27(3): 2017–32.

O'Brien, F. (1999), *The Third Policeman: A Novel*, London: Dalkey Archive Press.

Orbaugh, S. (2017), 'Killer Kitsch: Kamishibai in Japan's Fifteen Year War, 1931–1945', *Far East/Dálný Vychod*, 7(1): 46–60.

Orenstein, C. (2015), 'Women in Indian Puppetry: Negotiating Traditional Roles and New Possibilities', *Asian Theatre Journal*, 32(2): 493–517.

Orenstein, C., and T. Cusack (2023), *Puppet and Spirit: Ritual, Religion, and Performing Objects: Volume I. Sacred Roots: Material Entities, Consecrating Acts, Priestly Puppeteers*, London: Routledge.

O'Sullivan, S. (2001), 'The Aesthetics of Affect: Thinking Art beyond Representation'. *Angelaki: Journal of the Theoretical Humanities*, 6(3): 125–35.
Oussoren, J. (2020), 'Shadow Theatre and Older People', *Applied Theatre Research*, 8(1): 143–8.
Pallasmaa, J. (2009), *The Thinking Hand*, London: Wiley.
Parsons, C. (2022), 'YETI LAMBE-LAMBE: How Brad Shur Took Puppetry's Smallest Form and Built a Whole Village', *Puppetry Journal*, 73(2): 28–9.
Parsons, L. (2007), 'Thompson's Rubbish Theory: Exploring the Practices of Value Creation', *Advances in Consumer Research - European Conference Proceedings*, 8: 390–3.
Peacock, L. (2009), *Serious Play: Modern Clown Performance*, Bristol: Intellect Books.
Pearson, M. (2019), 'How Does Theatre Think through Things?', in *Thinking through Theatre and Performance*, 115–29, edited by M. Bleeker, A. Kear, J. Kelleher and H. Roms, London: Methuen.
Peterson, V. (2017), 'Plato's Allegory of the Cave: Literacy and "the Good"', *Review of Communication*, 17(4): 273–87.
Philpott, A. R. (1977), *Puppets and Therapy*, Boston: Plays.
Plato (2017), *The Republic*, London: Penguin.
Polansky, S. G. (2014), 'Freedom to Experiment: The Coherence and Complexity of Federico García Lorca's Puppet Theater', *Hispania*, 101–12.
Posner, D. N., C. Orenstein and J. Bell (2014), *The Routledge Companion to Puppetry and Material Performance*, London: Routledge.
Poster-Su, T. (2020), 'A Grotesque Act of Ventriloquism: Raising and Objectifying the Dead on Stage', *Applied Theatre Research*, 8(1): 45–56.
Poster-Su, T. (2021), 'Sculpting China: Critical Puppetry and the Formation of Diasporic Identity in Chang and Eng and Me (and Me)', *Critical Stages* (24). https://www.critical-stages.org/24/sculpting-china-critical-puppetry-and-the-formation-of-diasporic-identity-in-chang-and-eng-and-me-and-me/ (accessed 22 November 2022).
Powers, R. (2019), *The Overstory*, London: Vintage.
Prentki, T. (2015), *Applied Theatre: Development*, London: Bloomsbury.
Purcell-Gates, L., and E. Fisher (2017), 'Puppetry as Reinforcement or Rupture of Cultural Perceptions of the Disabled Body', *Research in Drama Education: The Journal of Applied Theatre and Performance*, 22(3): 363–72.
Purcell-Gates, L., and M. Smith (2020), 'Applied Puppetry: Communities, Identities, Transgressions', *Applied Theatre Research*, 8(1): 3–11.
Rahn, S. (2013), *Rediscoveries in Children's Literature*, London: Routledge.
Rancière, J. (2010), *Dissensus: On Politics and Aesthetics*, London: Continuum.
Rayner, A. (2006), 'Presenting Objects, Presenting Things', in *Staging Philosophy: Intersections of Theater, Performance, and Philosophy*, edited by D. Krasner, and D. Z. Saltz, 180–99, Ann Arbor: University of Michigan Press.
Riccio, T. (2004), 'Kenya's Community Health Awareness Puppeteers', *Performing Arts Journal*, 76:1–12.
Richards, P. (2019),'Living Objects: Introduction', *Living Objects: African American Puppetry Essays*, 2. https://opencommons.uconn.edu/ballinst_catalogues/2 (accessed 24 April 2023).
Ridout, N. (2009), *Theatre and Ethics*, London: Palgrave Macmillan.
Robazza, G., and M. Smith (2022), 'Co-design as Play: Junk Sounds and Architecture in Urban Space', in *Cities' Identity through Architecture and Arts*, 121–39, edited by N. Mohareb, A. Cardaci, S. Maruthaveeran and N. Cavalagli, Cham: Springer International.

Rosenthal, M., S. Rainbird and C. Schmuckli (2004), *Joseph Beuys: Actions, Vitrines, Environments*, London: Menil Collection in association with Tate Publ.

Roth, P. (1995), *Sabbath's Theatre*, London: Vintage.

Royal Shakespeare Company (RSC) (2019), 'We Are to Conclude Our Partnership with BP', https://www.rsc.org.uk/news/archive/we-are-to-conclude-our-partnership-with-bp (accessed December 17, 2022).

Salverson, J. (2008), 'Taking Liberties: A Theatre Class of Foolish Witnesses', *Research in Drama Education*, 13(2): 245–55.

Sartre, J. P. (1989), *No Exit and Three Other Plays*, New York: Vintage.

Scanlan, J. (2005), *On Garbage*, London: Reaktion Books.

Schneider, R. (2003), 'Performance Remains', *Performance Research*, 6(2): 100–8.

Schweitzer, M., and J. Zerdy (2014), *Performing Objects and Theatrical Things*, London: Palgrave Macmillan.

Schwenger, P. (2006), *The Tears of Things: Melancholy and Physical Objects*, Minneapolis: University of Minnesota Press.

Sennett, R. (2008), *The Craftsman*, London: Penguin.

Sheriko, N. (2017), 'Patchwork Play: Nineteenth-Century Toy Theater and Participatory Media Culture', *Nineteenth Century Studies*, 30: 25–43.

Silanka, P. V. (2019), 'Kenyan Women in Puppet Theatre', in *Women and Puppetry: Critical and Historical Investigations*, 173–8, edited by A. Mello, C. Orenstein and C. Astles, London: Routledge.

Silk, D. (1986), 'The Marionette Theatre', *Conjunctions*, 9: 42–52.

Smith, M. (2008), 'PickleHerring and Marlsite Projects: An Interdisciplinary Approach to Junk Music-Making', *International Journal of Community Music*, 1(2): 159–68.

Smith, M. (2009), 'Puppetry as Community Arts Practice', *Journal of Arts & Communities*, 1(1): 69–78.

Smith, M. (2014), 'Towards a Definition of Applied Puppetry', in *EUROPSKE ODREDNICE POJMA LUTKE I STRUČNO LUTKARSKO NAZIVLJE, (European Definitions of the Puppet Concept and Professional Puppetry Terminology)*, 83–94, edited by L. Kroflin, Osijek: Academy of Arts in Osijek.

Smith, M. (2015), 'The Practice of Applied Puppetry: Antecedents and Tropes', *Research in Drama Education*, 20(4): 531–6.

Smith, M. (2016), 'Thinking through the Puppet Inside Immigration Detention', *Applied Theatre Researcher*, 4(2): 147–59.

Smith, M. (2018), 'Hand to Hand: The Dynamic Situation of Applied Puppetry', in *Dolls and Puppets: Contemporaneity and Tradition*, 88–93, edited by Kamil Kopania, Warsaw: Aleksander Zelwerowicz Academy of Dramatic Art in Warsaw (The Department of Puppetry Art in Białystok).

Smith, M. (2020), 'The Sentient Spoon as Broken Puppet: Celebrating Otherness with Performing Objects', *Journal of Applied Arts & Health*, 11(1–2): 49–58.

Smith, M. (2022), 'Applied Puppetry – Principles and Practice', in *Applied Puppetry in Education, Development, and Therapy: Theory and Practice*, 13–28, edited by L. Kroflin, Osijek: Academy of Arts and Culture and UNIMA Education, Development and Therapy Commission.

Sontag, S. (2008), *On Photography*, London: Penguin.

Sontag, S. (2009), *Illness as Metaphor and AIDS and Its Metaphors*, London: Penguin.

Speaight, G. (1970), *Punch & Judy: A History*, London: Studio Vista.

Speaight, G. (1955), *The History of the English Puppet Theatre*, London: Harrap.

Sussman, M. (2014), 'Notes on New Model Theatres', in *The Routledge Companion to Puppetry and Material Performance*, 268–78, edited by N. D. Posner, C. Orenstein and J. Bell, London: Routledge.
Taylor, J. (2014), 'From Props to Prosopopeia: Making after Cardenio', in *The Routledge Companion to Puppetry and Material Performance*, 230–44, edited by N. D., Posner, C. Orenstein and J. Bell, London: Routledge.
Taylor, J. (2016), 'The Varieties of Secular Experience: Magical Thinking, Occult Economies, and Puppetry', Unpublished seminar paper, Centre for Humanities Research & Department of History, University of the Western Cape South African Contemporary History and Humanities Seminar.
Taylor, J. (2017), 'Subjects and Objects: Puppetry in the Western Cape', *Puppetry International*, 41: 29–31.
Taylor, J. (2018), 'Barrydale Renosterbos Festival', http://www.chrflagship.uwc.ac.za/renosterbos-barrydale-festival-2017 (accessed 17 January 2018).
Thill, B. (2015), *Waste (Object Lessons)*, London: Bloomsbury.
Thistlewood, D. (1995), *Joseph Beuys: Diverging Critiques*, Liverpool: Liverpool University Press and Tate Gallery, Liverpool.
Thomas de la Peña, C. (2009), 'A Saccharin Sparrow (Circa 1955)', in *The Object Reader*, 506–9, edited by F. Candlin and R. Guins, London: Routledge.
Thompson, J. (2022), *Care Aesthetics: For Artful Care and Careful Art*, London: Taylor & Francis.
Thompson, M. (1979), *Rubbish Theory: The Creation and Destruction of Value*, Oxford: Oxford University Press.
Thornton, N. (2019), *David Nash: 200 Seasons at Capel Rhiw*, Cardiff: Amgueddfa Cymru – National Museum Wales.
Tomko, M. (2007), 'Politics, Performance, and Coleridge's Suspension of Disbelief', *Victorian Studies*, 49(2): 241–9.
Torley, K. (2020), 'Community Puppetry in Ireland', *Applied Theatre Research*, 8(1): 149–52.
Tizzard-Kleister, K., and M. Jennings (2020), '"Breath, Belief, Focus, Touch": Applied Puppetry in Simulated Role-Play for Person-Centred Nursing Education', *Applied Theatre Research*, 8(1): 73–87.
Tsitou, F. (2012), 'Puppetry in Museum Interpretation and Communication', doctoral dissertation, Royal Holloway, University of London.
Turner, V. (2008), *The Ritual Process: Structure and Anti-structure*, London: Aldine Transaction.
Walsh, M. (2013), 'I Object Maria Walsh on Art and the New Objecthood', *Art Monthly – London* (371): 9–12.
Wiame, A. (2016), 'A Thought without Puppeteer: Ethics of Dramatization and Selection of Becomings', *Deleuze Studies*, 10(1): 33–49.
Wiame, A. (2016), 'Deleuze's "Puppetry" and the Ethics of Non-human Compositions', *Maska*, 31(179–80): 60–7.
Winnicott, D. W. (1953), 'Transitional Objects and Transitional Phenomena: A Study of the First Not-Me Possession', *International Journal of Psycho-Analysis*, 34: 89–97.
Winnicott, D. W. (2010), *Playing and Reality*, London: Routledge.
Woynarski, L. (2020), *Ecodramaturgies: Theatre, Performance and Climate Change*, London: Palgrave Macmillan.

Woodyer, T., and S. Carter (2020), 'Domesticating the Geopolitical: Rethinking Popular Geopolitics through Play', *Geopolitics*, 25(5): 1050–74.

Woodward, S. (2020), *Material Methods: Researching and Thinking with Things*, London: Sage.

Woo, Y. L. (2016), 'Performance Artist Explores Female Sensuality', *Korea Herald*, https://www.koreaherald.com/view.php?ud=20160829000395 (accessed 5 December 2022).

Index

Abed, Husam 29–30
ACT project 82–4
actants 36, 39, 52, 59–60, 150–1, 163
Actor Network Theory (ANT) 57, 59, 149
Aebes, Martha 113
affect 5, 27–8, 41, 62, 66, 151
agency 30, 43, 48, 58, 76, 120, 133–4, 137, 149–50, 156
animism 44, 56, 131, 150
anthropocentrism 38, 40–1, 66
anthropomorphism 11–13, 24, 54, 106
Apollo and Daphne 42–3, 60
Applied Puppetry definition 1–2, 5–6
arboreal feminism (Sandilands) 60
Arons, Wendy 7, 35, 38
artificial others 24, 124
assemblage 13, 54–5, 64, 103–4, 145–50, 157, 163
Astles, Cariad 4, 27
attunement 15, 19, 39–42, 48, 107, 153, 158
automata 72, 154
autonomy 13, 45–8, 58–9, 61, 84, 92–3, 112, 118, 122–3, 149

Baird, Bil 2, 8, 14, 69, 72–6
Banyan theatre 8, 22, 54
Barba, Eugenio 7, 99, 163
Barthes, Roland 7, 9, 43–4, 53
Bass, Eric 23–4
Bell, John 7, 49, 59, 66, 71
Bennett, Jane 44, 145, 149–51, 154–5, 163
Beuys, Joseph 7, 38, 91, 94–5, 104–5, 109
bio object (Brown) 52
bioperformativity (Woynarski) 38
biopower 69, 71–4, 77, 111, 113, 121, 124, 151
Blumenthal, Eileen 2, 117
Boal, Augusto 4, 7, 20, 23, 30–1, 84, 156
Bogost, Ian 7, 163
border 9–10, 30, 77, 111–12, 117–18, 120, 125, 162

Bread and Puppet Theatre 99–100, 108, 162
Breath, Belief, Focus, Touch (BBFT) 24
Brecht, Bertolt 22–3, 75, 85
Broken Puppet Symposiums 4, 27
Brown, Bill 7, 14, 51–3, 55–7, 67, 87
Bunraku/ Ningyo Joruri 9, 43–4
Burvill, Tom 119

cancer 42, 48
Cappelletto, Chiara 48–9
care 23–4, 25–7, 30–2, 41, 57, 141
cathexis 36, 41, 152, 157
chair games 14, 154
Chesterton, G. K. 127, 140, 142
children's workshop 91–2
chimaera 3, 54, 65, 106, 163–4
cities 10, 127, 133–7, 138–42
Cohen, Matthew 63
Coleridge, Samuel Taylor 7
communion 99–100
Communitas (Turner) 122–3
community 2, 5–7, 25–6, 28, 66–7, 74, 76–9, 82–4, 93–4, 116, 158, 162–3
community arts 5, 91
Contractor, Meher, Rustom 2, 71
Craig, Edward Gordan 51, 128
Critchley, Simon 120–2
Crone, Rosalind 62–3
Crothers, Jessie 70–1, 81
cyborg 153, 163

Dafa Puppet Theatre 29–30
Dakroub, Karim 4, 29
Deák, Réka 29–30
decentring 59, 127, 151, 156–7
Deleuze, Gilles 7, 150, 154, 165
Delijani, Clare Finburgh 7, 153–4
Derrida, Jacques 7, 116
détournement 102, 160
devising 6, 64
disability 4, 27–8, 138, 141

Dissensus (Rancière) 120-1, 125
Dolls 7, 128, 134, 137
doubleness 23, 131
Droomtheater 31

Earth Arts 154-5
eco performance 11-12, 38-9
ecology 10-12, 37-41
Educational Puppet Association (EPA) 1-2
embodiment 6, 16, 27, 39, 41-2, 48, 62, 115, 118
empathy 12, 23-4, 78, 128, 135, 164
enchantment 26, 92-3
enmeshed 8, 13, 38-9, 41, 58, 115, 133, 163
entanglement 40, 44-5, 59, 62
enzyme project 54-5, 109, 164
ephemeral 37, 48, 119, 121, 159-160
estrangement 115-6, 125
ethics 21, 26, 37, 67, 76, 111-13, 117-21, 123-4
expanding foam 13, 145, 155

face to face 14, 117-18, 121, 124-5
feminist art 7, 13, 92-3, 163
Fisher, Emma 4, 27
flat puppetry 130-1
fluid materiality 161-2
foolish witness 119-120
forum theatre 4, 32
Foucault, Michel 7-8, 56, 69, 71-3
freedom 58, 64, 72, 76, 123, 131, 133, 141
Friedman, Gary 8, 77

Gablik, Suzi 13, 92-3, 104, 109, 113, 158
gaps 77, 121-2, 125
garbage, trash 87-90, 92, 96-7, 108
gender 28, 63, 77, 119, 128, 137, 140-1
Geum-Hyung, Jeong 8, 39
gift 116-17, 124
Goodlander, Jennifer 10, 28, 133
Grant, David 19, 22-3, 31
Gray, John 7, 131, 133, 141
Gross, Joan 75, 83
Gross, Kenneth 7, 64, 112

Hall, Stuart 76, 79-80
hand to hand 14, 111-13, 116-18, 120, 123-5

hands 112-13, 124
Handspring Puppet Theatre 8, 25-7, 31, 36
haptic experience 25, 62, 66, 123, 156
Harman, Graham 7, 40, 57-8, 64-5, 149, 151-2, 154
Health Action 75, 77-8
Heart of the Beast Puppet and Mask Theatre 99-100
Heidegger, Martin 40, 53, 151
heritage 57, 63, 84, 92, 97, 101, 108, 112, 122, 133, 162
heteroglossia 75, 80, 83
historical tropes 69-72
HMP Haslar IRC 10, 14, 49, 61, 111-25, 157
Holocaust 52, 56
hospitality 7, 111, 113, 115-16, 124
Hughes, Jenny 145, 153
humour 121-2
hyper objects 11, 59, 100, 153, 158

identities 10-11, 28, 66, 69, 72-4, 76-7, 79-80, 84, 117, 133, 137, 141
immersive 82, 97, 99-100, 103, 105, 122, 128, 131
immigration 10, 30, 61, 111, 116, 118-20
India 2, 7, 60, 69-74
Indian Puppetry 71, 115
inertia 43, 158
inner life (of objects) 24, 45, 56, 61-2, 65, 149, 152
intersectional 13, 28, 38, 48, 58, 74, 92-3, 157
interstitial 38-9, 45, 53, 121-5, 151, 153, 163
irreverence 87, 92, 101, 106, 137

Japan 9, 43-4, 130, 161
Jeffers, Alison 117
Jennings, Matthew 23-5
junk music 82, 102-4, 108, 134
Jurkowski, Henryk 2, 7, 70

Kamishibai 8, 130-1, 142, 162
Kantor, Tadeusz 7, 51-2
Kenosis (Morton) 41
Kentridge, William 7, 26-7, 159-60
Kenya 76-83
Kershaw, Baz 7, 13, 37, 49, 88, 94

Kiki (monkey puppet) 55–6
Kleist, Henrik von 131, 133, 141
Kohler, Adrian 36

Laakkonen, Riku 30–1
Lacy, Suzanne 7, 92–3
Lambe Lambe 128–9, 142, 162
language 79–83
Latour, Bruno 36, 57, 59, 149–51
Lavery, Carl 7, 153–4
Lebek, Karolina 161
Levinas, Emmanuel 7, 111, 118–21, 123–4
liminal space 16, 76–7, 80, 84, 99, 121, 153
lip sync puppetry 82–3, 87
listening 31, 35, 40, 93, 108, 113, 157–8
litany 155, 157, 163
Little Amal 9–10, 161–2
Little Angel Theatre 4, 46
ludic space 3, 10, 107, 113, 127, 131, 133–4, 136, 138, 145, 149

magic 14, 26, 32, 41, 47, 102, 131
magic realism 11, 42, 97, 128, 148
mainstream culture 94, 161
Malinowska, Anna 161
Margolies, Eleanor 138
Marlsite 3, 13–14, 37, 87–109, 153, 159
Marneweck, Aja 12, 25–6
materialism 6–7, 12, 14, 19, 38, 51, 150–1, 161
materiality 21, 28, 37, 41, 55, 95, 108, 145, 150–3, 159–63
May, Theresa 7, 35, 38
McCarthy, James 70–1
medical mannequins 22–5
Mesh theatre (Kent) 39, 48
meshing 38–9, 45, 105, 161
meta object (Brown) 52, 54
metaphor 9, 21, 30, 35, 42, 45, 48, 54, 72, 99, 102, 131, 133, 141, 152
Metaxis (Boal) 23, 31
Miller, Daniel 12, 17
missionary 70–3, 75, 78, 81
more-than-human (Abram) 8, 13, 38, 48, 51, 59, 145, 153–5, 161
Mori, Masahiro 7, 40, 49

Morton, Tim 7–8, 11, 14, 35, 39–42, 48, 88, 100, 154, 157
museum puppetry 55–7

Nakamura, Aya 127, 130–1
Nash, David 12, 36
Nelson, Victoria 61
new materialism 6, 8, 12, 14, 28, 51, 65, 149, 154
Nicholson, Helen 116, 145, 153
non-human ensemble 8, 145, 152
nursemaid 23–4

object speculations 19–21
object theatre 7, 30–1, 40, 55
Object-oriented ontology (OOO) 7–8, 39–40, 57–8, 64–6, 88, 149, 154, 163
Objectboundaryhood 95–6
objecthood 6, 55, 58
objects as enablers 14, 23, 153
Objects with Objectives project 4, 19, 22, 28, 32, 49
occupy puppets (Graeber) 162
Odin Theatre 99–100
othering 58, 77
otherness 11, 27, 30, 119, 120–3, 151

pain 61, 117–18, 123, 130
Paiva, Duda 38–9
paradox 37–8, 47–9, 58, 61–3, 88, 133
pareidolia 3, 13, 90, 97
participation 37, 39, 59, 91, 94, 97, 125, 138, 141
performance remains (Schneider) 11, 56, 60–1, 152, 159
performing object (Bell) 7, 59
Pearson, Mike 7, 35–6
Peterson, Valerie 158–9
Philpott, Alexis 2, 70–1
plastic 54–5, 87–8, 90, 92, 104–9, 145, 160, 164
Plato's Cave 7, 158–9
play 6, 14, 22, 29, 48, 60, 62–3, 97, 113, 123, 127–42, 148, 152, 157
popular materialism 161
population control 2, 69, 72–5, 77
Poster-Su, Tobi 58, 76, 80
power 2, 8, 51, 58, 61, 69, 71–2, 74, 141–2, 156–7

propaganda 70–1, 73–4, 130, 162
prosopopoeia 36
prosthesis 36, 48
psychogeography 133–4, 137, 140–1
punch 7, 43, 62–3, 162
punctum 53–4, 153
Puppet City 10, 133–42
puppet history 2, 56, 70, 81
puppet surrogates 10, 117, 135
puppethood 37, 48
Purcell-Gates, Laura 27–8, 41

race 28, 58, 77, 84, 137
reciprocity 116, 161–2
recycling 3, 10, 90, 92
refugees 9, 29–30, 117
remote puppetry 14, 64, 69, 76–7, 83–4
representation 40, 61, 67, 72, 75–80, 83–4, 117, 120–1
resistance 41, 44, 48, 72, 74, 150, 154
rhizomatic 145, 150
Richards, Paulette 58, 76
risks 64, 66, 120, 122
robots 40, 72, 128, 160, 164
root 12–13, 15, 23, 37, 48–9, 61, 145, 147–157
Royal de Luxe 11, 161–2
Royal Shakespeare Company (RSC) 158, 161
Rubbish theory (Thompson) 87–8

scale 11, 127–9, 134, 141–2, 162
Scanlan, John 88
Schweitzer and Zerdy 59, 152
semiotics 7, 9, 44, 79–80, 84
sensitization 78, 80, 82
shadow puppetry 2, 7, 31, 42, 57–8, 82–3, 112–13, 119, 158, 162, 164
Shawky, Wael 7, 61
Silk, Dennis 56
simulation role play 23, 25
socially engaged art 7, 72, 92, 94, 96, 153–4
solidarity 40, 117
Sontag, Susan 42, 158
South Africa 4, 8, 12, 19, 21, 23, 25–6, 28, 63, 77
Spanish Civil War 67, 70, 130
Speaight, George 2, 63
stillness 36, 45, 61, 65, 102, 156, 158

street theatre 47, 59, 105, 107–8, 128, 162
surrealism 53–4
Sussman, Mark 142
sustainability 26, 153

Talisman 28, 57, 64, 102
Taylor, Jane 26, 33, 36, 48
technology 27, 164
Theatre and Performance Research Association (TAPRA) 13, 145
Theatre for Development (TfD) 14, 69–70, 74, 76, 80–1, 84
therapy 4–5, 12, 29–31, 66
thingness 36, 53–5, 57, 67
Thomas de la Peña, Carolyn 62
Thompson, Michael 87–8
time 57, 65, 88, 95, 135, 152
Tizzard-Kleister, Karl 23–5
Torley, Karen 22–25, 32, 54
touch 39, 45, 112, 118, 123–4
toy theatre 127–9, 131, 134, 136–7, 142
transcendence 41, 55
transformations 14, 26, 43, 99
transgressions 28, 123, 137
trashability (Thill) 88
trauma 23, 27, 29–30, 42, 56, 63, 119–24, 130
trees 38, 60, 106–7, 157
trickster 7, 16, 66, 84, 117, 131
TUPUMUE project 78–82, 84

Übermarionette 51, 131
uncanny 6–7, 36, 39–40, 44, 54, 66, 125, 128, 156
ur-object 88, 90

veering 39, 41
ventriloquism 21, 57, 75
vibrant matter (Bennett) 38, 149–151, 154, 163
vibrant witness 23, 52, 56–7
violence 26, 43, 58, 62–64, 66–7, 123–4
Vogel, Nina 129

Walker, Kara 7, 58
Walsh, Maria 58–9
War Horse 3, 8, 25–6, 36, 160–1
waste 3–4, 10, 13, 87–8, 90, 92–3, 96–106, 108–9, 150, 153, 157, 159–160

Wayang 2, 162
welcome 113, 116–17, 120, 124
Welfare State International (WSI) 7, 37, 47, 93–94, 99, 102
Wiame, Aline 154
Winnicott, D. W. 66
witness puppets 26–7, 57, 119–20
Woodward, Sophie 44, 48

workshop design 63–4, 91–2, 160
workshops 6, 12–14, 37, 48, 53, 60, 62–67, 74, 91–92, 111–13, 115, 116–25, 129–30, 154, 156, 160
Woynarski, Lisa 7, 38

Yas-e-Tamam Theatre Group 128
Young, Jeff 11, 46